THE MEDIA MONOPOLY

Other books by Ben H. Bagdikian

Caged
Double Vision
The Effete Conspiracy, and Other Crimes by the Press
The Information Machines
In the Midst of Plenty
Man's Contracting World in an Expanding Universe (editor)
The Shame of the Prisons (with Leon Dash)

THE MEDIA MONOPOLY

Sixth Edition

Ben H. Bagdikian

With a New Preface on the Internet
and Telecommunications Cartels

Beacon Press   Boston

Beacon Press
25 Beacon Street
Boston, Massachusetts 02108-2892

Beacon Press books
are published under the auspices of
the Unitarian Universalist Association of Congregations.

05 04 03 02 01 00   8 7 6 5 4 3 2 1

Library of Congress Cataloging-in-Publication Data
Bagdikian, Ben H.
The media monopoly / Ben H. Bagdikian—6th ed.
p. cm.
ISBN 0-8070-6179-4 (pbk.)
1. Mass media—Economic aspects—United
States. 2. Monopolies—United States.
I. Title.
P96.E252U625 2000
338.4'7302223'0973—dc21   96-29825

CONTENTS

ACKNOWLEDGMENTS

MANY YEARS AGO a fellowship from the John Simon Guggenheim Foundation permitted me to suspend news reporting for a year in order to study changes in family ownership of newspapers. Later the John and Mary Markle Foundation supported extensive research on factors that make for failure and success in newspapers, a study that led to a great deal of illuminating information and made clear that a fundamental change was occurring in media industries. Annual grants from the Committee on Research of the Academic Senate of the University of California at Berkeley and a sabbatical leave granted in 1980 and again in 1988 were indispensable.

Many research assistants helped along the way: Marian Bryant, Amy Troubh, Suzanne Donovan, Alyson Pytte, Dan Wohlfeiler, Fred Goff, Zoia Horn, Lyn Heffernan, Gail Nichols, and the Data Center.

My son, Chris, and his wife, Patti Keller, who are not to be blamed for the contents of the book, were invaluable in administering long-distance therapy to my computer.

I have special thanks for my wife, Marlene Griffith, whose warm support did not dim her penetrating eye and incorruptible logic.

I recite the cliché of acknowledgments in order to protect the innocent: many helped but I alone am responsible for the final result.

Ben H. Bagdikian

PREFACE TO THE SIXTH EDITION

AS THE UNITED STATES ENTERS the twenty-first century, power over the American mass media is flowing to the top with such devouring speed that it exceeds even the accelerated consolidations of the last twenty years. For the first time in U.S. history, the country's most widespread news, commentary, and daily entertainment are controlled by six firms that are among the world's largest corporations, two of them foreign.

Even with the dramatic entry of the Internet and the cyber world with their uncounted hundreds of new firms, the controlling handful of American and foreign corporations now exceed in their size and communications power anything the world has seen before. Their intricate global interlocks create the force of an international cartel.

There are pernicious consequences. While excessive bigness itself is cause for economic anxieties, the worst problems are political and social. The country's largest media giants have achieved alarming success in writing the media laws and regulations in favor of their own corporations and against the interests of the general public. Their concentrated power permits them to become a larger factor than ever before in socializing each generation with entertainment models of behavior and personal values.

The impact on the national political agenda has been devastating. For years, the mainstream news has overdramatized its reporting of congressional and White House debate on the national debt and deficit beyond their intrinsic importance. Politicians raised the issue, but it was seized upon and overblown by the major media—media that politicians use as a bellwether on what issues will get them the most public attention and partisan advantage. During these crucial years, the American economy was undergoing an astonishing phenomenon that the mainstream news left largely unreported or actually glamorized in its infrequent references: the largest transfer of the national wealth in American history from a majority of the population to a small percentage of the country's wealthiest families.

The handful of dominant corporations have pursued quick, ever-higher profits, mainly by producing more trivialized and self-serving commercialized news. Their entertainment, with its powerful impact on the popular culture, has become further coarsened and brutalized. As each use of shock-as-attention-getter becomes bolder, more barriers have fallen.

Main media talk shows and entertainment have vulgarized language as a ratings technique, introducing changes that go beyond the inevitable evolution of all language in modern societies. New terms have always emerged for new phenomena and experiences. The cyber world, for example, has invented words because the Internet and its offshoots need new words to describe what never existed before. Advertisers and adolescents have always invented their own novel jargon. But today that normal process is artificially escalated. In the race for ever-higher profits, each of the dominant media owners tries to outdo competitors in the once-private language of barroom fights and locker-room sexual boasts.

Fortunately, not everything in the new mass media is dismal. There are positive changes. In mainstream news, the general level of reporters' education and writing has risen, and there are more stories reported with appreciation of context and supportive factual data. The *New York Times,* for one, has looked at some social phenomena it had ignored in the past. In both television and movies there are admirable and sometimes even stunning presentations of drama and history, as well as agreeable entertainment. When the Internet is added, those with the technical equipment and motivation have gained unprecedented and growing access to information and self-expression.

Nevertheless, the money rewards for advertising's drive for mass audiences have escalated so sharply that the repeated use of stereotyped trivial and brutal material has overwhelmed what is positive in printed and electronic mass media. The unprecedented billions to be made by the commercial media themselves and the resulting revenues for their sponsors have made both resistant to growing pleas by parents, educators, and social scientists to lower the level of demeaning and violent content.

The Internet, with its chaotic vastness, has brought sweeping changes for industry and individuals, from selling books to midnight stock market trading at home. It is an effective instrument for personal expression, a formidable source of information and entertainment, and of instant electronic mail for the minority currently equipped to use it. But it has been overblown as the final liberation of the individual from "the system." Advertising and other corporate promotion on the Internet seem to grow exponentially, with "the system" becoming more fully embedded in the cyber world each day.

The American population is remarkably diverse in background, politics, geography, and tastes, and has always needed this variety reflected in a parallel diversity in its public information and entertainment. But more than ever, the major media have treated the public as a homogeneous mass with low taste and limited intelligence. With the country's widest disseminators of news, commentary, and ideas firmly entrenched among a small number of the world's wealthiest corporations, it may not be surprising that their news and commentary is limited to an unrepresentative narrow spectrum of politics.

The Intertwined Six

Six firms dominate all American mass media. Each is a subsidiary of a larger parent firm, some of them basically operating in other industries. The six parent firms are General Electric, Viacom, Disney, Bertelsmann, Time Warner, and Murdoch's News Corp. Bertelsmann is based in Germany and News Corp in Australia, the other four in the United States. All the parent firms are listed in *Fortune* Magazine's 1999 Global 500 of the largest corporations in the world. Other giant firms in other industries clearly were on the prowl for new mass media in order to join the Big Six—like Sony, a Japanese hardware firm; Seagram's, a Canadian liquor firm; and AT&T, a telephone company traditionally providing one-to-one (not mass) communication.

The top six firms, ordered solely on their annual media revenues, are Time Warner, Disney, Viacom (an amalgam of CBS and Westinghouse), News Corp, Bertelsmann, and General Electric. These six have more annual media revenues than the next twenty firms combined.

The number of dominant firms remains six, even with an announcement in early 2000 that stunned the country's businesses and all computer-users—the world's largest Internet service provider, America Online, Inc., said it would acquire the world's largest media company, Time Warner, to form AOL Time Warner, Inc. Consequently, while six firms still dominate all mass media, the largest of those six would become a corporation valued at $350 billion. It would be history's largest merger, in the media or in any other enterprise.

(If the new merger prevails, references elsewhere in this

Preface to "Time Warner" should be read as "AOL Time Warner.")

Barring government anti-trust intervention or other unforeseen events, the new company, like all mammoth players in a field, is likely to force other giant media firms, like Disney, Viacom, and News Corp, to make similar mergers with Internet and communication giants like Microsoft, AT&T, and MCI World, affecting commonly known cyber operations like Yahoo, Amazon.com, and eBay. The prospect is for a giantism and concentrated power beyond anything ever seen. Advertising becomes even more dominant and inescapable in the human landscape. AOL Time Warner becomes what the computerized news service MSNBC described on January 10, 2000, as "the most powerful global advertising force across all media, including Internet, publishing, television and music."

What was clearly the focus of the top executives of AOL and Time Warner in their joint announcement of the merger was a shopping mall of global dimensions in which media and other products could be promoted, displayed, and ordered instantly with a click of the computer mouse or interactive television set. In the midst of the executives' expected rhetoric about the wonders of their joined enterprises, the two leaders' stress was on instant merchandizing. AOL, for example, already owns Compuserve and Netscape and has a strategic alliance with Sun Microsystems that gives it enhanced entry into the burgeoning e-commerce.

The merged firms will have more than 100 million global subscribers, 20 million cable homes, AOL access to Time Warner's 30 magazines and 75 million homes that receive the cable networks CNN, TBS, and TNT. Expected annual revenues are $40 billion. Given Time Warner's vast holdings in all media, the ordinary citizen, whether a reader, TV viewer, movie-goer, or Internet user, would be forced to deal with a communications cartel of a magnitude and power the world has never seen before.

The lasting social and political implications are sobering. Mergers of this size further dwarfs news as merely another industrial byproduct. As dramatized by the case of the *Los Angeles Times,* the new mergers deepen the dangers of more deterioration of news as a handmaiden of its owners' corporate ambitions, endangering the future of the independent and diverse public information on which democracy depends.

The immense size of the parent firms means that some of their crucial media subsidiaries, like news, have become remote within their complex tables of organization. That remoteness has contributed to the unprecedented degree to which the parent firms have pressed their news subsidiaries to cross ethical lines by selecting news that will promote the needs of the owning corporation rather than serve the traditional ethical striving of journalism.

Symbolically, *the* largest corporation in the world, General Motors, has now entered the mass media field. GM has acquired the three largest satellite TV broadcasting companies and has received $1.5 billion from the Internet's America Online, Inc., in a joint race for high-capacity speed in the expanding cyber world.

The power and influence of the dominant companies are understated by counting them as "six." They are intertwined: they own stock in each other, they cooperate in joint media ventures, and among themselves they divide profits from some of the most widely viewed programs on television, cable, and movies.

News reporting and commentary controlled by mainstream media companies are the most politically narrow in the democratic world. Their presentations and analyses are limited to the center-right, ignoring political views held by almost a third of American voters. In 1999, the Roper Center for Public Opinion Research surveyed the political ideologies of Americans, offering the choices "very liberal," "somewhat liberal," "lean liberal," "moderate," "lean conservative," "somewhat conservative," and "very conservative." The first three choices received a combined 31 percent self-identification. Thus, almost a third of the respondents seldom see news and commentary selected to meet their political interests and concerns.

Political narrowness in the media reportage and commentary inevitably leads to a narrow range of genuine choices at elections, and since meaningful voter choice is vital to sustain any democracy, to that extent, the contemporary mass media's constricted politics weaken the foundation of the democratic process.

Major industries, including those controlling the media, have always been more comfortable with conservative politics. Now that these industries own the country's daily printed and broadcast news, it is not surprising that their newly acquired staffs have come to understand that they remain in their employers' good graces by downplaying or keeping unwanted ideas out of the printed and broadcast news. With time, this shrunken social-political range becomes the accepted definition of what is news. The emerging picture has overtones, subtle or otherwise, of an Orwellian Big Brother, Incorporated.

Such concentrated private power is not what the creators of the American democracy had in mind when they created the First Amendment guaranteeing free speech and free press. They could not foresee that two hundred years later, by the twenty-first century, the sacred First Amendment guaranteeing every citizen free speech would, to an appalling degree, become dependent upon the "speaker's" wealth.

Enter: The Internet

In the beginning, the Internet was celebrated as a welcome liberation of the individual from powerful mass media systems. Anyone with a computer and a modem connection to the outside electronic world has access to the growing vastness of the new medium. Individuals expressing themselves on the Internet are provided gratification of being one voice among thousands. Civic bodies and an unlimited variety of propagandistic groups and individuals can display their goals and values at less expense than ever before and have a potentially large—if mostly anonymous and uncertain—audience. Internet's e-mail, with its own cyber address system for each participant, permits private messages that are close to instantaneous and permits replies at the same speed.

But with each passing month, the balance in favor of the individual looks less reassuring. Thanks to the Internet's heavy presence of corporations, intrusive advertising, and other highly orchestrated business displays designed to be seen by millions, the individual's private Internet space is continually invaded by electronic sales pitches. And on-line commerce has its share of fraudulent or ludicrous ads, like ads for the nonexistent vitamins F, P, T, and U, presented as cures for everything from sexual dysfunction to leg cramps.

Internet capabilities have also raised serious problems of copyright protection, since any anonymous person can place copyrighted articles, book chapters, photographs, recordings, and other intellectual property on the Internet that other anonymous users can copy and reissue.

Whatever its final form, the present and future power of the Internet remains formidable. Though by century's end, only a minority had home modems, it most certainly will become a future large majority. Except for television fifty years ago, few technological devices have acculturated society as rapidly as the computer-plus-Internet.

The Internet's growth and versatility—10,000 new sites every day—have created anxieties among the older media. Printed news media, with their complex production and manual distribution on daily, weekly, or monthly schedules, fear the Internet's immediacy and twenty-four-hour operations. They fear that an on-line source might possibly contain a news break that has not been verified by good journalistic standards. As a result, most metropolitan and smaller printed newspapers also place their dailies on the Internet.

At the same time, the Internet has created its own version of the older printed forms, like its family of magazines designed solely for the Internet, called "zines." Unlike their slower, hierarchically organized, printed grandparent, the zines can change content at any time. They can be started without buying press time, distributors, or mailed delivery, and can be created by anyone with the urge, either with or without training in traditional disciplines. Many zines are private gossip and rumor fountains. Their lack of concern with accuracy periodically creates mischief and injustice for individuals and groups. Consequently, along with new content that is broadening, practical, and beneficial, the zines also spread messages that are hateful, socially destructive, and plainly psychotic, and all directed at the same potential large audience.

Nevertheless, despite their awareness of capricious Internet standards, printed papers, fearful of electronic scoops, have become Internet-watchers. An Internet gossipmonger, Matt Drudge, who admits he isn't worried about accuracy, was the first to hint at the Clinton sex scandal. Drudge's account caused a *Newsweek* reporter to rush his story onto the Internet, even though his print editors wanted another week to verify facts. Clearly, the competition to sell news has encouraged print sources to lower their standards of what is fit to print.

The U.S. Postal Service has also been significantly affected by the Internet, which has its own electronic "post office" for e-mail. Uncounted thousands now prefer e-mail to first-class letters sent through the Postal Service. But while individuals enjoy the speed and lower costs of the Internet, they lack the protections of the U.S. Postal Service's severe penalties for violations of first-class mail privacy, use of the mails to defraud, extort, or threaten, and other advantages of what Internet jargon denigrates as "snail mail."

The new medium marches on, constantly gathering new uses. By mid-1999, for example, at least three firms were selling groceries over the Internet, with deliveries made from central warehouses. Airline and other transportation ticketing is growing, as are computer software sales. It is creating a radical change in the distribution and sale of books. For those who have learned the skill, the Internet offers an incomparable source for research. It can supply documents and reports whose depth and breadth no bricks-and-mortar library can match (which is why computers are often the first objects seen upon entering libraries).

By mid-1999, though fewer than half of homes, schools, and offices had access to the system, the Internet contained 2.8 million sites (individual displays), the equivalent of 800 million traditional "pages." The 35 percent of Americans using the Internet used it to complete more than $500 million a year in credit card purchases and spent even more annually in monthly fees for Internet services, like Yahoo or Infoseek, that facilitate finding particular locations in the vast arrays of information and displays. Though the total potential audience for each site is never predictable, advertisers have flocked to the new medium, paying far more than usual rates per potential (but unguaranteed) numbers of viewers. They do it because they recognize that the Internet, when combined with interactive television-computer sets, has created unmatched opportunities for impulse buying by merely pressing a button. On-line marketing is growing so fast that a British market research firm estimates it will be over $5 billion by 2003 (with "adult," that is, sex-oriented, material accounting for more than half the sales).

Technology and Monopoly

Thanks to the new electronics, including the Internet and interactive cable, the lines between traditional forms of the media—like newspapers, television programs, and movies—have become blurred. By owning all these media, a few large corporations have mass communications power that far exceeds the capabilities of smaller firms, social action organizations, and individuals.

Under the folklore of capitalism, even giant firms would compete forcefully against each other. But through mutual cooperation, interlocked directors, and shared partnerships in media operations, contemporary capitalist competition has become more like a cooperative cartel.

As noted throughout this book, media power is political power. Politicians hesitate to offend the handful of media operators who control how those politicians will be presented—or not presented—to the voters. Media political power has always been a fixture in American history. But today the combination of the media industry and traditional corporate power has reached dimensions former generations could not match.

There is another ominous difference between characteristics of today's major news media and those of a century ago, a difference that profoundly influences the nature of American politics. As this book documents, in the nineteenth century the most significant mass media were important newspapers and magazines that covered a far wider range of political points of view than their modern counterparts. In the nineteenth century, major newspaper chains promoted labor unions and higher wages for ordinary workers.

Inclusion of the left within those earlier major media was instrumental in the enactment of the country's first abolition of the worst abuses of workers, initiation of national policies to protect the natural environment, and development of safer and more sanitary communities for working people. It was their status as major media that informed a large enough portion of the electorate that these new laws and regulations were important for the future of social justice in the nation.

Today, that political variety among the mainstream media has disappeared. As the country enters the twenty-first century, the news and analyses of progressive ideas and groups are close to absent in the major media. Similarly absent is commentary on the dangers of this political one-sidedness to American democracy. For other countries, it's different. A March 16, 1997, *New York Times* story noted, "The concentration of power in the hands of a relatively few—along with the linking of big money, big media and government power—has raised searching questions about Russia's young democracy." The same statement about "big media, big money" could justifiably be applied to the United States today, but it never is within the "big money, big media."

Positive accomplishments of labor unions, for example, continue to be rarely reported in the standard news. Even added pay for workers is depicted as a "problem." In April of 1998, the *New York Times* reported that full employment created a serious "problem" for industry, which was having difficulty in enlisting more workers. Successful corporate strategies to avoid raising worker pay were reported sympathetically. Apparently, in the main media the bedrock capitalist doctrine of prices responding to supply-and-demand does not extend to human labor.

The fifth edition of this book described how each of the leading firms has acquired firms that together represent all three crucial steps in mass communications. Each of the dominant six firms now owns the major companies that create the content of the mass media, like newspapers, magazines, book publishing houses, and movie and TV production studios. Each of them has also acquired the next step, the national delivery systems for the programming they control or lease, like broadcast networks and cable. And finally, each has acquired or shared ventures with the ultimate delivery mechanism into each American home and office, the telephone company lines, cable systems, and satellite dishes.

Whom Do the Media Watchdogs Watch?

Vertical integration was once looked upon with alarm by government. It was understood that corporations which have control of a total process, from raw material to fabrication to sales, also have few motives for genuine innovation and the power to squeeze out anyone else who tries to compete. This situation distorts the economy with monopolistic control over prices. Today, government has become sympathetic to dominant vertical corporations that have merged into ever larger total systems. These corporations, including those in the media, have remained largely unrestrained.

In 1998 alone, there were 12,000 mergers valued at more than $1.5 trillion. In 1999, the Viacom-CBS merger, valued at $37.3 billion, was the largest merger in world history. In many of the mergers, the chief beneficiary is neither the public nor, ironically, sometimes even the ordinary stockholders but the executives and investment houses arranging the merger. Less than a year after Viacom-CBS became "the largest merger in the world," the AOL–Time Warner deal was almost ten times larger.

"Globalization" has become the all-purpose excuse for acts of corporate irresponsibility, like displacement of American workers in favor of miserably paid and often abused workers in poor countries. A significant portion of that overseas replacement of American workers is paid by American taxpayers through the U.S. Export-Import Bank and the American contributions to the World Bank, money often used to encourage U.S. firms to move abroad.

For example, the economic crash of the "Asian tigers" in the 1990s was fueled by some of the leading U.S. lending institutions pouring trillions into foreign regimes known to the world as shaky and corrupt. Yet, time after time, after the predictable collapses, the bankers have been rescued from their folly and greed by the American government, using special funds whose origins are ordinary

American taxpayers. Yet most mainstream news media continue to report the transactions as an unfortunate element of international financing, with no mention of its unfairness to American taxpayers.

When new legislation or regulatory action desired by big business is pending, mainstream business news quotes "Wall Street analysts" concerned with impacts on corporate share prices, and does not look at prices or the past history of the impact of such deals on the ordinary consumers. On June 2, 1999, a full-page AT&T ad in the *New York Times* proclaimed that AT&T, already the owner of TCI, the largest cable company in the country, had acquired yet another, MediaOne. The ad stated prominently, "American consumers will be winners." Papers can accept such ads, but they are also obligated to look at the fate of similar promises in parallel events. Examination would show that the record of such corporate promises has been dismal. After the Telecommunications Act of 1996, which promised more competition and lower rates, there has been no general reduction of residential phone or cable bills. In most places, the bills have gone up, but that rise did not become important news. If, however, predicted rises in major new stock offerings have failed to materialize time after time, the mainstream financial news regularly reports it emphatically and even derisively. But failed corporate promises to ordinary consumers most often are met with main media amnesia.

Richer Six, Poorer Public

The leading media firms have so penetrated the law-making and regulatory machinery of Washington that it is close to a literal fact that these firms can directly and indirectly write our communications laws. According to the *Wall Street Journal,* the freshman Republican members of the 1994 Congress, key to a new Republican majority of House and Senate, invited heads of major telecommunications firms to a closed conference to ask what the media leaders wanted in communications laws. The Congress then delivered the desired legislative package to the industry, with White House acceptance, in the Telecommunications Act of 1996. That disastrous Act rewrote more than sixty years of communications law and opened the floodgates to the largest and greatest number of industrial mergers in American history.

The American public, by law, owns the airwaves, but that is news to most people who watch television and listen to radio. Public ownership was merely a whisper in the news when the Congress and

White House gave the broadcast industry a free gift worth $70 billion for high-definition television frequencies. To pour salt on the wound, the gift to industry will force the public to buy expensive new television sets or attachments to receive the new service.

Today, the Federal Communications Commission, the Federal Trade Commission, the Anti-Trust Division of the Department of Justice, the Congress, and a newly conservative federal court system favor a free market philosophy. They have all but retired from protecting the public from excessive private power and exorbitant prices.

The irony becomes more bitter because the fabulous riches achieved by the media giants arise to a large degree from new communications devices, like the Internet and satellites, that were originally invented and made practical with taxpayers' money.

Disneyland

When one large firm controls all forms of the major media, it becomes the delight of Wall Street's love of "synergy," a combination of two or more forces that creates a result greater than the sum of the individual parts. Each part of such a firm feeds business to other parts of the same corporation.

The Disney Company, for example, describes its Consumer Products division as offering "a dazzling array of toys, books, apparel, magazines, computer software, animation art, and collectibles to Disney fans around the world." Just one example is that the once gentle appeal of A. A. Milne's Pooh Bear has now been parlayed into a major Disney product, with five hundred different Pooh books, eleven Pooh magazines, and a line of LEGO toys based on Pooh. More than fourteen hundred worldwide Disney retail stores sell Disney memorabilia, from Pooh to Cinderella, from *The Lion King* to the father of them all, Mickey Mouse (when the copyright on Mickey runs out in 2003, the public might see more mouse ears than ever). In a Disney retail store, one can buy a Mickey Mouse trinket for a dollar or a painted art scene from *The Lion King* for $2,500.

The twenty-two major subsidiaries of the Disney Company— daily newspapers (the company's *Women's Wear Daily* and *W* were sold to Condé Nast in 1999*)*, magazines, books, radio, television, videos, movie studios, cable companies and programs, record labels, cruises, two thousand Disney character dolls, children's clothes (with Disney characters on them), theme parks, comics—bring the company more than $23 billion in revenues a year. It owns 43 percent of the Internet companies Infoseek, and its ESPN sports sites are available on all Disney cruise ships.

Disney's impressive commercial market power is exceeded only by the corporation's power to socialize new generations, a longer lasting effect than the firm's annual harvest of dollars, euros, and yens. The problem is not that Disney is evil, unlovable though its internal politics may be. Most Disney media images, in fact, stress cuteness, gentleness, and adventure. Nor is it because there is no place in an affluent society for toys, games, films, media entertainment, and other Disney products. The problem is a system that permits a single corporation to have such overwhelming power, not just over the media marketplace but over youth culture in the United States and globally. That power is so concentrated, ubiquitous, and artful that, to a degree unmatched in former mixtures of entertainment, it dilutes influences from family, schooling, and other sources that are grounded in real-life experience, weakening their ability to guide growing generations.

Every generation has had this problem, from the nineteenth-century "penny dreadfuls" to twentieth-century comic books. But today the power of an almost inescapable modern multi-media in the hands of a few giant entrepreneurs has reached dimensions that deserve serious public pressure to arouse government regulatory agencies from their prolonged hibernation.

Some of the dominant media firms like General Electric and the pre-CBS Westinghouse (which became Viacom) are major owners of heavy industry, a corporate world where employees are expected to obey without question when ordered, and executives are often outraged that their newly acquired journalists like to think of themselves as independent professionals whose first loyalty is to the public.

Others, like Disney, Time Warner, and Viacom come from entertainment and have further spread the repellent hybrid of news-as-entertainment and its equally repellent vocabulary of now-common "infotainment" and "advertorials."

When the first edition of this book was published in 1983, fifty corporations dominated most of every mass medium and the biggest media merger in history was a $340 million deal. At that time, the strategy of most of the fifty biggest firms was to gain market domination in one medium—to have the largest market share solely in newspapers, for example, or in magazines, or broadcasting, or books, or movies, but not in all of them. By the time the second edition was published in 1987, the fifty companies had shrunk to twenty-nine. By the third edition in 1990, the twenty-nine had shrunk to twenty-three, by the fourth edition to fourteen. By the fifth edition in 1997, the biggest firms numbered ten and involved the $19 billion Disney-ABC deal, at the time the biggest media merger ever. But "the biggest" of 1983, worth $340 million, would give way seventeen years later to AOL Time Warner's $350 billion merged corporation, more than 1,000 times larger.

There was reason enough, even then, for concern that so small a number of dominant firms had such a disproportionate influence on American culture, commerce, and political power. That shrank the status of the individual and more personal groups as voices in society. But today there is an even smaller number of dominant firms—six— (even excluding the AOL–Time Warner deal), and those six have more communications power than all the combined fifty leading firms of sixteen years earlier. It is the overwhelming collective power of these firms, with their corporate interlocks and unified cultural and political values, that raises troubling questions about the individual's role in the American democracy.

At each step, the leading firms' dominance in one medium gave them the money, power, and the enthusiasm of Wall Street investors who encouraged and supported them in dominating other media. Today, the six firms are so large and control so many enterprises that their prosperity is seen as necessary to prevent a slide into a Wall Street disaster.

The Shadow of Giants and Coarsened Culture

As the dominant corporations' increasing global scale enlarged their importance in the stock market, Wall Street analysts and leading investment houses became a factor in deciding how much and what kind of news and entertainment will reach the public. Wall Street lives and dies by daily stock levels, so pressure on media companies has increased not only to achieve ever-higher profits and stock levels, but also to do it rapidly. This process is at odds with healthy and durable growth in media industries. Newspapers, broadcasting, and book publishing all need long-term stability to accumulate and retain talent, to nurture creativity, and to maintain steady audiences. It is a slow process keyed to the public, and not to the daily stock market report.

The new mass media have had some positive and socially exciting impact, as mentioned earlier. But there is a darker side that increasingly overshadows its positive attributes, a dark side that for decades has rebuffed the changes advocated by consumer groups and civic organizations. The broadcasting industry has even ignored laws mandating change, as in its initial circumvention of the 1996 law requiring networks to air three hours a week of children's educational programming.

Corporate interlocks may cause big media firms to cooperate, but in one conspicuous way they compete and compete ferociously. They fight each other for the biggest possible share of the $80 billion a year in advertising, a reflection of their advertisers' own competition for the more than $6 trillion a year in consumption spending by the U.S. population. For the media this means competing for that elusive but golden commodity in modern life—human attention. The seeming paradox of cooperation at the corporate level but all-out competition in the race to capture audience attention is less paradoxical than it seems: the losers in this competition still make a great deal of money. But in the corporate ethos, the goal is not just high profit, but to make the highest profit, to be Number One.

In the frenetic race for attention, media companies adopt any means to freeze viewers' eyes in order to prevent viewers from changing channels. Their pursuit of the huge commercial rewards for this instant fixation has produced significant social and political changes in the country's culture and social values.

The pressure to capture instant attention has trivialized printed and broadcast news. It has coarsened popular culture with increasing use of gutter talk and other devices designed to shock. The result is obnoxious not just because it is crude and vulgar, though it is that. Its ultimate effect is to diminish reliance on talent, ideas, and inherently attractive entertainment. Instead, it substitutes every possible permutation of violent destruction of human beings, endless gratuitous sex scenes, and overuse of four-letter words and toilet humor more appropriate for adolescents giggling in seventh-grade restrooms.

As usual, Rupert Murdoch, with his bottomless contempt for his audiences, has led the way with his Fox network and movies. Worth an estimated $3.2 billion, Murdoch spent $800,000 on Washington lobbying and obtained waivers from U.S. law denied others. Murdoch's firm is News Corp, based in Australia. He owns Fox network and many of its affiliated stations even though the law says no foreign-based firm may own as much as 25 percent of a broadcasting station. Through his satellite and cable units, he will be able to reach more than three-quarters of the wired world. According to *The Economist,* his British holdings have had $2.1 billion profits, but by creative bookkeeping and political influence, he has not paid a shilling in British taxes.

But for all his contempt for public taste and his ruthlessness in getting what he wants, Murdoch grovels if it will make him richer. When China protested, Murdoch's HarperCollins book contract with Chris Patten, retiring as governor of Hong Kong after Hong Kong reverted to China, was canceled. Murdoch issued an abject apology to the Chinese government. When the Chinese expressed irritation with the BBC for its China coverage, Murdoch canceled the BBC on his news service. It appears that when Murdoch had to balance the world's largest potential market against his own highly conservative politics, he would not offend a communist government.

The trend in violence and crudity has become contagious. Today in movies and mainstream TV, for example, "comic effects" have been achieved by a teenager masturbating with a pie, a talk show host vomiting on air, and a character in a film drinking excrement. Talented scriptwriters are replaced by scripts so unfunny and tawdry that they would have been turned down by the greedy managers of pre–World War II New Jersey burlesque houses.

For advertisers whose corporate goods are promoted by such acts, violence and sex are literally cheap, that is, less expensive than creative, original, artistic programming. The violence is cheaper than ever, thanks to modern computerized effects that can impose digital images of massive explosions and Armageddons of slaughter.

Meanwhile, Back at Reality . . .

Television has been called "a weapon of mass distraction." Unfortunately, the power to keep politics distracted from the real business of a democracy is not limited to television.

In the 1990s, the nation saw its main news media increasingly obsessed with scandals and the lives of celebrities. The most dramatic and unrelenting episode of this growth in sleazy news stemmed from Independent Prosecutor Kenneth Starr's grand jury investigation and the orchestrated leaks to the news media involving intimate episodes between self-indulgent President Clinton and a libidinous young White House intern named Monica Lewinsky. Prosecutor Starr is not the first puritan who would wallow endlessly in sexual detail under the protective claim of serving a higher purpose. The possible impeachment for the President's lying about the affair gave the prosecutor a socially acceptable excuse for months of emphasis on erotic acts, all their possible variations, the precise location and physical positions of the partners, whether they had been orgasmic, and other tours of erotica.

But if the Office of the Independent Counsel seemed obsessed by details of consensual sex acts, the country's news media did not need to make them the top news for almost a year. The private lust of presidents has dotted U.S. history, but in the past it did not displace the nation's serious business in the news. Yet Starr's interminable investigation and leaks dominated most news outlets, including the *New York Times,* usually reported on page one and usually without attribution to any identifiable source. The Associated Press assigned twenty-five reporters to the story. On network television for 1998, there were six stories about the Oval Office encounters for every one story on that year's election campaign. Along the way, there were comically pretentious arguments over whether the United States Constitution's provision of "high crimes and misdemeanors" for removal of a President included concealment of consensual oral sex. The major media seemed as obsessed with sex as the President and Prosecutor Starr.

In the midst of the extended reporting, commentary, and solemn analyses of the whole affair, an editor of the supermarket checkout-counter scandal sheet *National Enquirer* said plaintively, "The *New York Times* isn't leaving anything for us."

The media sex obsession further lowered public respect for the major news media. The public watched the proceedings avidly, but they knew it was a sleazy substitute for important news. From start to end of the coverage of the scandal, public opinion surveys seldom varied from showing that 50 to 70 percent of those surveyed said that whether or not the sex stories were true, the news should turn to more serious issues.

The prolonged fixation on private sex acts in the White House was the product of more than fifteen years of degraded news standards in the major media. The *American Journalism Review* quoted the editor of a midsize Illinois daily paper as saying, "If a story needs a real investment of time and money, we don't do it anymore." In the void, media firms poured in sex, back-alley language, private-life gossip, and a general lowering of journalistic standards.

That process quickly enveloped political reporting. Private lives became substitutes for candidates' political ideas, past voting records, and proposals on important relevant issues. Voters too often came to know a candidate's choice of breakfasts and bedmates, but not his or her thoughts on the most pressing public issues.

All the News That's Fit to Print?

There is another landmark in the degradation of news: the increasing insertion of a news company's own business goals as a selection factor in what news the readers will be permitted to see—or not see.

Letting those who buy commercials influence the news has been rampant in local television news for years and was never totally absent in the daily printed news. But whenever this has been proven and publicized, it has been met with public disapproval, embarrassment by the offending media company, and condemnation by professional journalists. Within journalism, the ideal policy has always been proudly referred to as "The Wall of Separation Between Church and State." The newsroom was the Church, and the business side of the news company, the secular State.

But now demolition of the Wall has become an open and boasted policy by one of the country's most influential daily newspapers, a boast soon followed by other papers that, for the first time, confessed that they let advertisers influence the news and, more important, insisted that it was justified. The dramatic landmark of this change came in 1997 when Mark Willes, former president of a cereal company, became CEO and board chair of Times-Mirror Company and publisher of its flagship paper, the *Los Angeles Times,* one of the country's most powerful dailies. After he took over, Willes announced that from now on there would be no more Wall of Separation of Church and State in the *Los Angeles Times.* He was quoted in the *American Journalism Review,* "Every time they point it out, I get a bazooka and tell them if they don't take it down, I'm going to blow it down."

Willes radically reorganized every section of the paper, including the main news section. For the first time in modern newspaper history, the news no longer would be assigned by journalist-editors but by co-editors, one of them from the business department of the paper.

Willes did increase circulation slightly, at a time when other big dailies were losing daily sales, but did so by cutting the price to 25 cents. (The *New York Times* had a newsstand price of 60 cents in New York City and $1.00 elsewhere.) He said he would increase circulation by 50,000 in the next year, but it turned out to be no more than 17,000, and his paper lost 11 percent in revenues.

But clearly, Wall Street loved Willes's move. Two years later, Times-Mirror stock had tripled in price.

Nevertheless, a few months later, in November 1999, Otis Chandler, former publisher of the paper, who, with other members of his family, is a beneficiary of a trust that controls a majority of the company's stock, wrote a damning letter that called the latest news staff's involvement in a special corporate advertisement an "unbelievably stupid and unprofessional act" and "the most serious single threat to the future survival and growth of this great newspaper." Chandler had the letter read to the newsroom staff, which broke out in cheers.

When it was revealed that the *Los Angeles Times* had made a deal to split advertising profits of a regular editorial section with an outside business, it became the last straw for the paper's angry news staff. Management agreed to let the paper's media reporter, David Shaw, conduct an unobstructed investigation of how the profit-sharing deal with a news source had happened. Furthermore, it agreed that the full report would be edited by a recalled retired editor and printed in a regular edition of the paper without the normal editors and top management seeing the report. The result was a step-by-step dissection of a process and an attitude that has been seeping into the news business ever since non-news corporations have gained control of news outlets. The *Los Angeles Times* investigation report was an extraordinary fourteen-page insert in the December 20, 1999, edition of the paper. In effect, the report demonstrated that once the chairman of the board, Mark Willes, had flamboyantly shredded the separation between news and advertising, even good editors operating within Willes's quagmire had lost their ethical map. The result, in Mr. Shaw's words, was: ". . . a tangled tale of ignorance and arrogance, of blind loyalty and bad judgment, of deadened sensibilities and diminished standards."

The Separation represents centuries of tension between purity of news and greed of publishers. Before Willes, hardly anyone in journalism denied that pandering to advertisers in the news has been a sin that ethical editors regard as corruption. Consequently, his swaggering assertion had a historical impact. He "gave permission." A sin was now a virtue. Papers around the country—in Florida, Texas, Minnesota, Arizona, Kansas, Colorado, and Massachusetts, for example—followed the Willes policy openly and proudly. In 1999, the Fall River (Mass.) *Herald News* told advertisers that for every inch of advertising, the advertiser would get an inch of staff-written "news" items about the advertiser's business.

Willes did not replace pure virtue with pure evil. After his bazooka, his paper did not become a two-hundred-page throwaway shopper. It continued to report important stories, often admirable ones. But he had changed the public ethics of newspapering for a wide range of his fellow publishers. And his policy deepened public cynicism toward the news and its producers.

The contamination spread to magazines. In 1999, Sony, Philip Morris, Mercedes-Benz, and Starbucks began newsstand magazines that looked like all the others, and charged a cover price, but in fact consisted of articles written to boost the publishers' products.

Surveys show public trust of the news at record lows. When a nation's public no longer trusts the public information it receives, the society has become vulnerable to all the pitfalls of a cynical citizenry. The leader of the *Los Angeles Times* had let the moneylenders into the temple and had proclaimed loudly and proudly that this is where they belong.

The News That Wasn't There

It has been a truism, often issued with pride by the main media themselves, that the national news has a major impact on the national political agenda. What the main media emphasize is what politicians attend to. Whatever is not given steady emphasis in the news is more safely forgotten by those who make laws and regulations. Consequently, the media race for quick and easy profits that pushed the real issues into the shadows has imposed a high cost on American voters: it becomes easier for politicians to distract the public with false or exaggerated issues.

The years from 1995 to 1998 were a time of almost hysterical national and legislative debate on the "crisis" that seemed to demand drastic reduction of the national deficit and debt by a fixed, arbitrarily selected year and do so by cutting social programs. Most of this "crisis" was a false one, easily solved by even a minor restoration of past levels of a genuinely progressive income tax.

It is a necessary function of the news media to report what the government is doing. But it is equally essential to report reputable authorities who express views and realities that are contrary to the rhetoric of Congress, and to make clear the best known reliable information from independent authorities.

Robert Heilbroner, a respected, middle-of-the-road economist, demonstrated that the federal deficit during this "crisis" period was in no unusual relationship to the current size and growth of the national economy. Furthermore, he pointed out that the entire debt was in the form of Treasury bills held by citizens and banks, an important part of the economy. But his findings were not discussed in the mainstream media.

During the period of congressional obsession with cutting government programs, the country's wealth was really being transferred from the middle class and working poor to the richest levels of the population. Economist Lester Thurow, of the Massachusetts Institute of Technology, wrote in 1999 that the shift was so great in magnitude that probably no other country in history had experienced such a redistribution of its wealth without a revolution or losing a war.

At the time Thurow made that observation, the United States had and today still has the widest gap between its rich and nonrich of any industrialized democratic country. The heated "crisis" distracted the media and public from this disturbing fact. Here are some additional significant developments that should have influenced the congressional debate on cutting social programs to solve the deficit "crisis." All were enumerated through publicly available data and were reported in August of 1999 by *EXTRA!*, the publication of FAIR (Fairness and Accuracy in Reporting):

1. Thirty years ago, the top 1 percent of households owned 20 percent of the national wealth. While the "crisis" was hitting headlines, the top 1 percent had doubled its share of that wealth.

2. Thirty years ago, 10 percent of American households had no net worth or were in debt. During the "crisis," the number of households with zero or negative wealth had doubled.

3. During the congressional debate, blue-collar workers were making less in real dollars than they did thirty years ago, and four-fifths of all American households had lost the value of their net worth,

while the magical 1 percent at the top owned more wealth than the entire bottom 95 percent combined.

Less than two years after the debate had raged in Congress, some of the politicians who had insisted most strongly that a spending cap was needed to save the Republic were just as insistent on passing a budget that went well beyond their own bitterly established spending cap. And now they insisted that it be done in ways most beneficial to the rich.

Something else was occurring and went largely unreported in the mainstream news while cutbacks were made in social programs and welfare benefits for the poor. During this time, large corporations continued to get "corporate welfare" from the taxpayers—$125 billion worth—the equivalent of the total income taxes paid by 60 million individuals and families. This was in the form of tax forgiveness and actual payments to corporations for transferring their industries to foreign countries. Some of the corporate beneficiaries were AT&T, General Electric, and General Motors (all major owners in the media business), as well as other big industries. During this same period 300,000 jobs for working people disappeared within the United States.

This was revealed in a *Time* magazine special report in which two of the best-known investigative reporters in the country, Donald Barlett and James Steele, reported on the subject. To *Time*'s credit, it included a box in which the magazine announced "We Play the Game Too" and gave figures for money Time Warner had received from local governments. The article said Time Warner and other large corporations, including six substantial media firms, were asking New York City for "large incentives" to build new headquarters in Manhattan.

If this kind of information about the nonexistent "debt crisis" and continuing corporate welfare—all readily available at the time— had been in the main news during the national debate, it would have altered the debate and bettered the lives of the majority of Americans. It would have helped protect the poor, who in the false "crisis" lost food stamps and saw Head Start classes cut back to levels where they remain limited today.

Making More and Reporting Less

As dominant media firms became larger and more profitable, they cut the quality of their news in another important category: foreign news. Until the Serbian genocidal war against Kosovo generated large-scale continuous reporting, the major media companies had spent years shrinking their coverage of foreign news.

In 1998, the television networks carried half the international news they did in the 1980s. Peter Arnett, the veteran correspondent, writing in the November 1998 *American Journalism Review,* said: "I'll put it simply: International news coverage in most of America's mainstream papers has almost reached the vanishing point. Today, a foreign story that doesn't involve bombs, natural disasters, or financial calamity has little chance of entering the American consciousness. . . ."

The main news media have had other profound flaws in the recent past. During most of the Cold War, major media news followed the official U.S. government line almost as closely as the Soviet media of the time followed the Kremlin line. Where foreign forces failed to follow desired U.S. ideology and politics, they were reported as terrorist threats that required opposition by the United States. Thus, in Nicaragua, El Salvador, Guatemala, East Timor, and throughout most of the Latin American dictatorships, regimes were committing frightful atrocities against dissenters with the financial and military support of the United States. Such violence was described repeatedly by the mainstream media as part of a noble American effort to preserve democracy.

The main media have done little to repair their self-censorship. The 1999 detention of General Pinochet in England, for example, was front-page news in America for weeks as Spain demanded his extradition so that he could be tried for his death squads and the terror in Chile committed during his regime. But there was almost nothing in the American mainstream media that reported that Pinochet's violence against dissenters had been supported by the United States through this nation's help in destabilizing the leftist regime of the democratically elected Salvador Allende government and support of Allende's assassination in 1973, both of which made way for seventeen years of Pinochet and his terror squads.

American responsibility for terror in Guatemala has been similarly underreported by the main media. It was still possible for the *New York Times* of February 7, 1999, to print in its Sunday magazine an 8,500-word article describing the fate of a Guatemalan village in wrenching details—the murders, kidnapping of children, and mass disappearances of dissenters by government-sponsored death squads—

with only a six-word subordinate phrase in the sixth paragraph to let the reader know that, in the name of suppressing leftist regimes, those atrocities had received the financial support of the United States. Nor did the article report that leaders of the "security forces" (death squads) had been brought to the United States for training in the U.S. Army's "School of the Americas." When Congress closed the "School" in 1999, it was reported in a brief item on the second page of the *New York Times* and largely ignored in other main media.

Not until twenty years after these events had occurred in Guatemala, in August of 1999, did the *New York Times* describe in more than a phrase how the United States had trained and supported torture and "disappearances" by Latin American "security forces." Most of the rest of the media kept this ugly part of the American record an obscure footnote, if they reported it at all.

If the news is the first rough draft of history, the major American news organizations have a disreputable Cold War record of distorting the first draft, and then years after the Cold War's end, the second draft of their country's own history. This is not a promising record in the light of the old dictum that those who ignore the mistakes of history are destined to repeat them.

Print, Radio, and TV Survive

Ever since the adoption of popular radio, the death of print has been regularly intoned by those who find it hard to see how printing words on paper, with its slow, cumbersome, and expensive process, could possibly survive in a world of instant electronic information. Media corporations themselves sometimes abandon print. Disney, for example, has sold many of its newspapers and magazines (but to other large print media). Nevertheless, the new cyber world, as with most earlier technological innovations through history, has not caused older established devices to disappear, even if the older media forms are faced with relinquishing center stage.

Daily newspapers are learning that evolution. The "cyber-electronic twenty-first century" begins with the print world still alive and more profitable than ever, though understandably filled with anxiety. Average daily circulation of U.S. dailies has been dropping for years, even as the number of households climbs. In 1970, people bought 62 million daily papers a day at a time when there were 63 million households. By 1999, daily newspaper circulation had dropped to 52 million but there were 100 million households. The growth of non-newspaper homes was dramatic. Big-city afternoon papers died as people listened to radio news while they drove home from work and then watched evening television. Nonetheless, among all mass media, newspapers continue to get the highest percentage of dollars spent on advertising, and newspaper industry profits average more than 20 percent.

The ownership of newspapers, like other media, went through a radical reversal after World War II. In 1946, three-quarters of all dailies were owned by local families and associates. Today, less than 2 percent of the country's fifteen hundred dailies are family owned. Most of the rest are owned by large national chains, whose top companies, in rank of total circulation, are Gannett, Knight Ridder, Newhouse, Dow Jones, Times Mirror, New York Times Co., and Hearst. Ninety-nine percent are monopolies in their own cities.

These same "newspaper companies" are, without exception, also owners of electronic media and are well aware that their television and cable properties pay even higher profit margins than their newspapers. Many observers predict that readers and owners will soon abandon dailies. But, as described later in this book, the United States, uniquely among major nations, leaves a multitude of vital questions to local voters. Since most local television news is disreputably void in daily coverage of civic bodies, except when melodramatic camera shots are possible, and since no other medium even attempts systematic reporting on local schools, taxes, policing, land use, and other relevant civic news, it is likely that members of today's young cyber-oriented generation will still read daily papers when their children are born.

In the past, local alternative weeklies did for their communities what liberal journals like *EXTRA!*, *The Nation*, and *The Progressive* do nationally. In the 1960s, these weeklies were the only local source of the antiestablishment news and commentary not seen in their nearby metropolitan dailies. But by the end of the 1990s, most alternative weeklies had been bought up as chains for maximizing profit, usually without their past political values. Only a few remained vigorous supporters of the underdog and critics of the local mainstream press.

Magazines have continued to enjoy their charmed life in the history of American printed media. In 1999, magazines as a whole had $11 billion in revenues and were enjoying 4 percent annual growth. Many behaved like recombinant DNA molecules, a single big-name magazine giving birth to several specialized offspring bearing parental surnames. *National Geographic* gave birth to *National Geographic Adventure,* and *Sports Illustrated* to *Sports Illustrated for Kids.* As individual publications, *TV Guide* continued to have the largest circulation, while *People* ran second, and *Sports Illustrated* third. In August of 1999, when Disney sold its Fairchild group to Condé Nast, it further concentrated the magazine field among the three leading conglomerates, Time Warner, Condé Nast, and Hearst.

TV Set versus the Computer?

The impression that all of young America has abandoned radio and television in its obsession with the Internet is not strictly true. The "classical" three networks—ABC, CBS (now a division within Viacom), and NBC—have maintained most of their traditional audiences and still get 40 percent of all television revenues. They average 25 percent profit a year, and the top twenty-five owners of television stations control 36 percent of the country's 12,000 commercial stations. But major network audiences are getting older, and the favored target of advertising is the youth market, which brackets people between the ages of eighteen and thirty-four, and in recent years has been expanded to those as ancient as forty-nine years old. These are the viewers and listeners most apt to spend the most money. During the last five years, network broadcasters' share of audience went from 69 percent to 55 percent, with most of the loss being gained by cable. This outcome has heightened the energy and deepened the angst of broadcasters and cable operators fighting for younger viewers.

There are now six networks: Fox, UPN (United Paramount Network, also owned by Viacom), and WB (Warner Brothers), plus the older three, ABC, CBS, and NBC. The increase fuels their fight for shares of a total TV audience that shrank by 9 percent in the 1998–99 broadcast season. The ten largest cable systems have three-quarters of the 67 million households connected to cable. The top cable company is AT&T, followed by Time Warner, Comcast, and Cox. The fifteen largest radio broadcasters have 42 percent of the television audience. Though many of the young seem to prefer their computers, TV ads in 1999 would bring in almost $37 billion, $11 billion for cable, and $16 billion for radio, money none of these media are ready to abandon.

Profits for networks and their affiliates remain almost obscenely high, especially for local stations, given how little effort they expend to make their money. Mainly, they throw a switch for a satellite feed from a network or programming syndicate, and on their own give the briefest local news, while going overboard on weather and sports. Barry Diller, chief of USA Networks, has said of local TV stations: "This is a business where if you are a birdbrain you have a thirty-five-percent margin. Many good broadcasters have a forty-to-sixty-percent margin. And you get it for free. . . . "

Advertising money flows lemming-like to major sports events. Before the 1999 Super Bowl XXXIII, Fox, which had the franchise for the football game, said it would charge $53,333 per second for commercials.

Commercial radio has become mainly a set of about half a dozen fixed formulas heard uniformly throughout the country. That is one reason why the number of households tuning in to stations financed by the Corporation for Public Broadcasting has doubled in the last five years. The largest (but not the only) noncommercial radio, National Public Radio, has seven hundred stations broadcasting NPR programs during most of their broadcast day. In addition, there are growing informal networks of alternative radio stations and individual broadcasters who create "networks" by mailing studio-quality audiocassettes to hundreds of stations.

Noncommercial television and radio continue to endure despite congressional hostility, suspicion, and niggardly federal appropriations. Though the noncommercial stations have far smaller audiences than the large commercial broadcasters, their collective audiences can still raise ratings enough to cause commercial stations to lust after them. Their appeal is undoubtedly increased by the hysteria that occurs in commercial broadcasting when surveys show even fractional differences among the contenders. Even more important than their audience size is the fact that the content of noncommercial broadcasts reminds the public that there are interesting, nonstereotyped, and often superior programs seldom heard or seen in the mainstream commercial airwaves. Furthermore, the major noncommercial stations draw some of the most desirable audience in terms of average income, education, and influence.

At century's end, that now elderly medium, motion pictures, is still making a great deal of money, though less than before the advent of television. In 1946, the motion picture industry sold 4.7 billion admission tickets, or thirty-three per capita. By 1999, the ticket sales were 1.3 billion, five per capita, with five theater chains getting most of the business: Regal, Loew's Cineplex, Carmike, SMC, and United Artists. The big production studios are now part of the major media empires, Time Warner (Warner Brothers movies), MGM, Viacom (Paramount), Sony, Disney, and 20th-Century Fox (Murdoch's News Corp). The industry still has $6 billion a year in revenues. Time Warner makes the most money, followed by Disney, Viacom, Sony, 20th-Century Fox, and MGM. In 1999 there were 26,000 screens in the United States, most of them multi-screen complexes within the same building or drive-in. They have added to their movie revenues by a total of $30 billion from follow-up showings on cable and $19 billion from home videocassette sales and rentals (Viacom, for example, owns the Blockbuster chain), not to mention their significant income from popcorn and soft drinks sold in theater lobbies.

Most big media companies have cashed in on tie-in sales with their movies. They frequently and deliberately insert saleable commodities into the scripts and scenes. Delay in release of the movie *Babe: Pig in the City* in 1998 created a crisis for Viacom's Universal Studios because the timing had been closely tied in with a hundred companies around the world that were opening their sales of pig babies, pig dolls, pig CD-ROMs, and talking pigs.

The top owners of another older medium, recordings, are the same corporations that control other media. The big five are Seagram's Polygram (with 25 percent of the U.S. and European markets), Sony, Time Warner, Bertelsmann, and Universal.

In the midst of growth and excitement about the Internet and the cyber revolution, the "old" media survive and, for the most part, produce the highest profits in their history.

Violence Still Raises Its Ugly Head

No matter what else may change in the world of television and cable, violence, with its proven social damage, remains as the attention-grabber-of-choice for commercial broadcasters who remain deaf to pleas from broad segments of the public. And in the absence of FCC action or congressional mandate, the broadcasters do their killing both on the screen and at the bank. They take both their money and their licenses for granted. They ignore survey after survey of parents, like one sponsored by the Benton Foundation in which 87 percent of parents wanted to limit commercials shown during children's programs, and 85 percent wanted more adult and community college courses offered on television.

The *Journal of the American Medical Association* has said that children between the ages of two and seventeen watch an annual average of 15,000 to 18,000 hours of television, compared with 12,000 hours spent per year in school. Children are also major targets for TV advertising, whose impact is greater than usual because there is an apparent lessening of influence by parents and others in the older generation. Prof. William Damon, director of the Stanford University Center on Adolescence, has said, "There has never in the history of the civilized world been a cohort of kids that is so little affected by adult guidance and so attuned to a peer world." Whole neighborhoods are adultless as single or both parents work during the day or much of the evening. Television increasingly has become the national educator, sex instructor, voyeur, baby-sitter—and substitute parent.

A report of a commission of the American Psychological Association has stated: "There is absolutely no doubt that higher levels of viewing violence on television are correlated with increased acceptance of aggressive attitudes and increased aggressive behavior." And the Committee on Communications of the American Academy of Pediatrics has reported, "By age 18, the average young person will have viewed an estimated 200,000 acts of violence on television alone. Video game violence, children's cartoons, and music lyrics have become ever increasingly graphic. In movies, action films depict anatomically precise murders, rapes, and assaults; with each sequel, the number of deaths increase dramatically. Although media violence is not the only cause of violence in American society, it is the single most easily remediable contributing factor. . . . At young ages, children . . . quickly learn that violence is an acceptable solution to resolving even complex problems, particularly if the aggressor is the hero." According to the Academy, children under age two should not watch television at all because at that age, brain development depends heavily on real human interactions. Nevertheless, $1 billion a year is spent on ads and commercials directed at children.

Books—Grandfather of Them All

In the age of the Internet, books, for more than 2,300 years the foundation for all mass media, remain alive, though annual sales increases have become more modest in recent years.

Even so, conventional books, both hardcover and mass market paperbacks, along with texts and specialized books, have $50 billion annual revenues. Books continue to sell to a generation seen as image-oriented and no longer interested in words printed on paper.

Between 1982 and 1997, book sales rose from 1.7 billion to 2.2 billion volumes, with prices that rose an average of almost three times per book. The dominant firms had most of the profits; 80 percent of smaller companies had gross revenues of less than $2 million a year each.

The five largest book publishers are Bertelsmann, by far the largest with 10 percent of all English-language book sales in the world, followed by Time Warner, Disney, Viacom (owner of, among other firms, Simon & Schuster), and News Corp. Thus two of the firms are based abroad, Bertelsmann in Germany and Murdoch's News Corp in Australia.

Bertelsmann's power in the marketplace is unmatched. It is the world's third largest conglomerate, with substantial ownership of magazines, newspapers, music, television, on-line trading, films, and radio in fifty-three countries. It has a major stake in the U.S. Internet service provider America Online (AOL) and a 50 percent interest in barnesandnoble.com. By purchasing Random House, it acquired a publisher that already had under its wing fifty formerly independent publishing houses and imprints, among them Knopf, Pantheon, Crown, Fawcett, Ballantine, Vintage, Anchor, Bantam, Doubleday, Dell, and Delacorte.

With each succeeding consolidation of publishing houses, the merged publishers cut back on the number of titles each had published while independent. Contracts with authors have been canceled and books in process eliminated or shredded.

Andre Schiffrin, former director of the once prestigious Pantheon Press, has said that since their emergence as consolidated giants, none of the three leading book firms has published a book of serious history, scientific inquiry, or translation. Medium and small publishers still publish serious books, but they lack the power to produce and promote books at a level that is competitive with the major firms, and they lack equal access to the global sales machinery.

There could be turbulence ahead. Electronic firms have announced models of "electronic books," one of them a handheld computer that measures four and one-half by three inches, and can hold the equivalent of ten four-hundred-page novels, each "page" turned by pressing a button.

Bertelsmann and News Corp demonstrate that their disproportionate market power is not just in the marketplace to dominate what the public will read. They can decide what the public will not read. As mentioned previously, Murdoch did it in the case of China. Bertelsmann, with its multimedia control, especially in Germany, successfully concealed a Nazi past that it had previously minimized or denied. When German sociologist and writer Hersch Fischler looked into the archives, he discovered that despite its claim of resistance and suffering under Hitler, Bertelsmann, throughout the Nazi period, had published anti-Semitic tracts for Hitler's Brown Shirts and members of the German army, praising Hitler and the Nazi movement, and also a book, *People Without Space*, a work that justified Hitler's invasions of nearby countries. Fischler could not get his findings published in Germany, given Bertelsmann's influence there. They were published by a Swiss magazine and ultimately in the United States in *The Nation*.

Selling Books

Once a staid and genteel business, even touchy about being called "a business," bookselling has become a cut-price, cutthroat operation as competitors fight for the largest share of the more than $26 billion book market in the United States. It is a scramble so wild, convoluted, and interlocked with the Internet that it now resembles a serpent eating its own tail.

In the melee of big corporate chain stores and the Internet competing to sell books, independent local bookstores, once the mainstay of the business, are now fighting for their lives. Andy Ross, owner of Cody's Book Store in Berkeley, California, one of the largest independent bookstores in the country, says that as recently as 1990, independent stores like his accounted for 32 percent of all national book sales, but by 1999 this figure has dropped to 19 percent.

The bookselling world has seen its residents supplanted by ever greater giants and would-be giants. Crown was followed by B. Dalton and Walden Books, which were followed by Barnes & Noble, the biggest bookstore, followed by Borders, the second largest in the country. The scene was thrown into a new spasm by the appearance of an Internet phenomenon called Amazon.com. Amazon.com claimed to be the planet's largest "bookstore" because you could sit at a computer and order a book from a list of three million titles and have it delivered in a few days by the U.S. Postal Service.

The race was also in price cutting. Barnes & Noble offered 50 percent discounts for books from the *New York Times*'s best-seller list. The *New York Times Book Review* entered into a financial agreement with Barnes & Noble. It agreed to place after each review in the paper's Internet version an electronic link to barnesandnoble.com. This presented the consumer with an instant way to order from one favored bookseller a book that the *Times* had just reviewed. The Barnes & Noble Internet site, claiming 4.5 million titles, also made a sales alliance with Microsoft's MSN. Borders by this time also offered 50 percent discounts on the *Times* best-seller list.

After Bertelsmann paid $200 million for a 50 percent interest in Barnes & Noble's Internet site, Books-a-Million, another Internet bookseller, agreed to be the exclusive supplier of discount books for Wal-Mart, the country's largest retailer (with bricks-and-mortar stores in bricks-and-mortar communities), with a discount of 55 percent on *New York Times* best-sellers.

Rebellions in the Ranks

Rebellions against the major media have become more numerous and dramatic. They protest the mainstream media's indifference to serving basic public needs. The protests also reflect frustration with government regulatory agencies that have ignored widespread public demands for less violence on television and more access by local groups to the broadcast stations in their own communities.

The rebellion in radio practiced a new technological form of civil disobedience. In 1993, Stephen Dunifer, a Berkeley, California, electrical engineer, assembled a low-power radio station in his van, drove to the nearby hills, and began broadcasting "Radio Free Berkeley." When the FCC warned Dunifer, he simply drove his van to new hillside locations. He was finally charged with broadcasting without a license, a federal offense. His lawyer noted in court that for the last twenty-eight years, the FCC had failed to grant any license for low-powered stations of 1,000 watts or less. Low-powered stations, like those permitted in Canada, Japan, and other countries, make it possible to limit range to neighborhoods and individual communities. Instead, the FCC typically issued 50,000-watt licenses, mostly to commercial stations, permitting them to reach broad regional retail trade zones, a large area that greatly increases profits from commercials. The FCC did not require the powerful stations to offer authentic public services or grant access to local groups.

Dunifer's prosecution brought to light a large underground of "pirate," or unlicensed, low-powered, community-range stations, perhaps as many as 1,000 in cities and neighborhoods around the country. As secret operations, their precise numbers are unknown, but the FCC formally closed 360 such stations.

The rebellion had its effect. In 1999, the FCC proposed new rules for lower-powered stations with 1,000-watt licenses.

On another front, there have been decades of unending and futile complaints by parents, educators, psychologists, two different surgeons general of the United States, and even a plea from the president of the United States against pervasive violence on television and movies. A new form of protest appeared in a number of full-page ads in the *New York Times.* Typically, one displayed a large photograph of Steve Allen, the popular entertainer and broadcaster, with the large-type heading: "Parents . . . Grandparents . . . Families . . . This is for YOU—TV IS LEADING CHILDREN DOWN A MORAL SEWER . . . How You and I Can Stop It." The sponsor of the ad was listed as the Parents Television Council, based in Los Angeles.

There has also been an ideological rebellion. As noted earlier, major media news and commentary are heavily concentrated on center-to-right politics, with an almost total absence of progressive views. Organizations attempting to correct the imbalance or other inadequacies include, among many others, the Center for Media Education, in Washington, which monitors telecommunications laws and regulations in order to alert the public to measures that attempt to further limit diversity and that show indifference to the needs of children and serious adult viewing. The Institute for Public Accuracy, in San Francisco, performs analyses of the conservative think tank data and public relations on which mainstream news outlets rely heavily. A number of progressive interview programs, like "Alternative Radio," based in Boulder, Colorado, have arisen, using audio Q&As for rebroadcast around the country and internationally. The International Media Project, based in Portola Valley, California, performs a similar function by forming a worldwide coalition of like-minded radio reformers. The Cultural Environment Movement, based in Philadelphia, also is forming worldwide coalitions.

For more than thirty years, various academics, national foundations, and media reform groups have proposed new ways to provide ample, nonpolitical funding for national noncommercial radio and television networks. They have advocated financing by various fixed excise taxes to replace the Corporation for Public Broadcasting, which lives in constant fear that its appropriations will be blocked by members of Congress who are seeking to protect commercial broadcasters and conservative views.

The drastic shrinkage in the number of independent bookstores in the face of competition with big chains and their Internet sales has led the American Booksellers Association to fight back by creating its own web site, BookSense, to serve eleven hundred independent bookstores. The ABA hopes this move will stop or reverse the loss of independent stores, whose number has gone from 5,200 to 3,300 in the last several years.

The once quiet world of scholarly and scientific research articles has experienced its own rebellion in reaction to steep price increases imposed by two large Dutch firms, Reed Elsevier and Wolters Kluwer, and a few other similar consolidated companies. The higher costs have forced libraries, especially university research libraries (and their faculties), to drop subscriptions drastically. After the major corporate consolidations, average prices charged for journals rose 20 to 30 percent, though in some individual instances it has been even more. The journal *Brain,* for example, more than doubled in price to $15,000 a year. It is these articles and books that lie at the heart of university research and the ability of scholars and scientists to keep abreast of current developments in their fields.

Dr. Michael Rosenzweig, a sociologist at the University of Arizona at Tucson, and his wife, Carole, started the rebellion in scholarly publications in 1986 when the journal in their field that he had helped create, *Evolutionary Ecology,* raised its subscription price to $8,000 a year. Key to the authority of any scholarly journal is its board of editors, and when the Rosenzweigs started their own *Evolutionary Ecology Research,* with an annual subscription price of $353, the whole board of editors from the former journal defected with Dr. Rosenzweig. More than a hundred libraries joined, including some of the most prestigious in the country, like Harvard, Yale, Columbia, and the

University of California. Their new organization is SPARC (Scholarly Publishing and Academic Resources Coalition).

Even the commanding role of Bill Gates's Microsoft is challenged by programmers of the original noncommercial breed who have invented Linux, an operating system that can be downloaded without charge to replace major functions of Windows and other commercially sold systems.

Can It Be Changed?

For the last thirty years, government agencies and the Congress have been wedded to the "free market," an oxymoron when it describes political and corporate tolerance of conglomeration and monopoly. In past decades, the most common remedy for excessive market domination has been the Anti-Trust Act, which is supposed to break up alliances and mergers that reduce competition.

Contrary to the present conventional wisdom that antitrust law cannot work, when it became an almost established fact that the big bookseller Barnes & Noble would merge with Ingram, the country's largest supplier of books to bookstores, an intense campaign by independent booksellers caused lawyers in the Federal Trade Commission to murmur that they were considering legal action to block the merger. The two corporate parties abandoned their plan. But it was a rare murmur and a rare victory.

The most effective remedies require congressional and White House approval, and most fail because the telecommunications industry is the fourth largest contributor to political campaigns. The recent Gore Commission on the future of broadcasting entered the field like a lion. But after the head of CBS threatened a "declaration of war" if Gore recommended specifics for "serving the public interest," Gore's report emerged like a lamb. The problem is money. Viacom's CBS and its allies in broadcasting have a great deal of money. (Subsequent chapters in this book describe the swift evolution by which the major mass media in the United States began their race toward their present power.)

Government indifference to the immense and still growing power of major media corporations has left the task of protecting consumers from exploitative prices and harmful media content to individual and citizen action groups. These groups have done and continue to do vital service to keep the public informed and to keep alive the struggle for a better media world.

But no citizen action group has the money to match the private corporate funds that flood the American political system. On lobbying alone, more than $1.4 billion a year is spent in Washington. This breaks down to $2.7 million and 38 lobbyists for each of the 535 members of Congress. By far, most of the money comes from corporations; most of the lobbyists work for corporate interests.

Consequently, there is a fundamental need for basic and sweeping campaign reform and drastic curtailment of money used for lobbying. That happens to be an issue that major newspapers editorially support, and one in which they can play a dramatic role, if in their coverage of crucial issues with wide public consequences they would list by name each member of Congress with an influential role in the fate of the measure and every source and amount of financial contributions from any entity with a clear stake in the outcome. This would make it explicit if private money is in danger of prevailing and help illuminate the insidious, behind-the-scenes buying of the country's laws.

There is convincing evidence that the relationship between big money and political votes already angers most voters. An aroused public can make a difference. The environmental movement that transformed the legislative and natural landscape began as a grassroots movement without initiative from the standard political parties and with powerful opposition from industry. When conservatives in Congress moved to abolish public broadcasting, House and Senate members were stunned and retreated when citizens, Republicans and Democrats alike, rose in unison in anger against the move.

Voters are rebelling. As public complaints escalate, more of the public expresses open disgust. New parties slowly gather strength. The general public is more vocal than ever about irresponsible mass media. The two standard parties are hemorrhaging votes to a vague and growing category entitled "Independent." Many voters have stopped voting or are electing candidates formerly considered unelectable, or others that are bizarre nonentities. These changes reflect growing voter rejection of contemporary politics, the same kind of dismissal as implied by Ralph Nader's proposal of a ballot line that offers "None of the above."

The power of corporate money to stop reforms cannot continue without further erosion of the relevant and responsible public information needed to sustain the American democracy.

It is true that corporate money in politics acts with swift and arrogant certitude. An informed public responds more slowly, but it does make the final decisions on election day.

In the fabled race between the swift-and-overconfident hare and the slow-but-steady tortoise, it helps to remember who crossed the finish line first.

The race is not always to the swift.

Notes

The *New York Times* was used extensively as a source because it is regarded as the country's most authoritative and widespread source of foreign and domestic news and because hundreds of client papers throughout the country use its news service. Spot checks of other papers showed that most did far less than the *Times*. So major media failures or inadequacies in reporting public information needed for properly informed voters throughout the country is, if anything, understated. Important lapses or inadequate accounts frequently are attributed to the *Times* for the same reason, though such negative judgments are by no means limited to the *Times*. Note: earlier editions of *The Statistical Abstract of the United States* indexed data by page number, but more recent editions index by table number.

x   Six firms dominate. http://cgi.pathfinder.com/fortune/global500/500list2.html and http://www.forbes.com/tool/toolbox/privateasp/rankindex.asp?index=500.

x   The top six firms. wysiwyg://428/http://www.cjr.org/owners/ (Cjr=*Columbia Journalism Review*);*New York Times,* 8 September 1999, 1.

xii   Symbolically, *the* largest. http://cgi.pathfinder.com/fortune/global500/500 list2.html and *New York Times,* 16 July 1999, 1.

xii   The power and influence. *New York Times,* 29 February 1996, 3.

xii   News reporting and commentary. 1999 Roper Center for Public Opinion Research, Question ID: USMS. 99 Feb R20.022;*EXTRA!,* July/August 1997, 24.

xiii   But with each passing. *University of California Berkeley Wellness Letter,* June 1999, 8.

xiii   Internet capabilities have. *College English,* May 1999, 532; *National Writers Union Hearsay,* November 1998, 4.

xiii   The Internet's growth and. *Business Week,* 17 May 1999, 108.

xiv   Nevertheless, despite their. *New York Times,* 9 July 1999,13; *American Journalism Review,* March 1999, 28; and "Death of Print," *Columbia Journalism Review,* January/February 1999, 56.

xiv   The U.S. Postal. *New York Times,* 20 February 1999, A-15, and 27 May 1999, B-1; 10 July 1999, B-1.

xiv   The new medium marches. *New York Times,* 10 July 1999, B-1.

xv   By mid-1999. *San Francisco Chronicle,* 8 July 1999, B-1; *Hoover's Online: Internet/OnLine,* wysiwyg://700http://hovweb.hoovers.com, 2. The 35 percent.

San Francisco Chronicle, 25 March 1999, D-1. Though the total potential. "Intrusive Ads," *Brill's Content,* February, 1999, 64; On-line marketing is. *New York Times,* 25 February 1999, C-3.

xvi   Today, that political. *New York Times,* 16 March 1999, 3.

xvi   Positive accomplishments of. *New York Times,* 6 April 1998, 1.

xvi   The fifth edition of this. See *The Media Monopoly* (Beacon Press, 1997), ix–xxxv.

xvii   In 1998 alone. *New York Times,* 5 January 1999, B-1; *New York Times,* 13 December 1998, C-1.

xviii   When new legislation. *New York Times,* 2 June 1999.

xviii   The leading media. *Wall Street Journal,* 17 January 1995, B-4.

xviii   The American public. *New York Times,* Editorial, 26 December 1998, A-24.

xix   The Disney Company. http://disney.go.com/investors/annual98/consumer.htm, under "Disney Consumer Products." *Lion King* painting price, personal inquiry at Disney Store, 400 Post Street, San Francisco.

xix   The twenty-two major. 1998 Annual Report of the Disney Company, on Internet site, ibid. Sale of *Women's Wear Daily, New York Times,* 20 August 1999, C-1. Ownership of interest in Infoseek and ESPN, and ESPN on Disney cruise ships, 1998 Annual Report of the Disney Company.

xx   When the first edition. Beacon Press, 1983; 2d ed., 1987; 3rd ed., 1990; 4th ed., 1992; 5th ed., 1997.

xxi   As the dominant. *New York Times,* 8 July 1996, C-6.

xxii   Corporate interlocks may. *Wall Street Journal,* 31 March 1999, B-8; *Statistical Abstract of the United States 1998,* Table 721.

xxii   As usual, Rupert. *The Nation,* 8 June 1998, 18; *The Economist,* 20 March 1999, 73.

xxiii   But for all. *Columbia Journalism Review,* May/June 1998, 51.

xxiii   The trend in violence. *New York Times,* 19 July 1999, C-1.

xxiv   But if the Office. *Columbia Journalism Review,* March/April 1998, 19; *EXTRA!,* November/December 1998, 15.

xxiv   In the midst. Statement confirmed by personal call to an editor of *National Enquirer,* 6 April 1999.

xxiv   The media sex obsession. *The Nation,* 5 February 1996, 25; *Columbia Journalism Review,* May/June 1999, 35.

xxiv   The prolonged fixation. *Columbia Journalism Review,* July/August, 1998, 13.

xxv   The dramatic landmark. *Columbia Journalism Review,* January/February 1998, 20; *American Journalism Review,* October 1997, 13.

xxvi   Willes did increase. *Columbia Journalism Review,* January/February 1999, 54.

xxvi   Nevertheless. *Los Angeles Times,* 4 November 1999, C-1.

xxvi   The Separation represents. *Columbia Journalism Review,* March/April 1999, 28.

xxvii   The contamination spread. *New York Times,* 6 September 1999, C-6.

xxviii   Robert Heilbroner, a. Robert Heilbroner, "The Devil Words: 'Debt' and 'Deficit,'" *Center for Democratic Values,* 1997.

xxviii During the period. Lester Thurow, *Building Wealth* (New York: HarperBusiness, 1999).

xxviii At the time. *FAIR,* July/August 1999, 9.

xix Less than two years. *New York Times,* 31 July 1999, 1.

xix Something else was. "Corporate Welfare," *Time,* 9 November 1998, 34; *New York Times,* 8 December 1998, C-27; *Takeover Magazine,* June 1999, 13.

xix As dominant media. *American Journalism Review,* November 1998, 51; *New York Times,* 8 September 1999, 1. In 1998, the television networks *FAIR, Inside the New York Times,* undated, Summer 1999, 1; Committee for the Study of the American Electorate, reported in *New York Times,* 6 November 1998, A-22; Peter Arnett, *American Journalism Review,* November 1998, 51.

xxx The main media have done. *The Progressive,* 30 February 1999, 28.

xxx American responsibility for. *New York Times,* 23 February 1999, D-1; *The Nation,* 22 March 1999, 5; *New York Times,* 31 July 1999, 2.

xxxi Daily newspapers are. *Morton Research, Inc.,* January–June 1997, Table 8; *Columbia Journalism Review,* July/August 1998, 28; *Hoover's Online,* 15 March 1999, 1; In 1970. *Historical Statistics of the U.S., Vol. II,* 809; *Statistical Abstract of the United States, 1998,* 572, Table 915.

xxxii The ownership of. *American Journalism Review,* June 1998, 20. Most of the rest. *Hoover's Online,* 15 April 1999, 1 (ranking of top companies by total circulation).

xxxii In the past. *The Nation,* 29 June 1998, 10.

xxxii Magazines have continued. *Hoover's Online,* 15 April 1999, 15 April 1999. 1. *San Francisco Chronicle,* 13 August 1999, B-1; *New York Times,* 20 August 1999, C-1.

xxxiii The impression that. *New York Times,* 17 May 1998, A-17; *Standard & Poor's Industrial Survey, Broadcasting and Cable,* 2 July 1998; *New York Times,* 8 June 1999, C-10.

xxxiii There are now six. *New York Times,* 17 May 1998, A-17; *Standard & Poor's Industrial Survey, Broadcasting and Cable,* 2 July 1998; *New York Times,* 21 December 1998, sec. 3, 1.

xxxiv "This is a business. *The New Yorker,* 9 November 1998, 34.

xxxiv Advertising money flows. *New York Times,* 28 January 1999, C-1.

xxxiv Commercial radio has. *New York Times,* 5 April 1999, C-5.

xxxiv At century's end. *Hoover's Online,* "Industry Zone, Movies & Music," 5 April 1999, 1. *Hoover's Online,* 15 April 1999, 1.

xxxv Most big media companies. *San Francisco Chronicle,* 30 November 1998, D-5.

xxxv The top owners of another. *New York Times,* 21 December 1998, B-1.

xxxv No matter what else. Lake Snell Perry & Associates, 14 January 1999, 2.

xxxvi The *Journal of the American Medical. University of California, Berkeley, Wellness Letter,* July 1988, 1; *New York Times,* 30 May 1999, B-1.

xxxvi A report of a commission. *New York Times,* 9 May 1999, 23; American Academy of Pediatrics, *Media Violence (RE9526),* June 1995, 949–951; *New York Times,* 19 April 1999, C-1.

xxxvi   In the age of. *Hoover's Online,* "Publishing & Printing," wysiwyg://673http: //hoovweb.hoovers.com/features/industry/publish.html, 15 April 1999.

xxxvii   Between 1982. *Statistical Abstract of the United States, 1998,* Tables 425, 428; *Hoover's Online,* ibid.

xxxvii   The five largest book. *New York Times,* 1 January 1999, C-1.

xxxvii   Bertelsmann's power in. *New York Times,* 24 May 1999, C-1.

xxxvii   Andre Schiffrin, former. *The Nation,* 5 July 1999, 10.

xxxvii   There could be turbulence. *New York Times,* 10 May 1999, C-1.

xxxviii   Bertelsmann and News Corp. When a German sociologist. *The Nation Digital Edition,* www.thenation.com/issue/981228/1228fisch.htm; accessed 16 April 1999.

xxxviii   Once a staid. *Statistical Abstract of the United States, 1998,* Table 425.

xxxviii   In the melee of. *Cody's Book Store News,* March 1999 Calendar.

xxxix   The race was. *Holt Uncensored,* No. 96, 8 June 1999; *San Francisco Chronicle,* 5 June 1999, D-1; *New York Times,* 9 December 1998, B-1; *New York Times,* 8 December 1998, C-6.

xxxix   After Bertelsmann paid. *Holt Uncensored,* No. 73, 5.

xxxix   The rebellion in radio. Federal Communications Commission v. Stephen O. Dunifer, Northern District of California, Case No. C-943542 CW.

xl   The rebellion had its effect. *New York Times,* 29 January 1999, C-1; *American Journalism Review,* June 1998, 46.

xl   On another front. *New York Times,* 23 May 1999, 18; *New York Times,* 15 August 1999, 35.

xl   There has also been. *EXTRA!,* July/August 1997, 24.

xli   The drastic shrinkage. *Holt Uncensored,* No. 57, 3 May 1999, 3. *Book Passage,* "Books on the Brink," Corte Madera, California, February 1999; *San Francisco Chronicle,* 24 May 1999, B-1.

xli   The once quiet world. *ARL,* Association of Research Libraries, December 1998, 3-7; *New York Times,* 8 December 1998, D-2.

xli   Dr. Michael Rosenzweig. *New York Times,* 8 December 1998, D-2.

xlii   Even the commanding. *New York Times Magazine,* 21 February 1999, 34.

xlii   Contrary to the. *New York Times,* 3 June 1999, C-1.

xlii   The most effective. *COUNTDOWN,* Center for Media Education, 20 November 1998; Civil Rights Forum and Project on Media Ownership, 18 December 1998, 2.

xlii   Government indifference. Center for Responsive Politics, 29 July 1999, 1.

PREFACE TO THE
FIRST EDITION

AS A YOUNG REPORTER in Providence, R.I., I used to drop by for tea in the back room of a secondhand bookstore run by Mary and Douglas Dana. Douglas, a rosy-cheeked Scot, would pull out his latest find in first editions and Mary would predict that he would keep the book and never sell it. One Saturday afternoon, Douglas showed me a first edition that made a difference in my reportorial life. It was *The Letters of Sacco and Vanzetti,* edited by Marion Denman Frankfurter and Gardner Jackson.

I knew that there had been a "Sacco and Vanzetti Case." I had been seven years old when the two men were electrocuted at Charlestown Prison in Boston. I never heard anything except certitude that the two Italians were murderers and that when the switch was thrown on their electric chair there was such a powerful flow of electricity that in my hometown of Stoneham, fifteen miles away, and in all of eastern Massachusetts, the electric lights blinked. I had no childhood reason to doubt their guilt and I remember no seven-year-old's reservations about the death penalty. But I was awed by the phenomenon of thousands of homes where a flicker of darkness recorded the deaths of two criminals.

That was all I knew about Sacco and Vanzetti when I first saw Douglas Dana's book, with its good, clear type and solid binding. As I flipped through the pages my eye caught the recurring name of Alice Stone Blackwell. A feminist editor and writer, daughter of Lucy Stone, Alice Stone Blackwell, it was clear from the book, had befriended the two prisoners. I remembered seeing a poem my mother wrote and dedicated to her friend Alice Stone Blackwell. I was interested in Alice Stone Blackwell, so Douglas Dana reluctantly sold me the book.

Reading the letters of Sacco and Vanzetti started a reportorial pursuit that took much of my spare time for the next several years. It led me to a tantalizing brush with a definitive solution to the crime for which Sacco and Vanzetti were falsely convicted and killed. I learned that it was untrue that lights blinked anywhere when the men were electrocuted. But from endless readings of the trial transcript, post-trial affidavits and appeals, official reports, interviews with principals still living, and the books that even now, sixty years later, are still being written about the case, I also learned something about the social role of newspapers.

Sacco, a shoe repairman, and Vanzetti, a fish peddler, were arrested for the killing of a paymaster and his assistant in South Braintree, Mass., in 1920. It was a cold-blooded murder on a sidewalk in daylight by five men who drove off in a car. Sacco and Vanzetti were Italian immigrants and anarchists. Their arrest came during a national hysteria, whipped by fear of the Russian Revolution a few years earlier, by an endemic bias against all "foreigners," by an uninformed public notion about anarchists, and by A. Mitchell Palmer, attorney general of the United States, who used the Department of Justice to attack all radicals in mass arrests known as "the Palmer Raids," which had become almost a national sport.

At the time of the arrests, most newspapers supported the Palmer Raids and, despite the overwhelming evidence of gross improprieties of justice, were enthusiastic about convicting Sacco and Vanzetti. The press is a mirror of sorts, which might account for its reflection and promotion of the hysteria. But in its great numbers and variety, it is also supposed to be a kind of balance wheel, bringing reason and diversity of opinion to its reporting and commentary. The balance wheel had failed.

By the time Sacco and Vanzetti were to be electrocuted in 1927, most of the serious press had changed its mind. Reporters confirmed the state had been dishonest and suppressed evidence. Editors had become convinced that there had been a grave miscarriage of justice. It was too late. By that time the pride of the Commonwealth of Massachusetts had become attached to the need to electrocute the two defendants. The state, frozen in its attitude, resisted a commutation because, in the words of Herbert Ehrmann, an admirable lawyer in the case, it would have "signaled a weakness within our social order."

In the United States we depend on our mass media to signal, among other things, "weakness within our social order." In 1921, when Sacco and Vanzetti were tried, the newspapers failed to send that signal, though there was ample evidence to support one. By 1927, when the men were electrocuted, a significant portion of the press had changed its mind. The change did not save the two men, but it said something about the media.

The lesson repeated itself during my subsequent work as a reporter. The news media are not monolithic. They are not frozen in a permanent set of standards. But they suffer from built-in biases that protect corporate power and consequently weaken the public's ability to understand forces that create the American scene. These biases in favor of the status quo, like the ones operating during the Sacco-Vanzetti case, do not seem to change materially over time. When Senator Joseph McCarthy gained demagogic power, he did it, as did A. Mitchell Palmer thirty years earlier, with the enthusiastic support of most newspapers. The newspapers had to abandon disciplines of documentation and critical judgment in order to promote McCarthy, but they did it.

During the emergence of the civil rights movement in the 1950s, most of the best regional papers, in the North and the South, would tell me when I dropped in for the traditional "fill-in" for outside journalists, that there was no serious problem in their "colored districts." Yet in city after city there came racial explosions that surprised even the local media.

When I was reporting on structural poverty in the early 1960s, once again in the newsrooms of some of the best papers I was told that there was no significant problem. But a few years later it was clear that not only was there a problem, but it had existed for a long time.

Yet if I asked these same papers about welfare cheaters, low-level political chicanery, or failings of almost any public agency, their libraries were full of clippings.

There was, it appeared, a double standard: sensitive to failures in public bodies, but insensitive to equally important failures in the private sector, particularly in what affects the corporate world. This institutional bias does more than merely protect the corporate system. It robs the public of a chance to understand the real world.

Our picture of reality does not burst upon us in one splendid revelation. It accumulates day by day and year by year in mostly unspectacular fragments from the world scene, produced mainly by the mass media. Our view of the real world is dynamic, cumulative, and self-correcting as long as there is a pattern of even-handedness in deciding which fragments are important. But when one important category of the fragments is filtered out, or included only vaguely, our view of the social-political world is deficient. The ultimate human intelligence—discernment of cause and effect—becomes damaged because it depends on knowledge of events in the order and significance in which they occur. When part of the linkage between cause and effect becomes obscure, the sources of our weakness and of our strength become uncertain. Errors are repeated decade after decade because something is missing in the perceptions by which we guide our social actions.

My personal associations, professional experience, and research tell me that journalists, writers, artists, and producers are, as a body, capable of producing a picture of reality that, among other things, will signal "weakness in the social order." But to express this varied picture they must work through mainstream institutions and these institutions must be diverse. As the most important institutions in the production of our view of the real social world—newspapers, magazines, radio, television, books, and movies—increasingly become the property of the most persistent beneficiaries of mass media biases, it seems important to me to write about it.

INTRODUCTION

*The dream of every leader, whether a tyrannical despot or a benign
prophet, is to regulate the behavior of his people.*

Colin Blakemore,
Mechanics of the Mind

IT IS SAID THAT Goethe would not read newspapers until they were
a month old because it helped him avoid merely passing events. Mimi
Bird King, an eccentric dowager in Houston, Texas, who preferred
living in the past, had her butler pick up a paper each morning, file it
in her cellar, and bring her that date's paper from twenty years earlier.
Napoleon said he was in favor of delaying the printing of news until it
didn't make any difference, which means delaying it forever.

Contemporary Americans have different needs. They are not, as
Goethe was, fed and clothed by Duke Charles Augustus. Nor do many
of them have servants who let them live in the past, like Mimi King.
Or if they hate the news, as Napoleon did, they nevertheless need information that cannot be postponed—about their children's schools,
changes in their work life, local and national politics that determine
their future, international events that may take away their gasoline
and their sons. Or a nuclear war that might satisfy Napoleon by finally ending anything for the news to report.

Men and women in the 1980s live in a world changing so
rapidly that continuous and timely information is indispensable.
Their environment is not Goethe's aristocratic shelter in the Court of
Saxe-Weimar or Mimi King's mansion, or Napoleon's exile on Elba.
We live in a dynamic world where ignorance of economic and political change is destructive of democracy and fatal to intelligent decision making.

Americans, like most people, get images of the world from their newspapers, magazines, radio, television, books, and movies. The mass media become the authority at any given moment for what is true and what is false, what is reality and what is fantasy, what is important and what is trivial. There is no greater force in shaping the public mind; even brute force triumphs only by creating an accepting attitude toward the brutes.

Authorities have always recognized that to control the public they must control information. The initial possessor of news and ideas has political power—the power to disclose or conceal, to announce some parts and not others, to hold back until opportunistic moments, to predetermine the interpretation of what is revealed. Leaders of democracies no less than medicine men, shamans, kings, and dictators are jealous of their power over ideas, as eager to control information as they are to control armies.

Controlled information has a morbid history. It is not morbid solely because it violates the ideology of democracy, though it does that. It is morbid because it is usually wrong. Unchallenged information is inherently flawed information. If it is in error to begin with, it is not open to correction. If it is correct at the time, it will soon be obsolete. If it changes without uninhibited response from the real world, it becomes detached from the real world. For a realistic picture of society there is no such thing as a central authority.

But the righteousness of power is irresistible. Every authority figure in the Western world once knew for certain that the world was flat and silenced anyone who pointed out the error. The authorities knew the earth was the center of the universe and constructed ill-fated philosophies based on the illusion. When the bubonic plague decimated the population of Europe, the authorities burned not guilty rats but guiltless "witches." For two thousand years the best doctors treated fevers by draining the patients' blood and kindly killed more human beings than the most murderous cannon.

The authorities were wrong. Their errors created intellectual sterility and immeasurable human misery. But they were not wrong because they were always unintelligent or evil. They were wrong and they remained wrong because their information, which they sincerely believed, was not effectively challenged by open and competitive ideas.

The Age of Enlightenment created a new kind of society. It rejected dictators and kings. It celebrated democracy and individual freedom. It acknowledged that the democratic consent of the governed is meaningless unless the consent is informed consent. Controlled information has survived in the twentieth century's grim parade of dictatorships, but these dictatorships have been the enemies of democracy and they have ultimately failed. The first amendment of the most sacred document in the quintessential democracy of the Enlightenment, the United States, guarantees freedom of expression. Diversity of expression was assumed to be the natural state of enduring liberty.

Modern technology and American economics have quietly created a new kind of central authority over information—the national and multinational corporation. By the 1980s, the majority of all major American media—newspapers, magazines, radio, television, books, and movies—were controlled by fifty giant corporations. These corporations were interlocked in common financial interest with other massive industries and with a few dominant international banks.

There are other media voices outside the control of the dominant fifty corporations. Most are small and localized, and many still disappear as they are acquired by the giants. The small voices, as always, are important, a saving remnant of diversity. But their diminutive sounds tend to be drowned by the controlled thunder of half the media power of a great society.

The United States has an impressive array of mass communications. There are 1,700 daily newspapers, 11,000 magazines, 9,000 radio and 1,000 television stations, 2,500 book publishers, and 7 movie studios. If each of these were operated by a different owner there would be 25,000 individual media voices in the country. Such a large number would almost guarantee a full spectrum of political and social ideas distributed to the population. It would limit the concentration of power since each owner would share influence over the national mind with 24,999 other owners. The division of the market into so many companies would mean firms would be smaller, which would make it easier for newcomers to enter the scene with new ideas.

But there are not 25,000 different owners. Today fifty corporations own most of the output of daily newspapers and most of the sales and audience in magazines, broadcasting, books, and movies. The fifty men and women who head these corporations would fit in a large room. They constitute a new Private Ministry of Information and Culture.

Modern technology and social organization have intensified the problems of centralized control of information. In an earlier age citizen talked to citizen about public policies that affected them. Each community could gather in a hall or church to decide its own fate. Deciding its fate was real because in older, agricultural societies each community came close to self-sufficiency and remote events had marginal meaning. That method of politics disappeared long ago. In place of the small towns are huge urban complexes where no citizen can know most other members of the community. No town hall or church could possibly hold all the voters. Each citizen's fate is shaped by powerful forces in distant places. The individual now depends on great machines of information and imagery that inform and instruct. The modern systems of news, information, and popular culture are not marginal artifacts of technology. They shape the consensus of society.

It is a truism among political scientists that while it is not possible for the media to tell the population what to think, they do tell the public what to think about. What is reported enters the public agenda. What is not reported may not be lost forever, but it may be lost at a time when it is most needed. More than any other single private source and often more than any governmental source, the fifty dominant media corporations can set the national agenda.

The size of the dominant media corporation makes them participants in the world of international finance. Most are traded on the stock market, under pressure to compete with the most speculative investments around the world.

George Morris, corporate secretary of one of the fifty dominant media companies, RCA Corporation, owner of National Broadcasting Company (NBC), told a journalist: "You really have to go to bed with the big investors . . . One man in my office does nothing all year long but deal with the many institutions that hold RCA stock."

When Fred Friendly resigned as president of CBS News in 1966 because the network refused to cancel a fifth daytime rerun of "I Love Lucy" for a crucial Senate hearing on the Vietnam War, he was told that the loss of revenue from a delayed episode of "Lucy" was intolerable to shareholders, who would not accept any decrease in net profits.

Allen Neuharth, chairman of the board of the largest newspaper chain, Gannett Company, told an interviewer, "Wall Street didn't give a damn if we put out a good paper in Niagara Falls. They just wanted to know if our profits would be in the 15-20 percent range."

John Knight, an editor and publisher for sixty years, eventually headed a major newspaper chain, Knight-Ridder, and became a rare leader in building journalistic institutions. When his company prepared to offer shares on the stock market, its executives presented themselves to a meeting of the Wall Street analysts who help determine which corporations the largest banks and investment houses will support with block purchases of stock. Knight made the initial appearance:

> I made the first talk at the financial security analysts—the last talk I ever made. I was never invited again. My opening line was, "Ladies and gentlemen, I do not intend to become your prisoner." I told them why. I said, "As long as I have anything to do with it, we are going to run the papers."

For the first time in the history of American journalism, news and public information have been integrated formally into the highest levels of financial and nonjournalistic corporate control. Conflicts of interest between the public's need for information and corporate desires for "positive" information have vastly increased.

This book describes two alarming developments in the mass media in the last twenty-five years. One is the impact of concentrated control of our media by the fifty corporations. The other development is the subtle but profound impact of mass advertising on the form and content of the advertising-subsidized media—newspapers, magazines, and broadcasting.

The last twenty-five years have not seen unrelieved degradation of the media. Much has improved. Journalism has experienced growth in its social perceptions, fresh creativity in drama and art, and ingenious applications of communication techniques, sometimes for social good. But these improvements have been paralleled and often overwhelmed by the effects of the control of large corporations.

The fifty corporations in control of most of our media differ in policies and practices. Their subsidiaries' products vary in quality, some excellent, many mediocre, some wretched. The corporations are led by men and women who differ in personality and values. In the massive output of the fifty corporations there is a wide variety of kinds of stories, ideas, and entertainments, including information that sometimes is critical of giant corporations.

The problem is not one of universal evil among the corporations or their leaders. Nor is it a general practice of constant suppression and close monitoring of the content of their media companies. There is, in the output of the dominant fifty, a rich mixture of news and ideas. But there are also limits, limits that do not exist in most other democratic countries with private enterprise media. The limits are felt on open discussion of the system that supports giantism in corporate life and of other values that have been enshrined under the inaccurate label "free enterprise."

Many of the corporations claim to permit great freedom to the journalists, producers, and writers they employ. Some do grant great freedom. But when their most sensitive economic interests are at stake, the parent corporations seldom refrain from using their power over public information.

Media power is political power. The formal American political system is designed as though in response to Lord Acton's aphorism that power corrupts and absolute power corrupts absolutely. Media power is no exception. When fifty men and women, chiefs of their corporations, control more than half the information and ideas that reach 220 million Americans, it is time for Americans to examine the institutions from which they receive their daily picture of the world.

Part I

THE PRIVATE MINISTRY
OF INFORMATION

1

THE ENDLESS CHAIN

For where your treasure is, there will be your heart also.
Matthew 6:22

GEORGE ORWELL in his novel, *1984*, fictionalized Big Brother, intruder into privacy and the one big owner of all the mass media in his society. Big Brother used his control of news, information, and popular culture to achieve Big Brother's vision of a conforming society. Most critics understandably thought of Communist societies where, indeed, everyone was surrounded by One Big Owner of the mass media. Among the many social ironies of the 1980s is the change in the world's mass media. Many Communist societies have discovered that they are forced to move away from centralized control of information, though the change is slow and tentative. At precisely the same time the developed democracies of the world, including the United States, have begun moving in the opposite direction, toward centralized control of their mass media, this time not by government but by a few private corporations.

No single corporation controls all the mass media in the United States. But the daily newspapers, magazines, broadcasting systems, books, motion pictures, and most other mass media are rapidly moving in the direction of tight control by a handful of huge multinational corporations. If mergers, acquisitions, and takeovers continue at the present rate, one massive firm will be in virtual control of all major media by the 1990s. Given the complexities of social and economic trends, it is unlikely to result in one owner. It is, however, quite possible—and corporate leaders predict—that by the 1990s a half-

3

dozen large corporations will own all the most powerful media outlets in the United States. Given the striking similarity in the private political and economic goals of all of the owning corporations, and given the extraordinary combined power of all the forms of modern mass media, it is not particularly comforting that the private control consists of two dozen large conglomerates instead of only one.

Predictions of massive consolidation are based on extraordinary changes in recent years. At the end of World War II, for example, 80 percent of the daily newspapers in the United States were independently owned, but by 1989 the proportion was reversed, with 80 percent owned by corporate chains. In 1981 twenty corporations controlled most of the business of the country's 11,000 magazines, but only seven years later that number had shrunk to three corporations.

Today, despite more than 25,000 outlets in the United States, twenty-three corporations control most of the business in daily newspapers, magazines, television, books, and motion pictures.

The same dominant corporations in these major fields appear in other, often newer, media. It is the open strategy of major media owners to own as many different kinds of media as possible—newspapers, magazines, broadcasting, books, movies, cable, recordings, video cassettes, movie houses, and copyright control of the archival libraries of past work in all these fields. Rupert Murdoch says that is now his basic worldwide strategy of acquisition and takeovers. Lee Isgur, media analyst for the investment house PaineWebber, has said, "The good companies must be integrated." Major owners of cable systems are corporations also dominant in newspapers, magazines, books, and broadcasting. Increasingly they insist on owning part or all of the programs they transmit on their cable channels. After Sony bought CBS Records, it also purchased a company that had exclusive rights to 35,000 songs. Time Warner, the largest media corporation in the world, owns copyright to thousands of other songs, including "Happy Birthday."

An alarming pattern emerges. On one side is information limited by each individual's own experience and effort; on the other, the unseen affairs of the community, the nation, and the world, information needed by the individual to prevent political powerlessness. What connects the two are the mass media, and that system is being reduced to a small number of closed circuits in which the owners of the conduits—newspapers, magazines, broadcast stations, and all the other mass media—prefer to use material they own or that tends to serve their economic purposes. Because they own so many of the different kinds of outlets, they have that golden commodity they speak of with financial joy, a "guaranteed audience." But the term "guaranteed audience" is another way of saying "captive audience."

Why do the corporations fight for so much dominance, spending most of their executive time and billions of dollars in ferocious bidding battles, mergers, acquisitions, leveraged buyouts, and take-overs? The answer is an ancient one: money and influence.

Money: "Market dominant" firms simply make a higher percentage of profit out of every dollar than less dominant firms. A four-year study of 2,746 corporations by the advertising agency Backer Spielvogel Bates showed that companies with 1.5 times the sales of their nearest rival were 52 percent more profitable than market followers. And market leaders averaged 31 percent return on investment compared to 11 percent for those ranked fourth to fifth. It is not necessary to be an old-fashioned monopoly, the only firm in the business; one needs to be merely one of a small number of firms that have a larger proportion of the business than all the others combined. The study adds, "It is not sufficient to have superior quality."

Influence: "Market dominant" corporations in the mass media have dominant influence over the public's news, information, public ideas, popular culture, and political attitudes. The same corporations exert considerable influence within government precisely because they influence their audiences' perception of public life, including perceptions of politics and politicians as they appear—or do not appear—in the media.

Few investors believe that the process of tightening control will stop soon. An investment banker, Christopher Shaw, chairman of Henry Ansbacher, Inc., has negotiated more than 120 media acquisitions. When asked where it will all stop, Shaw likes to quote a client, saying that by the year 2000 all United States media may be in the hands of six conglomerates. Robert Maxwell, a British publisher, said in 1984, "In ten years' time, there will be only ten global corporations of communications. I . . . would expect to be one of them." J. Kendrick Noble, media analyst of PaineWebber, believes that by the end of the century the largest media properties in the country will be owned by a half-dozen huge companies.

If executives of dominant media corporations are personally silent about dangers of concentrated ownership, it is not surprising: the process benefits them in terms of both money and power. But the media they control also are silent. The silence is not convincing evidence that the media never reflect the corporate and political interests of their owners.

Today, the chief executive officers of the twenty-three corporations that control most of what Americans read and see can fit into an ordinary living room. Almost without exception they are economic conservatives. They can, if they wish, use control of their newspapers, broadcast stations, magazines, books, and movies to promote their own corporate values to the exclusion of others. When their corporate interests are at stake—in taxes, regulation, and antitrust action—they use that power, in their selection of news, and in the private lobbying power peculiar to those who control the media image—or non-image—of politicians.

In a democracy, the answer to government power is accountability, which means giving voters full information and real choices. In the media business it is not different; monopoly and concentrated control diminish real choices. Dominant corporations in the media usually claim that the merger process improves the country's media. The record of improvement of media quality after their acquisition by big firms or Wall Street takeovers is not impressive.

A few newspapers under major corporate ownership have been improved in journalistic quality, but not most. The largest chain owner in terms of circulation is Gannett, whose new chief executive officer has said in 1989 what others in the business have long recognized, that many of the chain's papers are journalistically "embarrassing," what *Business Week* magazine called "slick but . . . mediocre journalism." The largest chain in number of individual papers is International Thomson, whose papers a Canadian parliamentary commission called "a lackluster aggregation of cashboxes." The deterioration of quality, after takeovers by Rupert Murdoch, in newspapers, magazines, television, books, and movies, descending, almost without exception, to ever more sex and violence, is now legendary. After the Wall Street turbulence in changing ownership of the national television networks by Capital Cities/ABC, General Electric's purchase of NBC, and real estate operator Lawrence Tisch's takeover of CBS, all suffered dismantling of experienced news staffs and draconian layoffs and loss of journalistic and entertainment quality.

When a corporation buys a local monopoly or market domination, few can resist the spectacular profits that can be made by cutting quality and raising prices. This is not what they talk about in public. But in private Christopher Shaw, the merger banker, speaking at a session of potential media investors in October, 1986, said that a daily monopoly newspaper with a 15 percent annual operating profit, can, within two years of purchase, be making a 40 percent profit by cutting costs and raising advertising and subscription prices. The investors were told, "No one will buy a 15 percent margin paper without a plan to create a 25-percent–45-percent margin."

When large corporations claim, for example, that they bring superior management skills to the smaller media they buy, most of the time "management skills" means top-heavy administrative costs, and because they enjoy market domination, quick increases in prices to consumers, and quicker and easier content. Chain newspapers charge higher subscription and advertising rates than counterpart papers owned by independent companies. The television oligopoly of three networks has increased advertising rates despite reduction of their audience shares. After cable was deregulated, cable rates charged by dominant firms rose as much as 50 percent faster than production costs.

When the same corporations expand their control over many different kinds of media, they speak glowingly of providing richer public choices in news and entertainment. But the experience has been that the common control of different media makes those media more alike than ever. Movies become more like television series. Cable, once thought to be a fundamental alternative to programs on commercial television but now under control of companies also in television and other media, is increasingly an imitation of commercial television.

The claim that large corporations can better resist incursions of government into freedom of information can be true. Some—not all—have done so. But when they have to choose between, on the one hand, candidates who will dispense governmental favors in the form of corporate taxes and relaxed business regulation, or, on the other hand, candidates who support freedom of information, the record is not encouraging. The history of Big Government and Big Corporations is more one of accommodation than of confrontation. Richard Nixon and Ronald Reagan, during their terms in the White House, made the most severe attacks in this century on freedom of information and of the press. But both made extraordinary moves to support corporate concentration and increased profit-taking in the media; newspaper publishers overwhelmingly endorsed both Nixon and Reagan for reelection, and while in office President Reagan received stunningly uncritical coverage by the Washington news corps. (See chapter 4.)

The claim by corporate owners of greater resistance to advertiser pressures has mixed validity. Greater public sophistication and professional journalistic standards have reduced clumsy practices of the past in which many "news stories" were masqueraded publicity for advertisers (though the practice has not disappeared). Instead, the basic form and content in newspapers, magazines and television programs have been altered to create editorial content not primarily for the needs and interests of the audience but for the audience-collecting needs of advertisers. The added pages in the average American newspaper and magazine since World War II have been designed primarily to serve advertising. The basic strategy in designing programs on commercial television and cable is not primarily what is perceived as the highest needs and wants of the audience, but what is perceived as the most likely to attract advertising. That priority has become more intense under corporate ownership and its greater insistence on immediate, maximum profits. (See chapter 9.)

It is a favorite axiom of large media operators that, while they have great power, if they abuse it the public will reject them. But in order to have the power of rejection, the public needs real choices and choice is inoperative where there is monopoly, which is the case in 98 percent of the daily newspaper business, or market dominance of the few, which is the case with television and most other mass media. New corporate owners of newspapers and television stations commonly reduce staff and news space. Few build for long-term development of audience loyalty.

Even when the most blatant deterioration of news takes place the public has little power to force changes. In 1977, when the local paper was owned by the Panax chain, a respected editor in Escanaba, Michigan, was fired when he balked at obeying orders to run the owner's personal propaganda as news on page 1. The community— Republicans and Democrats, conservatives and liberals—were outraged. They formed an organized boycott of the paper. It failed. There was no other source of local news, advertisers would not or could not withdraw all their ads, and during the boycott the owner could subsidize the Escanaba paper with proceeds from his other newspapers.

Neither in practical improvement of service to the public nor in added independence from government is the record of corporate ownership of the media sufficiently impressive to counter the dangers of tightening control of public information.

There are conspiracy theories to explain the rapid concentration of media power, but in modern times actual conspiracy is not necessary. The absence of a conspiracy, however, does not mean that large media corporations lack power or fail to use it in a unified way. They have shared values. Those values are reflected in the emphasis of their news and popular culture. They are the primary shapers of American public opinion about events and their meaning. And through that, and their organization in large powerful corporate units, they are a major influence on government.

It is not accidental that one factor stimulating the growth of newspaper chains was a favorable government tax ruling. A company's accumulated annual profits enjoy a forgiving tax rate if the profits are for "a necessary cost of doing business," usually assumed to mean contingencies for future problems. But the Internal Revenue Service decided that a newspaper using its accumulated profits to buy another newspaper is "a necessary cost of doing business." Many media giants have grown through leveraged buyouts and junk bonds that burden their captured corporations with huge debt. The practice has the hidden economic effect of adding to the tax burden of the average citizen because the enormously increased corporate interest payments are deductible from corporate taxes. This is not the stuff of the mainstream news about mergers and acquisitions. The resulting public unawareness and the private lobbying power of the media corporations and their bankers have made Congress and the White House loath to alter it, though it is a significant factor in the continuing burden of "the budget deficit."

Historically, media power has been purchased by those who wished to use it for their personal political ambitions. There have been media owners who lusted after high office. William Randolph Hearst wanted to be president. James M. Cox, publisher of a paper in Ohio, became Democratic candidate for president in 1920, only to be defeated for the presidency by another Ohio newspaper publisher, Warren Gamaliel Harding. Today, the desire of most corporate leaders is not to become president of the United States; it is to influence the president of the United States. The magnitude of that influence depends on the magnitude of media power. The local publisher of the Coffeyville, Kansas, *Journal* (circulation 7,000) cannot expect to see the president of the United States or influential members of Congress anytime he or she wishes. But that access does exist for the chairman of the board of the corporation that owns the Coffeyville *Journal*, the Gannett Company, which also owns other newspapers with combined circulation of more than six million, and substantial broadcasting and television production power. (See chapter 5.)

Small media companies also want governmental favors. The local newspaper owner may have wanted tax and zoning favors from the local City Hall. But modern multinational corporations want them for their national and worldwide interests and for that they go to the heart of the national economic and the political system. Furthermore, many media owners have financial connections—through ownership, interlocking directorships, and banking partners—with defense production, banking, insurance, gas and oil. They have unified attitudes toward basic issues that separate policies favorable to large financial interests as opposed to those favorable to the individual taxpayer and consumer. President Eisenhower called attention to the ominous power of what he called the "military-industrial complex." The new corporate domination of the mass media has created a media-industrial complex.

Media lobbyists work the corridors of government as do lobbyists for other industries, but they speak with special power because politicians fear the media. Sheila Kaplan, writing in the *Washington Monthly*, wrote that the man who is president of the Magazine Publishers Association gave $12,000 to Republican candidates in a "Victory 88" fund. A vice-president of Gannett's billboard division made campaign contributions to members of the Senate committee that regulates billboards (Gannett makes about $200 million a year from its billboards, most of it from tobacco and alcohol ads). The National Cable Television Association gave $446,000 to federal candidates between 1985 and 1988, and the National Association of Broadcasters gave $308,000 in the same period.

When General Electric bought RCA in 1986 (and with it NBC News), it combined its media power with its other industrial and financial interests. General Electric is a major defense contractor—it manufactures and sells electronic, electrical generating, and nuclear systems worldwide, produces aircraft and spacecraft components, and is in the insurance and banking business, with sales exceeding $40 billion a year. Its multinational operations are sensitive to both governmental foreign policy and the news.

In 1986, the Wall Street acquisition expert, Christopher Shaw, told potential media investors two reasons they should buy newspapers, magazines, broadcast stations, or book publishing firms. The first reason was "profitability." The second was "influence."

Beginning in the mid-1960s, large corporations suddenly began buying media companies. It did not require a conspiracy. The trigger was Wall Street's discovery of the best-kept secret in American newspapering.

For decades American newspaper publishers cultivated the impression that they presided over an impoverished institution maintained only through sacrificial devotion to the First Amendment. The image helped reduce demands from advertisers for lower rates and agitation by media employees for higher wages. The truth was that most daily papers were highly profitable. But that was easy to conceal when newspapers were privately owned and no public reports were required.

The golden secret was disclosed by an odd combination: the fertility of founding families and the inheritance taxes.

Most of the country's established newspapers were founded in the late nineteenth century, including the *New York Times*, the *Washington Post*, and the *Los Angeles Times*. At the time of their formation they were modest, local operations. But by the 1960s, thanks to the country's population growth, affluence, heightened literacy, mass advertising, and local monopolies, they had become substantial enterprises. Papers started decades ago with small investments (Adolph Ochs bought the *New York Times* in 1896 with only $75,000 of his own money) were now worth millions.

Inheritance taxes for family owners can be avoided for three generations; a person could leave the estate in trust for grandchildren, but not beyond. By the 1960s, the three generation grace period for hundreds of papers was about to end and owners looked for a way to avoid overwhelming taxes (and possible forced sale of the paper) on the death of the third generation. One answer was to spread the ownership by trading shares on the stock market, thereby relieving family members of inheritance taxes on the entire property. Or the family could sell the paper outright to an outside corporation.

For some papers the transfer to outside investors came because the family ran out of heirs, or, given sexism in the trade, they ran out of that standard fixture in newspaper history, appropriate sons-in-law. In other cases, the heirs fought among themselves.

Typically, a paper was started by a strong patriarch, but by the third generation dozens of his descendants' families were living off the dividends. Most of the relatives were not emotionally involved in the paper and lavish offers for their inherited stock became irresistible. In Louisville, Kentucky, for example, the Bingham family had created one of the country's more distinguished papers. In 1986 their children quarreled over the properties and one daughter, who had been drawing $300,000 a year in dividends, sold her minority stock to the Gannett chain for $84 million. (Gannett eventually acquired the whole paper.) Major papers began offering their stock publicly in the early

1960s. Firms selling stock to the general public are required by the Securities and Exchange Commission to disclose company finances. Furthermore, Wall Street investment houses who make the major investments in such firms dislike mysteries about properties in which they may invest billions, so they demand even more inside information than the SEC. Suddenly in the 1960s the investing world discovered that the newspaper industry, like the legendary Hetty Green, had assiduously presented itself to the public in mendicant rags, but was now exposed, as Mrs. Green had been, as fabulously rich. The media race was on, and concentrated ownership followed.

(The high annual profit margins of individual local papers—often in the 20 to 40 percent pretax range—are still concealed by embedding them in general data for the parent corporation, and for the traditional purpose of preventing rebellions of local advertisers and employees. Curiously, most journalists, ordinarily skeptical of institutional secrecy, remain ignorant of the large profit margins of the papers and broadcast stations they work for.)

By the 1960s, television was already concentrated in ownership. The three networks and their wholly owned and affiliated stations continue to have more than two-thirds of the audience. Broadcasters enjoy a "natural monopoly" in the sense that there is a limited number of frequencies available in each community and the government protects each station's channel from competition.

Concentrated ownership was in broadcasting's corporate genes. The industry began as a private cartel in 1919 when the Radio Corporation of America (RCA) was formed as an umbrella monopoly under which General Electric, Westinghouse, AT&T, and United Fruit Company agreed to divide the newly emerging radio market among themselves. The National Broadcasting Company was their radio network. CBS did not enter the field until 1927, and not until 1943 did an activist Federal Communications Commission force RCA to divest itself of one of its two radio networks, thus creating ABC.

Television, in the jargon of Wall Street, is a "semimonopoly," not only because of the limited number of owners, but because in most cities the dominant stations have virtually guaranteed high profits; the ratings simply determine which company gets the most.

Recent events in broadcasting have further concentrated ownership in television. Initially, no company was permitted to own more than seven radio and seven television stations. Under the political drive for deregulation, the FCC in 1984 permitted each company to expand its holdings to twelve AM and twelve FM radio stations and twelve television stations.

Magazine groups became important when mass advertising did. A century ago, when the country's new mass production industries began turning out vast quantities of consumer goods, they needed sales promotion on a national scale. In the era before broadcasting, magazines were the only national advertising medium, since newspapers were strictly local. Magazines became the major carrier of expensive ads, a practice made easier because, unlike newspapers, they could produce quality color on heavy paper. As the magazines became high profit centers, they attracted larger operators who formed groups.

Magazines of general interest (*Life, Look, Saturday Evening Post,* etc.) died in the 1960s when the advertising power of color television replaced them, but specialized magazines, including those devoted to women, remain profitable. Like the other media that have become heavily concentrated in ownership, their rates of profit have increased—the result of market domination by a few corporations. In recent years, the dominant groups, notably Time Warner, have so increased their dominance that although there are 11,000 magazines in the country, three corporations have more than half the business.

Many book companies became properties of outside firms in the 1960s when major electronic and defense industries (IBM, ITT, Litton, RCA, Raytheon, Xerox, General Electric, Westinghouse, and General Telephone and Electronics) entered textbook publishing. At the time, these firms believed that instruction in American classrooms would soon be centered around computers; control of book publishing firms would put them in a position to sell schools and colleges the software for the new hardware, which some of them also sold. Computers have not taken over the classrooms to the extent expected, but the entry of outside corporations into the book world had begun.

Hollywood studios, long concentrated in ownership, remain so, and with added complexity. Conglomerates came to appreciate the power to create national styles and celebrities (and extra profits) when combinations of different media reinforced each other in unified promotional campaigns. Today, most of the leading movie studios are also owners in other media, and, thanks to the free-market amnesia about antitrust law, have once again started buying up movie houses to guarantee audiences for their own films and keep out competitors' pictures. In 1948 the United States Supreme Court found ownership of movie theaters by the major movie studios a violation of antitrust law. The U. S. Department of Justice in recent years has ignored that finding and by 1988 a few major studios had bought control of more than a third of all the movie screens in the country.

It is possible that large corporations are gaining control of the American media because the public wants it that way. But there is another possibility: the public, almost totally dependent on the media for such things, has seldom seen in their newspapers, magazines, or broadcasts anything to suggest the political and economic dangers of concentrated corporate control.

It is also possible that the public image of owners' selfish use of their media power is obsolete, based on the historical notoriety of the crudities of nineteenth-century "yellow journalism." Most owners and editors no longer brutalize the news with the heavy hand dramatized in movies like *Citizen Kane* or *The Front Page*. More common is something more subtle, more professionally respectable and more effective: the power to treat some unliked subjects accurately but briefly, and to treat subjects favorable to the corporate ethic frequently and in depth.

Another evidence of the change from the shrillness of a century ago is the periodic appearance of news or criticism that does not reflect owners' private values. With dramatic national news (though not local news) there is competition between local newspapers and broadcast stations, so omissions of obvious news breaks would be embarrassing and ineffective.

But there are two kinds of impact on public opinion, one brief and transient, the other prolonged and deep. The first is the single news item, soon obscured by dozens of new ones, each day tending to obliterate the impact of what went before. A compelling study of the ephemeral quality of isolated news accounts is Deborah Lipstadt's book, *Beyond Belief*, which reveals that American newspapers from 1933 to 1945 printed numerous reports showing that something horrendous was happening to European Jews under Hitler. But the news stories were brief, isolated, and seldom on the front page. They were not pursued with continuity, never drawn together to form a coherent picture, and newspapers did not press to discover the difference between official denials and reality. Consequently, the atrocities did not become important in the public mind and, probably as a result, they did not provoke strong government action. Far more effective in creating public opinion is pursuit of events or ideas until they are displayed in depth over a period of time, when they seem to form a coherent picture and therefore become integrated into public thinking. Continuous repetition and emphasis create high priorities in the public mind and in government. It is in that power—to treat some subjects briefly and obscurely but others repetitively and in depth, or to take initiatives unrelated to external events—where ownership interests most effectively influence the news.

In all the media, it is normal and necessary to decide what to include and what to exclude, what to treat with emphasis and what to relegate to minor display, when to treat something in depth and when to keep it superficial. It is the legitimate task of the professional editor. Because these discriminations are normal and necessary, it is difficult for the public, and often for individual journalism professionals, to detect when, among the elements that go into legitimate news selection, private ownership interests become a factor.

Fifty years ago, executive editors spoke openly to their staffs about owners' sensibilities. Today most editors do not—ironic confirmation of raised professional standards. When protection of an owning corporation's private interests intrudes into news decisions, other professionally acceptable reasons are given (such as "Nobody's interested"). The barrier is seldom absolute: there is merely a higher threshold for such stories. News stories that cast doubt on the corporate ethic must be more urgent and melodramatic than stories sustaining that ethic. Gradually, the total news picture of society is skewed in favor of corporate interests.

The central interests of owners are clear to executive editors who know that there are limits to their freedom and who thus perform varying degrees of self-censorship. Periodically, an executive editor takes literally an owner's encouragement to edit "without fear or favor," and periodically the editor is fired or squeezed out. There are always stories that will require the editor to exercise his or her unstated function of applying the second-hand weight of the owner's thumb on the scale of the news.

Some industrialized democracies have more concentrated ownership than the United States, but no other developed country has the peculiar need of the United States for a different pattern. Every other developed country has a national press and a relatively unimportant local press. In those countries the dozen or more national papers, headquartered in the national capital, are the only ones to carry serious political and economic news. They are available in every locality and—crucially important—each competing national paper is different in its political and economic orientation. Readers have a real choice among the differing papers, in which a wide spectrum of public issues is aired and debated and can thus enter the national discourse.

The United States has never had a true national daily press. American politics is more local than in other countries. Major decisions that are left to the national government in other countries—education, police, land use, property taxes, and much else—are voted on by local communities in the United States. No national news medium can, by itself, serve the American voter. Consequently, there are 1,600 local newspapers and no truly national ones. The *Wall Street Journal* comes closest to a national paper, but it is a specialized one. The *New York Times* is only slowly expanding toward general availability throughout the country. *USA Today* is a national paper but it is a daily magazine that does not pretend to be a primary carrier of all the serious news.

In the United States, unlike elsewhere, when a handful of corporations gain control of most daily newspapers, they are collecting local monopolies. Television (which does little systematic local reporting of the kind done by local newspapers) is a semimonopoly of the three affiliated stations. There is more competition in magazines, books, and motion pictures, but as their ownership has become more concentrated over the years, their social and political orientation has become more uniform.

For a few years radio has been in a state of rearrangement around the new and more popular FM stations. But now radio groups also are increasing in concentrated ownership. If broadcasting revenues and audience share are combined, as is done by many industry calculations, the three major television corporations still have most of the revenues and access to the total broadcast audience.

(An earlier edition of this book included radio owners, which led to the figure, at the time, of fifty corporations that had most of the business in all major media. Had radio been excluded in that edition, or combined with television as it is in this one, there would have been forty-six dominant corporations instead of fifty. Consequently, it is more accurate to compare the twenty-three corporations dominant in the media today with forty-six seven years earlier. If one combines the revenues of radio and television, as do some industry calculations, then the three networks—ABC, CBS, and NBC—still have a majority of the combined revenues.

There are fourteen dominant companies that have half or more of the daily newspaper business (seven years ago there were twenty), three in magazines (seven years ago there were twenty), three in television (seven years ago there were three), six in book publishing (seven years ago there were eleven), and four in motion picture production (seven years ago there were four). Today the dominant firms in each medium total thirty. But some corporations are dominant in more than one medium. For example, Newhouse and Thomson are dominant in newspapers, magazines, and books; Paramount Communications, Inc. (until mid-1989 called Gulf + Western)* in books and motion pictures; Time Warner in magazines, books, and movies; Murdoch in newspapers, magazines, and movies. Because of the dominance of some firms in more than one medium, the total number of corporations dominating all major media is twenty-three.

* Elsewhere in this book Paramount Communications, Inc., is referred to by its original name, Gulf + Western. The two dominant operations of the newly named corporation remain the same: Simon & Schuster books with its associated book houses, and Paramount Pictures.

If one considers total revenues from all media, including recordings, cable, and videocassettes, seventeen firms receive half or more of all that revenue. That calculation expresses the collective media power of the seventeen firms. But it does not show which corporations dominate each individual medium, which is the basis of this book.

The corporations listed in this book as "dominant" have control of half or more of all the activity in their particular medium. A few dominant firms always establish the nature of any market, and universally they do it with advantage to themselves—in pricing and distribution, in promotion, in obtaining sympathetic government policies, in increasing their control of product beyond consumer choice, and in overwhelming or preventing new competition.

It is claimed by defenders of dominant media firms that there are still many smaller firms, which is often the case. They like to cite the 25,900 different "publishers" listed in Bowker's *Books in Print*. A more realistic figure is closer to 2,500 if one counts only American firms that regularly issue one book or more in any one year. If half or more of the book business is held by six firms, each of the giants would, if equal in strength, have revenues of more than $500 million to enter the field; each of the remaining 2,494 firms would, if equal in strength, have less than $3.5 million with which to compete against the $500 million owners. If one uses the giants' preferred figure of 25,000 publishers then the monopoly power of the giants is even more overwhelming. It is clear which firms will win in the competition in what makes for effectiveness in the book business; credit from big banks for expansion and acquisitions, bidding for manuscripts, negotiating and paying for shelf space and window displays in bookstores which increasingly are owned by national chains, mounting national sales staffs, buying advertising, and arranging for author interviews in the broadcast media. Obtaining publicity for books and their authors is especially easy if the publishing house also owns television stations, newspapers, or magazines that print book reviews and stories about writers, a combination enjoyed by four of the six dominant book publishing corporations.

In any field, whether the media or detergents, when most of the business is dominated by a few firms and the remainder of the field is left to a scattering of dozens or hundreds of smaller firms, it is the few dominant ones who control that market. With detergents it means higher prices and lowered choice. With the media it means the same thing for public news, information, ideas, and popular culture.

The measure of half-or-more-of-the-business varies by medium. For daily newspapers, this book has used average daily circulation because the papers are all issued daily and their circulation is carefully audited by an independent agency. (If gross revenues per company were applied to newspaper companies, the dominance of the top corporations would be even more highly concentrated than if listed by circulation alone; but since accurate figures for the revenue for individual newspapers is seldom available, circulation has been used.) Magazines, on the other hand, are issued at different intervals, from weekly to quarterly, so varying circulations are not comparable as measures of strength; annual revenues, the standard of that industry, are therefore used. Television dominance is measured by audience reach, which is regularly surveyed by rating agencies; initial possession of revenues is also used for television and radio. Book and motion picture corporations are measured by annual revenues. Only the audiences and revenues of a particular medium involved are counted, not revenues of the parent firm, which may be in other media or in nonmedia enterprises. Many of the firms listed below are significant players in other media, but unless they are part of a group that has half or more of one medium, they are not listed as "dominant."

In recent years, ever-mounting levels of media conglomeration worldwide have made it more complicated to determine how much absolute equity each large corporation (or its bank and investment house) has in which combination of properties. The large magazine group, Diamandis, until its sale in 1988, was 70 percent owned by Prudential Insurance Company. It was once owned by CBS, which also had other businesses, including defense. Recently, Diamandis, in turn, was sold to the large French publishing firm, Hachette, whose chairman is also chairman of the largest defense contractor in France.

Some large firms remain private (Hearst, Newhouse, Reader's Digest Association) without legal need to make public financial filings. For them, market share comes from educated guesses by media specialists on Wall Street and by general knowledge of their audited circulation and advertising pages. Other firms, like Rupert Murdoch's News Corp. Ltd., have complex mixtures of private subsidiaries that operate in a number of different nations. More and more the dominant firms exchange properties to fill out their particular domination patterns or cooperate on mutually beneficial ventures. They have participated in the 1980s phenomenon of the creation of ambiguous forms of debt—junk bonds, preferred stocks treated as bonds, and other new forms of Wall Street paper.

The highest levels of world finance have become intertwined with the highest levels of mass media ownership, with the result of tighter control over the systems on which most of the public depends for its news and information.

Narrow control has advanced rapidly. In 1981, forty-six corporations controlled most of the business in daily newspapers, magazines, television, books, and motion pictures. Today, these media generate even larger amounts of money, but the number of giants that get most of the business has shrunk from forty-six to twenty-three.

The dominant twenty-three corporations are:

1. Bertelsmann, A.G. (books)
2. Capital Cities/ABC (newspapers, broadcasting)
3. Cox Communications (newspapers)
4. CBS (broadcasting)
5. Buena Vista Films (Disney; motion pictures)
6. Dow Jones (newspapers)
7. Gannett (newspapers)
8. General Electric (television)
9. Paramount Communications (books, motion pictures)
10. Harcourt Brace Jovanovich (books)
11. Hearst (newspapers, magazines)
12. Ingersoll (newspapers)
13. International Thomson (newspapers)
14. Knight Ridder (newspapers)
15. Media News Group (Singleton; newspapers)
16. Newhouse (newspapers, books)
17. News Corporation Ltd. (Murdoch; newspapers, magazines, motion pictures)

18. New York Times (newspapers)
19. Reader's Digest Association (books)
20. Scripps-Howard (newspapers)
21. Time Warner (magazines, books, motion pictures)
22. Times Mirror (newspapers)
23. Tribune Company (magazines)

Newspapers

Most of the fourteen corporations that dominate the daily newspaper industry have acquired additional daily newspapers (and other media) in the last seven years. The number of daily papers in the country has continued to shrink, from 1,763 in 1960 to 1,643 in 1989, but total national daily circulation has risen slightly from 62 million to 62.9 million and is dominated by a smaller number of firms, from twenty-seven years ago to fourteen today.

The fourteen, in order of their total daily circulation as of September 30, 1988, were:

Gannett Company: *USA Today* and 87 other dailies

Knight-Ridder, Inc.: Philadelphia *Inquirer*, Miami *Herald*, and 27 others

Newhouse Newspapers: Staten Island *Advance*, Portland *Oregonian*, and 24 other papers (Newhouse also owns Condé Nast magazines and Random House book publishing)

Tribune Company: *Chicago Tribune, New York Daily News*, and 7 others

Times Mirror: *Los Angeles Times* and 7 others

Dow Jones & Co.: *Wall Street Journal* and 22 Ottaway newspapers

International Thomson: 120 dailies and book publishing

New York Times: *New York Times* and 26 others

Scripps-Howard Newspapers: Denver *Rocky Mountain News* and 22 others

Hearst: *San Francisco Examiner* and 13 others

Cox: *Atlanta Journal* and 19 others

News Corp. Ltd. (Murdoch): *Boston Herald* and 2 others

Media News Group (Singleton): Dallas *Times Herald* and 17 others

Ingersoll Newspapers: New Haven *Register* and 36 others

Magazines

Tightening concentration was most dramatic in magazines, which from 1981 to 1988 went from twenty dominant corporations to three. The chief cause was the further enlargement of Time, Inc., which in mid-1989 merged with Warner to form Time Warner, the largest media firm in the world. Similarly, Rupert Murdoch's purchase of Walter Annenberg's Triangle Publications made him dominant in yet another field, when combined with his existing magazine holdings. The purchase price of $3 billion was a reminder of how the media field has become an arena open only to giants. In 1979 when Gannett Company bought Combined Communications Corporation (billboards, newspapers, and broadcasting) it was the largest amount of money ever involved in a media acquisition up to that time—$340 million.

The three dominant corporations, in order of estimated annual revenues, are:

Time Warner: *Time, People, Sports Illustrated, Fortune,* and others
News Corp. Ltd.: *TV Guide, Seventeen, New York,* and others
Hearst: *Good Housekeeping, Cosmopolitan,* and others

Television

The three television networks—Capital Cities/ABC, CBS, and NBC—despite mergers, attempted takeovers, extreme corporate turbulence, and declining prime-time viewing, still dominate the field. Cable and home ownership of VCRs has grown, but the three networks still have more than two-thirds of the audience. When all radio and television revenues are counted, the three networks still have most of the revenues. ABC is still owned by Capital cities, a rich but undistinguished newspaper chain. CBS, after incurring massive indebtedness in fighting off hostile takeovers, finished by being controlled by a real estate operator who instituted draconian cost-cutting and reduction of its most distinguished activity, news and documentary units. General Electric, the tenth largest United States corporation and a major defense contractor, bought RCA, owner of the National Broadcasting Company, for $6.3 billion.

Book Publishing
Book publishing, less driven by the commanding force of mass advertising on which newspapers, magazines, and broadcasting depend, is still highly concentrated. The 2,500 companies that regularly issue one or more books a year are dominated in revenues by six corporations that grossed more than half of book revenues.

In books, as in other media, there is the growing presence of corporations that dominate in other media. Of the six largest book publishing firms, five are active in other media.

The six companies are:

Paramount Communications (Simon & Schuster, Ginn & Company, and others)
Harcourt Brace Jovanovich (Academic Press and others)
Time Warner (Little, Brown; Scott, Foresman; and others)
Bertelsmann, A.G. (Doubleday, Bantam Books, and others)
Reader's Digest Association (Condensed Books and others)
Newhouse (Random House and others)

Motion Pictures
The motion picture industry has always been volatile in its corporate convolutions, but through it all the major studios, in one incarnation or another, have remained dominant.

In 1988, in terms of share of box office grosses for their films, there were four firms with most of the business:

Buena Vista Films (Disney)
Paramount Communications (Paramount Pictures)
20th-Century Fox (Murdoch)
Time Warner (Warner Brothers)

Like other large media companies, General Electric brings yet another complication that distinguishes it from small, local companies: it has, through its board of directors, interlocks with still other major industrial and financial sectors of the American economy, in wood products, textiles, automotive supplies, department store chains, and banking.

Under law, the director of a company is obliged to act in the interests of his or her own company. It has always been an unanswered dilemma when an officer of Corporation A, who also sits as a director on the board of Corporation B, has to choose between acting in the best interests of Corporation A or of Corporation B.

Interlocked boards of directors have enormously complicated potential conflicts of interest in the major national and multinational corporations that now control most of the country's media.

A 1979 study by Peter Dreier and Steven Weinberg found interlocked directorates in major newspaper chains. Gannett shared directors with Merrill Lynch (stockbrokers), Standard Oil of Ohio, 20th-Century Fox, Kerr-McGee (oil, gas, nuclear power, aerospace), McDonnell Douglas Aircraft, McGraw-Hill, Eastern Airlines, Phillips Petroleum, Kellogg Company, and New York Telephone Company.

The most influential paper in America, the *New York Times*, interlocked with Merck, Morgan Guaranty Trust, Bristol Myers, Charter Oil, Johns Manville, American Express, Bethlehem Steel, IBM, Scott Paper, Sun Oil, and First Boston Corporation.

Time, Inc. (before it became Time Warner) had so many interlocks it almost represented a Plenary Board of directors of American business and finance, including Mobil Oil, AT&T, American Express, Firestone Tire & Rubber Company, Mellon National Corporation, Atlantic Richfield, Xerox, General Dynamics, and most of the major international banks.

Louis Brandeis, before joining the Supreme Court, called this linkage "the endless chain." He wrote: "This practice of interlocking directorates is the root of many evils. It offends laws human and divine. . . . It tends to disloyalty and violation of the fundamental law that no man can serve two masters. . . . It is undemocratic, for it rejects the platform: 'A fair field and no favors.'"

As media conglomerates have become larger, they have been integrated into the higher levels of American banking and industrial life, as subsidiaries and interlocks within their boards of directors. Half the dominant firms are members of the Fortune 500 largest corporations in the country. They are heavy investors in, among other things, agribusiness, airlines, coal and oil, banking, insurance, defense contracts, automobile sales, rocket engineering, nuclear power, and nuclear weapons. Many have heavy foreign investments that are affected by American foreign policy.

It is normal for all large businesses to make serious efforts to influence the news, to avoid embarrassing publicity, and to maximize sympathetic public opinion and government policies. Now they own most of the news media that they wish to influence.

2

PUBLIC INFORMATION AS INDUSTRIAL BY-PRODUCT

One hand washes the other.

Old Country Saying

ONE DAY IN 1979 four people in a Manhattan office were performing a standard obstetrical operation in the life cycle of American publishing: A book was about to be born. The central figure was Nan Talese, senior editor for one of the country's most important book houses. The bearer of the new book was Mark Dowie.

Dowie is the investigative reporter who disclosed that the Ford Motor Company had knowingly produced dangerous gas tanks in its Pinto cars, having decided that it was cheaper to pay off heirs of the dead than to spend a few dollars per car to make the tanks safer.

The book he was proposing in 1979 would examine the history of this kind of corporate decision making. It would begin with Cornelius Vanderbilt, who rejected air brakes for his nineteenth-century trains, and move through contemporary examples like the Ford Motor Company and its unsafe gas tanks.

Talese was excited. One of the most respected editors in New York, she had produced a series of successes for her employer, Simon & Schuster. She told Dowie and his agent that the book was important and would sell. An atmosphere of celebration filled the room when Dowie, almost as an afterthought, said, "Do you think the title, *Corporate Murder,* will be acceptable?"

27

Talese then asked an odd question: "Is Gulf and Western one of the corporations?"

Gulf + Western is an intriguing firm, quite beyond the idiosyncrasy of having a plus sign instead of the usual & in its trademark. Begun in the 1930s as the Michigan Bumper Company, the company originally made rear bumpers for Studebakers. By the mid-1960s it had caught conglomerate fever, in which a company no longer concentrates on one kind of product but acquires a variety of unrelated industries as investments. Even more than most conglomerates, Gulf + Western soon had a reputation on Wall Street for lusting after any company that could be squeezed for profits or whose assets would expand its borrowing capacity for still more acquisitions. It became the owner of an extraordinary collection of more than 100 companies.

Gulf + Western was a leading producer of auto parts (in the United States, Western Europe, Mexico, Venezuela, and Puerto Rico), musical instruments, cigars (Dutch Masters, El Producto, La Palina, and others), rocket engineering, insurance (Providence Washington, Capitol Life), farm supplies, military air crew equipment, chemicals, shoes (Bostonian, Stetson, Jack Nicklaus), racehorses, traffic lights, suits and dresses (Kayser-Roth, Catalina, Cole of California, Jonathan Logan, Oscar de la Renta, Esquire), oil drilling, racetracks (Roosevelt Raceway), nuclear power plants, lingerie (Kayser, Halston, Fruit of the Loom), microprocessors, hosiery (Interwoven), loan companies (Associates Corporation, Budget Finance), oil and gas tankers, home furnishings (Simmons Mattresses), zinc mills, television production (Desilu Productions), carriers for nuclear waste, candy (Schraffts), tobacco (Mixture No. 79, Old Grand Dad, Heine's), sports teams (New York Knickerbockers, New York Rangers, Washington Diplomats), steel mills, pantyhose (No Nonsense, Mojud, Schiaparelli, Supphose, Jordache, Sheer Indulgence), mining (in North and South America, the Middle East, and Far East), and jet engine and missile parts. It once owned 50 percent of UPITN, which provided television news for networks in eighty countries, including ABC in the United States. It owned 8 percent of the arable land of the Dominican

Republic, where it had 100,000 acres of sugar cane and 50,000 head of cattle. It operates in every state of the Union and in fifty foreign countries. Perhaps appropriately, when the United States government manufactured coins, the molds were made by Gulf + Western.

There is hardly a major issue in the news that does not affect Gulf + Western. Almost every American buys the company's consumer goods. Federal and state regulatory agencies cover the corporation's industrial and consumer operations. U.S. foreign policy influences the fate of its large overseas investments. Military appropriations provide money for the corporation's defense industries. The national debate on nuclear power will determine the fate of the firm's nuclear supply operations. Environmental controls increase expenses in the company's mines and factories. And, of course, anything that might arouse public suspicion about big business or conglomerates jeopardizes its existence.

Gulf + Western had reason to be familiar with problems related to the public image of conglomerates. For one thing, the Securities and Exchange Commission once charged it with trying to conceal a $64 million profit in Dominican sugar. Periodically, Wall Street investors had become uneasy at the complexity of the corporation's wheeling and dealing. The company had to be concerned with its public image at every level of society. This led to its making history in 1979 with the largest magazine ad on record—sixty-four continuous pages in *Time* magazine at a cost of $3.3 million. The purpose of the advertising scheme was to associate the name Gulf + Western with respectability and honesty. Gulf + Western had yet another powerful lever on public imagery. It owned Paramount Pictures, one of the largest movie studios in the world. And it owned Pocket Books, a dominant paperback publisher, and Simon & Schuster, a leading book company.

So it is not surprising that in 1979, the year Gulf + Western felt compelled to place a $3 million ad to enhance its public image, an editor at a Gulf + Western subsidiary, Simon & Schuster, considering a book that would criticize big corporations, would ask, "Is Gulf and Western one of the corporations?"

When Dowie said the book did not mention Gulf + Western, Talese said, "Fine. I don't think we'll have any problem getting the title past our corporate people."

But she was mistaken. Even though she and her staff unanimously supported the book, neither the title nor the book itself was acceptable. Talese reported back, sadly, that the president of Simon & Schuster, Richard Snyder, was vehemently opposed to the manuscript because, among other reasons, he felt it made all corporations look bad.

If Simon & Schuster had been an independent book company, as it once was, Talese would not have asked an author the question she asked Dowie. It is also possible that Dowie's manuscript would now be available to the public, which, as of 1987, it was not.

Talese's question was, at least, direct and open. In contrast, no one can know how many editors of books, magazines, broadcasts, screenplays, and newspapers never say the words out loud but think about possible damage to the parent corporation and act accordingly. But a survey by the American Society of Newspaper Editors found that 33 percent of all editors working for newspaper chains said they would not feel free to run a news story that was damaging to their parent firm.

Among the motives for conglomerates to acquire a variety of industries is that one subsidiary can help another. Presumably Gulf + Western's ownership of zinc mills helps it operate a steel mill. As a producer of oil and gas tankers it can transfer technology and workers to its production of carriers of hazardous wastes. A producer of lingerie presumably would have some advantage in selling fashion apparel. One wholly owned company can act in symbiosis with another wholly owned company. One hand washes the other.

A corporation dependent on public opinion and government policy can call upon its media subsidiaries to help in what the media are clearly able to do—influence public opinion and government policy. At the very least, the corporation can make sure that one subsidiary does no preventable harm to another, which in this case means that even if the media subsidiary does nothing positive to help its corporate siblings at least it will publicize as little as possible anything that hurts them.

The capacity to propagate information and ideas is at the root of political power, and political power is essential to modern corporate ambitions. So is the power to suppress information and ideas. Among the less subtle demonstrations of the power to suppress was a scene in Atlanta at the annual convention of the American Booksellers Association on May 26, 1978. Like most conventions, this one was filled with the compulsive good cheer of people who have goods to sell to other people in the business of buying them, in this case books. But in the midst of this commercial camaraderie was an angry press conference.

Harold Roth, president of the book publishing firm Grosset & Dunlap, was upset. His firm, owned by a film and oil conglomerate, usually made its money on books like *The Bobbsey Twins, Nancy Drew, Tom Swift,* and *The Hardy Boys,* but now it was publishing the hardcover edition of the memoirs of ex-President Richard Nixon.

Roth had called the press conference to denounce a group who campaigned against the Nixon book by urging people to wait until it was remaindered at reduced prices. Publisher Roth saw this as something close to political censorship.

"It is incredible," he told the assembled reporters, "that anyone could suggest that a book not be published. If we abridge the freedom of any writer or publisher, we effectively abridge the freedom of all." History, Roth said, requires the publication of all points of view and "should not be censored because of one's political persuasion."

Sitting in the press conference was the man who had made the book possible. William Sarnoff, nephew of one of RCA's early presidents, David Sarnoff, was president of Warner Publishing, the book publishing subsidiary of the conglomerate Warner Communications. Warner, like many conglomerates, had modest antecedents: It had been a firm specializing in funeral parlors and parking lots. But in the tide of modern industry it had quickly become a $2-billion-a-year conglomerate with heavy interests in broadcasting, books, movies, cable, and records. It owned Atari video games, which were highly dependent on militaristic themes. It owned factories in West Germany, Brazil, and England which, with its overseas movie and television businesses, gave it high stakes in working with the federal government. Its corporate officers had intense personal interests in national politics, having been contributors to Richard Nixon, including the Committee to Re-Elect the President (CREEP) in 1972, the organization whose activities led to Watergate and the resignation of Nixon.

After Nixon left the White House, Warner executives approached Nixon with the idea of publishing the presidential memoirs. The price, according to the agent, Irving "Swifty" Lazar, would be $2 million. Lazar met with William Sarnoff and Howard Kaminsky of Warner Communications and Nixon's former press secretary, Ron Ziegler, and sealed the deal with handshakes. For the $2 million, Warner acquired world publication rights, including the hardback edition, which it licensed to Grosset & Dunlap.

When reporters at the Roth press conference discovered William Sarnoff in the audience, they tried to ask him about the Nixon deal. He declined to answer questions. As Sarnoff heard Roth speak about the sacred right to publish opinions of all kinds, it is conceivable that it brought to his mind an event five years earlier when Sarnoff played a crucial role in the fate of another controversial book.

A minor subsidiary of Warner Communications was Warner Modular Publications, Inc. It had been acquired when university enrollments and governmental education appropriations were rising and there had been a surge of interest in analyzing the country's institutions. Sarnoff, trained in business but unacquainted with book publishing, was chief of all Warner book operations, including this small one in Andover, Mass., close to Boston's intellectual and academic complex. Warner Modular produced monographs, pamphlets, and books that could be used as supplemental reading in university courses.

The publisher of Warner Modular was Claude McCaleb,

whose career had been spent in publishing books for universities. He was developing a list to meet the growing request for fresh analyses of national and world events. He perceived Watergate as a symptom of a larger deterioration of the morality of private and public power and planned a series to explore the idea. Part of the series was a small book called *Counter-Revolutionary Violence,* by Noam Chomsky of the Massachusetts Institute of Technology and Edward S. Herman of the Wharton School of the University of Pennsylvania. Their thesis was that the United States, in attempting to suppress revolutionary movements in underdeveloped countries, had become the leading source of violence against native people.

On Monday, August 27, 1973, McCaleb's Andover office received a telephone call from William Sarnoff in New York. Sarnoff had seen ads for the Chomsky-Herman book scheduled to be run in the *New York Times, New York Review of Books,* the *New Republic,* the *Nation,* and *Saturday Review.* The ads were to coincide with the New York meeting of the American Sociological Association whose members, the publisher hoped, would be interested in the book. Advance copies were scheduled to be delivered to the meeting in a few days.

Sarnoff posed a question stimulated by the ad copy that crossed his Manhattan desk: Was this another Pentagon Papers case that would embarrass the parent firm? The answer was no, this was an analysis of public material by two established academics.

Two hours later Sarnoff called McCaleb again. He wanted McCaleb to fly to New York that night with a copy of the book. McCaleb explained that the first advance copies of the book were just now being printed. Sarnoff ordered the publisher to hand-carry a copy of the manuscript. The next morning McCaleb deposited the manuscript in Sarnoff's office. He then went to the New York Hilton to be present when advance copies of the book arrived at the sociology convention. At the Warner Modular booth at the convention, McCaleb received a call from Sarnoff's office in Rockefeller Plaza: Report at once. In the corporate office, according to McCaleb, "Sarnoff immediately launched into a violent verbal attack on me for having published CRV [*Counter-Revolutionary Violence*] saying, among other things, that it was a pack of lies, a scurrilous attack on respected Americans, undocumented, a publication unworthy of a serious publisher."

Sarnoff agreed with McCaleb that there was no libel problem but, according to McCaleb, "He then announced that he had ordered the printer not to release a single copy to me and that the . . . [book] would not be published."

McCaleb said he was attacked by Sarnoff in terms he had never experienced in nineteen years of academic publishing. He reminded Sarnoff of the agreement they had made when McCaleb was hired—that the professional staff would select the books and their judgment would be measured by the success of their books in the marketplace. McCaleb said Sarnoff dismissed the agreement, saying "it did not cover pieces that were worthless and full of lies." Sarnoff complained that too many of Warner Modular books were by left-wing writers. McCaleb said that was inevitable, since the purpose of the series was to print critical analyses of existing institutions, but that he was also planning books by conservatives like Edward Banfield, Friedrich Hayek, and Milton Friedman.

Sarnoff canceled the ads for *Counter-Revolutionary Violence* and ordered the destruction of the Warner catalogue listing the Chomsky-Herman book and its replacement by a new catalogue with the book omitted. McCaleb, stunned, said that at that very moment 10,000 of the books were coming off the presses and to cancel them would shatter the staff and shock the academic world. According to McCaleb, Sarnoff answered that "he didn't give a damn what I, my staff, the authors, or the academic community thought and ended by saying we should destroy the entire inventory of CVR."

The books were destroyed; McCaleb and his staff resigned. Warner Communications sold Warner Modular to another firm and the small subsidiary disappeared shortly thereafter. When I wrote to Sarnoff asking if McCaleb's account coincided with his I received a one-word answer: "No!" He did not answer my request to elaborate.

It was five years later that Sarnoff attended the press conference in Atlanta and heard Harold Roth, president of Grosset & Dunlap, publisher of Warner's Nixon book, telling reporters in obvious sincerity that "if we abridge the freedom of any one writer or publisher we effectively abridge the freedom of all" and that points of view "should not be censored because of one's political persuasion."

It is not often that the public hears of such clear destruction of editorial independence. In most cases there is no visible imposition of the parent firm's policies, and the policies are not often absolute, conditioned as they are by the desire for profits. During the Vietnam War, for example, Random House published some antiwar books even though it was owned at the time by RCA, an important defense contractor. Simon & Schuster has not eliminated all books hinting that large corporations are less than perfect.

The problem is more subtle and profound. In a democracy only one condition justifies a private publisher's imposing his personal politics on the decision of what to print: that a wide spectrum of other ideas has equitable access to the marketplace. If a small number of publishers, all with the same special outlook, dominate the marketplace of public ideas, something vital is lost to an open society. In countries like the Soviet Union a state publishing house imposes a political test on what will be printed. If the same kind of control over public ideas is exercised by a private entrepreneur, the effect of a corporate line is not so different from that of a party line.

Detecting how most of the mass media impose political tests on what the public will see and hear is not as straightforward as the episodes in this book might make it seem. Political intervention in its most pervasive form is not open and explicit but is concealed under seemingly apolitical reasons. In the case of books, for example, every major publisher receives a daily avalanche of manuscripts and proposals; some publishers receive as many as 10,000 a year. Only a few of these manuscripts can be published. The others are rejected for a variety of legitimate and practical reasons: Some are devoid of ideas, some are badly written, some have poor sales prospects, and some may not fit the specialty of a particular publishing house. But it is also possible that some are instantly recognized as contrary to the personal politics of the owner or governing board of the publishing company. If that is the determining factor in a decision to reject a manuscript, a pragmatic reason will usually be given instead.

The same difficulty in confirming the influence of corporate politics in editorial decisions applies to all mass media. In 1982, for example, two highly popular television personalities, Walter Cronkite and Ed Asner (of the "Lou Grant Show"), had their programs canceled after each had made liberal public speeches that criticized an aspect of American foreign policy. The networks said the programs were killed because of low ratings. Asner said it was because of his personal politics. Cronkite said he did not think the reason given by the network was accurate. In both cases the network canceled the shows allegedly for low ratings, but it did not cancel other shows with low ratings. In neither the Cronkite nor the Asner case was it possible to find documentation that contradicted the official reason.

Most difficult of all to document is the implicit influence of corporate chiefs. Most bosses do not have to tell their subordinates what they like and dislike. Or if such an explanation is necessary, it is not necessary to repeat the lesson. Simon & Schuster, like most publishers, insists that personal or corporate politics plays no part in its decisions. So do most editors, at least in public. But it is possible that Nan Talese (no longer at Simon & Schuster) would not, after the Mark Dowie experience, need to be told explicitly in a formal memorandum which ideas will bring rejection at the corporate level.

Every year there is a distressing list of reporters and editors of newspapers and magazines who are fired or demoted because they stumbled on the private politics of their owner, or a list of television producers and writers who make professionally competent decisions that run counter to the politics of the corporation. Even when such firings and demotions are clear interventions of corporate politics into the editorial process, the worst damage is not in one particular incident but in the long-lasting aftermath in which working professionals at the editorial level behave as though under orders from above, although no explicit orders have been given.

In August 1982, for example, the *Wall Street Journal* reported that Earl Golz, a reporter for the *Dallas Morning News,* was fired, although he had worked as a reporter for thirteen years, and his editor, Wayne Epperson, was forced to resign because of a story Golz wrote that offended a major Dallas bank, the Abilene National Bank. Golz's story reported that the bank had loan problems so serious that it was in danger of failing, as another large bank, Penn Square National, had done a few days earlier. The Abilene National Bank chairman reacted with rage and the paper got rid of the reporter and his editor. Less than two weeks later the Golz story was confirmed when the bank failed and federal examiners found that the bank had loan losses far beyond its assets. The bank chairman who had denied it all was fired. But the reporter and editor were not rehired. No reporter or editor on that paper—and perhaps on other papers as well—will have to be told for a long time what the boss expects. There will be no need for memorandums or spoken words. Subordinates, to be safe, may go even further in self-censorship than the boss requires. But no official intervention will show.

A common defense of giantism in the media is that the big media corporations are strong enough to withstand improper pressure from nonmedia corporations asking for favorable treatment. But there are too many cases in which giant media firms and other giant corporations have a common political front. In addition, when giants clash, the possibility of fiscal bloodshed can be so overwhelming that, like nuclear nations, they find other ways to resolve their differences. The quiet alteration of the news or suppression of a book may seem preferable to placing corporate money and reputation in jeopardy. Such a case may be the dispute involving three large corporations, Du Pont, Time, Inc., and Prentice-Hall, on one side and on the other side a smaller entity, an author named Gerard Colby Zilg.

Zilg, a former congressional aide, spent five years writing a book about the Du Ponts and their company, *Du Pont: Behind the Nylon Curtain.* It was published by Prentice-Hall in 1974 and quickly sold its first printing of 10,000. The reviews were good. The *New York Times Book Review* said it was "something of a miracle, and that's just what this young man (25) has pulled off. It's hard to believe that this masterful book is Zilg's first . . . If you want to be picky, about every 50 pages you can find something trivial that shouldn't be there." *Publishers Weekly* said the book should "be useful . . . for future historians."

The Du Pont company did not like the book. It had been able, through a process of its own, to obtain a copy of the author's manuscript before it had even been set in type. The company decided to bide its time until Prentice-Hall, pleased with the book's rising success, signed an agreement that made it the selection of the Fortune Book Club. The Fortune Book Club belonged to Time, Inc. and was administered by Book-of-the-Month Club (which later was also bought by Time, Inc.). Du Pont complained to Fortune Book Club and Prentice-Hall. As a result, Fortune Book Club canceled its agreement with Prentice-Hall and Prentice-Hall ceased promoting the book.

William Daly, general counsel for Prentice-Hall, in a conversation with a representative of Du Pont, Richard H. Rea, said the book contract was canceled because Du Pont had threatened to remove its advertising from Time, Inc. publications if the Time, Inc. book club offered the Zilg book for sale. According to Rea's memorandum, written at the time and later entered in a lawsuit:

> Daly related that BOMC [Book-of-the-Month Club] . . . as of last Thursday (August 1) had notified Prentice-Hall that, after further pressure from Du Pont, they were cancelling their agreement. Daly said the pressure consisted of threats of litigation and cancellation of all of Du Pont advertising in *Time, Life* and *Fortune.*

Zilg sued Prentice-Hall and Du Pont for conspiracy to suppress his book and asked for damages under provisions of the First Amendment and antitrust laws against conspiracies in restraint of trade. After four years he won his suit against Prentice-Hall but not against Du Pont.

Books that make their subjects unhappy are legion. Sometimes public complaints against books are even desired or provoked by publishers because controversy draws attention to a book and can increase sales. Books that contain errors, as Du Pont claimed Zilg's book did, also are common, but this is seldom cause for withdrawal from publication. The difference in the case of angered subjects and alleged errors lies in the power of the offended subject. Du Pont, Time, Inc., and Prentice-Hall all understood the vocabulary of power and the preferred alternative of silencing an author's ideas and information rather than engaging in a struggle among giants.

The quick empathy that power centers have for each other seemed to be demonstrated when Kermit Roosevelt, a former Central Intelligence Agency (CIA) officer, wrote a book called *Countercoup: The Struggle for the Control of Iran.* It was the author's inside version of how intelligence agencies overthrew a left-leaning Iranian premier, Mohammed Mossadegh, in 1953 and reinstated the Shah. The issue was control of oil. The plot was called "Ajax," of which Roosevelt wrote: "The original proposal for Ajax came from the Anglo-Iranian Oil Company (AIOC) after its expulsion from Iran nine months earlier." The book was published by McGraw-Hill in early 1979. Books were on sale in bookstores and reviewer copies were already in the mails when British Petroleum, successor corporation to AIOC, persuaded McGraw-Hill to recall all the books—from the stores and from reviewers.

Large media firms may help each other, but they can also help themselves. The bigger they are, the more mechanisms they have to promote their own interests. Among these mechanisms is the power to leave out news that will reduce their income or embarrass the parent firm. A few uncelebrated examples illustrate the routine character of such self-serving acts.

- The *Los Angeles Times* is owned by Times Mirror Company, which also owns other newspapers, cable systems, book publishing houses, agricultural land, urban real estate, commercial printing plants, and other nonjournalistic operations. The *Times* over the years has been a persistent advocate for state and federal subsidy of agricultural water, most of which is used for agricultural land. In 1980, the *Times,* as it had for all such water projects over the decades, pressed for a new, $2 billion, tax-paid canal system. A Times-Mirror subsidiary would be a beneficiary, particularly a planned real estate and recreational project. Other papers, the *New York Times* and the *Bakersfield Californian,* reported the project and its dependence on the controversial canal, but the *Los Angeles Times* did not, saying it was not newsworthy.*

- In 1978 the Samuel Horvitz Trust owned five monopoly newspapers in Ohio and New York, cable systems in Ohio and Virginia, and construction firms in Ohio, and it was a major landowner in Florida. The trust was run by three sons of Samuel Horvitz plus a family employee. The trustees had a falling-out. One son, Harry R. Horvitz, who headed the news properties, sued the other three trustees in a business dispute. When the trial was scheduled, the three majority trustees issued orders to their newspapers: "Neither you nor any employee of the trust-owned corporations will engage either directly or indirectly in the reporting, publishing or disseminating anything whatsoever with respect to our pending litigation in probate court."

- In Atlanta on June 18, 1979, the major papers in Georgia printed as news the report of a speech by their publisher that a major media merger between the news empire, Cox,

---

* An earlier edition of this book said that the *Los Angeles Times* failed to report with normal prominence a state-ordered rebate of overcharges made by Pacific Telephone, for whom the *Times*'s subsidiary printed phone books. That statement, based on a television documentary, was incorrect. The *Times* printed the story of the rebate on page one.

and General Electric was improperly held up on the false assumption that there was a connection between the publishing entity of the newspapers, Cox Enterprises, and Cox Broadcasting. Any connection, the publisher said, was a "myth." His assertion was printed in his paper without further information. That same day Cox Broadcasting issued a proxy statement showing that the two Cox entities had the same chairman and shared two other directors and that the Cox family owned a majority of stock in one and 46.14 percent of stock in the other. Ordinarily, a news report failing to include such information would be considered incompetent.

- Media companies, large and small, have often demanded special favors because of their power over public information. The larger the media company, the larger the favors it can ask for. Rupert Murdoch, an Australian who controls papers in England, Australia, and the United States, is publisher of the *Post,* the only afternoon daily in New York City. He also owns an Australian airline. In 1980, after the staff of the Export-Import Bank of the United States rejected Murdoch's application for a taxpayer-subsidized loan for his Australian airline, Murdoch had lunch at the White House with then president Jimmy Carter and later with the president of the Export-Import Bank. Two days later Murdoch's *Post* endorsed President Carter in the crucial New York presidential primary, and six days after that the bank reversed its decision and awarded Murdoch his loan of $290 million at 8.1 percent interest.

A parochial myth that permeates all the media is that intervention of owners into the content of news is no problem. But it persists as a problem. Bruce Ware Roche, in his dissertation "The Effects of Newspaper Owners' Non-Media Business Interests on News Judgments of Members of News Staffs," listed numerous corporate interventions in newspapers. When Walter Annenberg, a dominant magazine publisher, owned the *Philadelphia Inquirer* he routinely banished from the news the names of people he disliked, including people normally reported. He used his newspaper to attack a candidate for governor who opposed action that would benefit the stockholders of the Pennsylvania Railroad, but Annenberg never informed the readers that he was the largest single stockholder in the railroad.

When the Du Ponts owned the dominant newspapers in Delaware they regularly censored news stories or ordered emphasis in display depending on how the stories would affect family interests, actions so blatant that a distinguished editor resigned rather than comply. The *Houston Chronicle,* owned by a powerful trust, also ordered stories killed if they would hurt the trust's banking, real estate, and other interests.

When General Electric bought stations KOA-AM, -FM, and -TV, it introduced constant promotions for General Electric. When the Amalgamated Clothing Workers tried to buy advertisements to explain why they were picketing the Marshall Field department stores, the *Chicago Sun-Times,* owned by Marshall Field Enterprises, refused to run the ads.

In the years after World War II, no standard newspaper in the country would accept ads from Consumers Union because its magazine, *Consumer Reports,* tested and reported, sometimes negatively, name brands advertised in newspapers. Television station KPIX in San Francisco is owned by Westinghouse, which became codeveloper of a large housing development in Half Moon Bay, Calif. KPIX-TV thereafter did several programs and documentaries on the housing development.

Perhaps the longest-lasting power of media companies is the power to create ideas and movements, which, if necessary, can reflect the strictly private desires of the media owner. Once public attention has been aroused, the media owner can pretend to be reporting a spontaneous public phenomenon.

In 1949, for example, William Randolph Hearst, head of one large publishing empire, and Henry Luce, chief of another,

Time, Inc., were both worried about communism and the growth of liberalism in the United States. They personally created an international personage who, for two decades thereafter, would become a powerful voice preaching doctrines they approved of. The voice was that of Billy Graham, an obscure evangelist holding poorly attended tent meetings in Los Angeles until the intervention of Hearst and Luce. Many rich and powerful people encourage evangelists like Graham, perhaps because those who have already made their money in the here-and-now don't mind urging everyone else to wait for their rewards in the hereafter. When the rich and powerful control overwhelming access to the public mind they can turn this impulse into a national movement.

Hearst and Luce interviewed the obscure preacher and decided he was worthy of their support. Billy Graham became an almost instantaneous national and, later, international figure preaching anticommunism. In late 1949 Hearst sent a telegram to all Hearst editors: "Puff Graham." The editors did—in Hearst newspapers, magazines, movies, and newsreels. Within two months Graham was preaching to crowds of 350,000.

In February 1950 Luce added his empire to the Hearst publicity. The impact was later described by Graham: *"Time and Life began carrying about everything I did, it seemed like. They gave me a tremendous push."* By 1954 Luce had put Billy Graham on the cover of *Time* magazine. Graham was preaching, "Either Communism must die, or Christianity must die," and the preacher became a public advocate of Senator Joseph McCarthy.

The massive Hearst media empire was also used to help create McCarthy. McCarthy, desperate for a campaign issue for reelection and observing the media support for anticommunism, made his historic speech in Wheeling, W.Va., in 1950: "I have here in my hand a list of 205 names known to the Secretary of State as being members of the Communist Party . . . still shaping policy in the State Department."

It electrified the country. The State Department and members of the Senate Foreign Relations Committee asked McCarthy for the names. William Randolph Hearst, Jr., who inherited the leadership of the empire from his father, was a personal friend and sympathizer of McCarthy. Recently he related: "Joe gave me a call not long after that speech. And you know what? He didn't have a damn thing on that list. Nothing."

It was a historic moment for a newspaper chain. Hearst had exclusive and authoritative information on the falsity of a declaration that was to paralyze American politics for five years. He did not put it in the news. Instead, he formed a cadre of Hearst journalists and researchers at the Hearst flagship paper, the *New York Journal-American,* to provide McCarthy with as much help as possible to keep the anticommunist hysteria alive.

The size of the Hearst and Luce empires had two negative effects on the quality of public discourse. The conglomerate power of their empires allowed them to create a national atmosphere if they wished. And if they focused largely on goals of large corporations, it had the effect, because of their dominance in the media, of undernourishing society of other news and ideas necessary for informed democratic decision making.

The result of the overwhelming power of relatively narrow corporate ideologies has been the creation of widely established political and economic illusions in the United States with little visible contradiction in the media to which a majority of the population is exclusively exposed. The illusions sustained by mass-media corporations are not minor ones. They often go to the heart of crucial public policy.

Two major themes in public life, for example, are the excessive burdens that taxes place on the vitality of corporations, and that labor-union-induced wages are a damaging drag on national productivity and thus on the economy. Both are false but both have been perpetuated by corporate-controlled media for decades.

The general public is largely unaware that from 1950 to 1984 corporations reduced their share of federal revenues from 25 percent to 8 percent. That shift, if reported in the news at all, has traditionally been depicted as a necessary move to improve the economy and decrease unemployment. It is doubtful that it has improved the economy—much of the savings to corporate life has gone into unproductive mergers and acquisitions, to lavish dividends at the expense of reinvestment to keep the industries competitive, and for transfer of jobs to foreign countries. But there is no doubt that the corporate shedding of a proper share of taxes has shifted heavier burdens to individual taxpayers. That fact is almost forbidden in news stories about taxes. Eventually, the corporate escape from taxes became intolerable by 1986—a generation late in the news.

The myth of union wages also is pervasive and its true perspective seldom reported in news stories about unions and national productivity. The truth is that productivity in unionized industries has risen. It has fallen in the non-unionized sectors that include white-collar and administrative workers.

The deeper social loss of giantism in the media is not in its unfair advantage in profits and power; this is real and it is serious. But the gravest loss is in the self-serving censorship of political and social ideas, in news, magazine articles, books, broadcasting, and movies. Some intervention by owners is direct and blunt. But most of the screening is subtle, some not even occurring at a conscious level, as when subordinates learn by habit to conform to owners' ideas. But subtle or not, the ultimate result is distorted reality and impoverished ideas.

3

"WON'T THEY EVER LEARN?"

There are still quite a few executive officers who are accustomed to giving orders and who resent the media for not taking them.

Kenneth A. Randall

AS JOSEPH PULITZER approached the end of his career he worried about the future of his newspaper. Would his heirs be competent and committed? Or would they sell to greedy new owners? He decided to follow the example of the *London Times* and to name trustees instructed by his will to operate the paper in the public interest.

The trustee device generally has failed. Voices from the grave seldom win debates; where there is a will there is a lawyer to break it. But 1904 was a more innocent age and Pulitzer set out to find distinguished citizens as trustees to preserve the integrity of his *New York World*. He was impressed with the character of the presiding justice of New York State's highest court, Morgan K. Stanley. He took the judge horseback riding and explained his plan. The judge seemed amenable. The two men tentatively agreed that Stanley would be a trustee. They rode on for a while before Pulitzer asked: "What do you think of the *World*?"

"It is a great paper. But it has one defect."
"What is that?"
"It never stands by its friends."

46

"A newspaper should have no friends," Pulitzer replied sharply.

"I think it should," the judge answered just as sharply.

"If that is your opinion," Pulitzer said, "I wouldn't make you one of my trustees if you gave me a million dollars."

Pulitzer was serious. In his newsroom a sign announced ominously, "The *World* has no friends."

But almost all news media have friends who are given preferential treatment in the news, who are immune to criticism, who can keep out embarrassing information, or who are guaranteed a positive image. In the newsrooms of America these friends are called "sacred cows." They frequently include the owner, the owner's family and friends, major advertisers, and the owner's political causes. Sacred cows in the news run the gamut from petunias to presidents. In one northeastern city the sacred cow is civic flowerbeds donated by the publisher's spouse, in another city it is an order that any picture of Richard Nixon must show him smiling.

The sacred cows in American newsrooms leave residues common to all cows. But no sacred cow has been so protected and has left more generous residues in the news than the American corporation. So it is ironic that in the last decade the most bitter attacks on the news media have come from the American corporate system. The irony becomes exquisite when, in the 1980s, the segment of American life that most hates the news increasingly comes to own it.

Large classes of people are ignored in the news, are reported as exotic fads, or appear only at their worst—minorities, blue-collar workers, the lower middle class, the poor. They become publicized mainly when they are in spectacular accidents, go on strike, or are arrested. Other groups and institutions—government, schools, universities, and nonestablished political movements—are subjected to periodic criticism. Minor tribes like athletes, fashion designers, and actors receive routine praise. But since World War I hardly a mainstream American news medium has failed to grant its most favored treatment to corporate life.

There has been much to celebrate in the history of corporate industry and technology. Great cities rose and flourished, material goods flowed to the populace, cash spread to new classes of people, in developed countries standards of living rose and life was prolonged.

There have also been ugliness and injustice in corporate wielding of power—bloody repressions of workers who tried to organize unions, corruption of government, theft of public franchises. But through it all, most of the mass media depicted corporate life as benevolent and patriotic.

In the late 1950s, ghosts appeared at industry's banquet. Raw materials had been extracted in astounding volumes and some were near exhaustion. Economic benefits of industrialization were spread unevenly, causing political turbulence. As ever, entrepreneurs contended for dominion over the earth's crust, this time wielding its bitter fruit—uranium. In some forms the ghosts were literally invisible. Since the start of the Industrial Revolution new vapors, 200 billion tons of carbon dioxide alone, were added to the atmosphere, changing climates and human organs. Thousands of new chemicals, like DDT, soon resided in every living tissue and, like radiation, created ominous biological alterations. By the 1980s some wastes of industry, 77 billion pounds a year, were so hazardous that it was not clear whether the planet could safely contain them. Corporate products and wastes began to poison drinking water, food, and in some cases whole communities. In the past itinerant merchants sold harmful products that could sicken or kill hundreds, but now great international organizations poured out avalanches of products which, if unsafe, threatened millions. One in four Americans came to die of cancer.

In earlier periods, death and disease were accepted as acts of God. If a tunnel collapsed on miners or textile workers died coughing blood, it was all the hand of God or random bad luck. But when industry's ghost of pollution and disease materialized in the last half of the twentieth century the problems drew attention not, as before, to the hand of God, but to the organizations that owned and operated most of industrial civilization—the great corporations.

Corporate unease became sharper when a president whom corporations considered their own, Dwight D. Eisenhower, left office in 1961 warning against the bloated power of what he called "the military-industrial complex." Later that same year twenty-nine major corporations, some with household names like Westinghouse and General Electric, were convicted of conspiracies in selling $7 billion worth of electrical equipment, and some executives actually served short jail sentences. More shocks to the corporate status quo came in quick succession. Racial tensions, suppressed for centuries, burst into a mass movement in the 1960s. The Vietnam War protests raised an additional specter of rebellion in the streets. Another president the corporations regarded as their champion, Richard Nixon, left office in disgrace in 1974, partly because of accusations of corruption involving prominent corporations.

When the twenty-nine corporations were convicted of conspiracy in 1961, a lawyer for one of the defendants told the judge the executives should not be punished because their acts were "a way of life—everybody's doing it."

The claim that "everybody's doing it" was a lawyer's exaggerated argument for leniency, but in the subsequent years mounting evidence showed that while it was not true that "everybody's doing it," an extraordinary number of large corporations were involved in shady practices. In 1979 the Department of Justice found that of the 582 largest American corporations more than 60 percent were guilty of at least one illegal action, including evasion of taxes, unfair labor practices, dangerous working conditions, price fixing, pollution, and illegal kickbacks. At the "West Point of capitalism," the Harvard Graduate School of Business Administration, the *Harvard Business Review* found that corporate ethical practices, poor in 1961, were even worse in 1976. Its survey of industrial leaders showed common practices like cheating customers, bribing political officials, and using call girls for business purposes. Two separate 1976 surveys of corporate executives by corporations themselves—Pitney Bowes and Uniroyal—found that a majority of business managers "feel pressured to compromise personal ethics to achieve corporate goals," including selling "off-standard and possibly dangerous items."

Nevertheless, nothing in government or law prevented the 200 largest corporations from increasing their control of all manufacturing from 45 percent in 1947 to 60 percent in 1979 or lessened corporate crime that produces $44 billion in losses a year compared with $4 billion in property losses resulting from crimes committed by individuals.

Courts have always been lenient with corporations though in recent years even that has not satisfied the corporate world. Conservative foundations give judges and their families all-expenses-paid trips to Miami so they can take courses in the laissez-faire doctrines of Milton Friedman, focusing on the necessity to leave corporations untouched by regulation and minimally touched by law. By 1980 one-fifth of the entire federal judiciary had taken the courses.

Added judicial sympathy would not have seemed necessary. In the 1961 conviction of the twenty-nine corporations involved in the electrical equipment conspiracy, all the cases had been delayed for ten years or more, some for twenty-five years, while the offenses continued. When the Aluminum Company of America was found guilty of illegal damage to competitors, massive legal defenses by the company delayed court action for sixteen years. Though the Internal Revenue Service regularly jails between 600 and 700 tax evaders each year, some for relatively small amounts, when the Firestone Tire & Rubber Company pleaded guilty to concealing $12.6 million income in two deliberately false tax returns and to conspiring to obstruct legal audits of their books, the corporation received a fine of only $10,000.

In addition to their ability to evade or soften the legal consequences of their actions, corporations are protected by their special positions in government. After laws are passed or before regulations are designed, outside advisory committees sit with government leaders to help shape official actions. In 1974, for example, AT&T had 130 positions on these advisory bodies, RCA 104, General Electric 74, and ITT 53. Defense industry executives sit on the Pentagon's Industry Advisory Council, oil executives sit on the National Petroleum Council, and some of the heaviest polluting industries have executives on the National Industrial Pollution Control Council. The most powerful business lobby, the Business Roundtable, has been able to use its membership on such committees to kill crucial legislation on the verge of passage, like the unexpected collapse in 1974 of a bill in the House of Representatives that would have established a consumer protection agency.

In universities, as in government, corporate values have steadily and quietly become dominant in the scientific research community. Corporate executives are the largest single group represented on governing boards of colleges and universities. In the public schools corporate materials have always been prominent and their presence is increasing. Only 1 percent of already tight school budgets are used for instructional materials, and industry has been quick to fill the gap with largely self-serving publications. Free classroom materials are produced by 64 percent of the 500 largest American industrial corporations, 90 percent of industrial trade associations, and 90 percent of utility companies. The materials concentrate on nutrition, energy, environment, and economics, almost all supplied by industries with a stake in their own answer to the problems posed in the materials. "Free marketplace" and nonregulation of business is the predominant classroom economics lesson, presented largely through materials from a business group, the Advertising Council. The only nonscholastic source of classroom material larger than corporations is the Department of Defense.

While corporate influence remained almost untouched in the last few decades, changes occurred at the grass roots. Fueled by the irreverence of the 1960s protesters, critical attitudes toward corporations for the first time in recent American history went beyond the small enclaves of the left and reached the middle class. In the early 1970s corporate abuse became an issue when an ecology movement cut across political and class lines. Government, responding to its demands, looked more closely at corporate crime. A new consumer movement, built around the nucleus of Ralph Nader and skilled university students, produced systematic data on dangerous consumer goods and unfair business practices. Slow-acting malignancies caused by asbestos and other carcinogens began raising morbidity and death rates among industrial employees, drawing attention to hazards in the workplace.

At about the same time Western capitalism entered a period of crisis. The spiral of prosperity faltered. In country after country, including the United States, standard remedies failed or made things worse. What seemed at first to be an isolated phenomenon of escalated oil prices became a more fundamental malaise. Undeveloped nations that were once docile sources of raw materials vital to the new industrial civilization became less docile. Leaders of business and finance had always insisted, at least in public, on the infallibility of the self-righting mechanisms of their marketplace. And yet the marketplace defied their pronouncements. That malfunction, too, turned the public's attention to the great corporations.

In most walks of public life, corporations are accustomed to a smooth path edged with indulgence. Criticism in the United States had tended to be short-lived if it came from government or established sources. Longer-lasting criticism came from public health authorities, social scientists, unions, liberal and left activists, and other specialized voices. In both cases, either criticisms failed to be reported in the mass media or the reports were brief or even neutralized by the media's criticism of the critics.

The standard media—mainstream newspapers, magazines, and broadcasters—had always been reliable promoters of the corporate ethic. Whole sections of newspapers were always devoted to unrelieved glorification of business people, not just in advertisements where corporations pay for self-praise but in "news" that is assumed to be dispassionate. Most business sections of daily papers seldom apply to corporations the same criteria of validation and critical judgment applied to other subjects. Most business pages consist of corporate propaganda in the form of press releases run without significant changes or printed verbatim. Each day millions of expensive pages of stock market quotations are printed even though only 2 percent of American households actively trade in the stock market. Editorially, corporate causes almost invariably become news media causes. Among the most commonly suppressed news items each year are stories involving corporations that are reported in minor publications but are not given serious attention in the major media. The integration of corporate values into the national pieties could not have been established without prolonged indoctrination by the main body of American news organizations.

In the years after 1970, mounting public anger at some corporate behavior does occasionally find expression in print and on the air, as when the public was asked to sacrifice warm homes and car travel during a gas shortage while the major oil companies reported their highest profits in history. Or local demonstrations against polluting industries became melodrama that met the criteria for conflict news. Or a spectacular trial, like the Ford Motor Company defense against criminal charges of neglect for its defective Pinto gas tanks, caught the media's attention. The barriers against damaging news about corporations were high but not impassable. Journalism had slowly changed so that in a few standard media, including, ironically, the daily bible of business, the *Wall Street Journal,* there were more than brief flurries of items about bad public performances of big business. There was still no significant criticism of the corporate system, simply reporting of isolated cases, but for the first time there was a breach in the almost uniform litany of unremitting praise and promotion of corporate behavior.

Corporate leaders were outraged. They criticized government agencies that reported corporate culpability. In their Political Action Committees they raised the largest campaign war chests in electoral history to defeat candidates they considered hostile to business, and in 1980 they elected a national administration dedicated to wiping out half a century of social legislation and regulation of business. They created intellectual think tanks to counter academic studies damaging to corporations. But the corporations reserved their greatest wrath for the news media. Hell hath no fury like the sacred cow desanctified.

Business had special advantages in its attack on the media. It had privileged access to media executives through common corporate associations and lobbies, and it could produce large-scale advertisements to counter antibusiness news and, increasingly, to use as threats of withdrawal against hostile media. And corporate leaders could invoke against the media that peculiar American belief (ironically created more by the media than by any other source) that to criticize big business is to attack American democracy.

Criticizing the media is neither unnatural nor harmful. The difference in the corporate attack was that the campaign attempted to discredit the whole system of American news as subversive to American values and to characterize journalists as a class of careless "economic illiterates" biased against business.

Some specific corporate complaints were justified. Throughout journalism there is more carelessness and sloth than should be tolerated. Most reporters are "economic illiterates" in the sense that they lack skills to analyze business records and they seldom have the sophistication to comprehend world economic forces. But the accusation that standard American reporting was biased against business was absurd. It was absurd, but beginning in the 1970s it was relentless.

In 1976 the vice-chairman of Bethlehem Steel, Frederic West, Jr., told the American Newspaper Publishers Association, "People in business have a lot of gripes about the press. Anytime a bunch of executives get together these days you can be sure somebody will start talking about what's wrong with the news media." In 1977 the president of Union Pacific said, "There is a basic bias that big business is bad." In 1981 the president of a major advertising agency, Needham, Harper & Steers/Issues and Images, said, "All too frequently some rather rabid anticorporate messages are aired as part of the regular daily news schedule . . . I assure you that I echo the sentiments of most people on the corporate side who've been stung repeatedly by the slanted coverage of their activities. Especially those stories about corporate profits."

A vice-president of Shell Oil complained to a Senate committee about bias in the news. He displayed headlines as evidence.

"I have brought along a few articles clipped from our daily newspaper as examples of what I mean." The headlines were

NADER CHARGES ENERGY SCARE DESIGNED TO DOUBLE OIL PRICES; ASPIN CLAIMS OIL COMPANIES GOUGING PUBLIC; SENATOR CLAIMS OIL SHORTAGE PUT UP JOB; JACKSON SAYS OIL FIRMS IRK PUBLIC WITH EVASIONS.

These news items usually originated with documented studies or with reports of established agencies. Lawrence K. Fouraker, dean of the Harvard Graduate School of Business Administration, echoing the complaints of those (including media companies and journalists themselves) who want only pleasant news about their work, said that business reporters "tend to be gullible about business, if it is not good news."

The same kind of corporate campaign against the news occurred at the local level. A. Kent MacDougall, probably the most sophisticated reporter of business among American newspaper journalists, reported in the *Los Angeles Times* that in Des Moines, Iowa, two dozen business leaders signed a public statement claiming bias because the local paper had published their salaries.

No other news sources, including high government officials, have been as effective as corporate executives in causing reporters to be fired, demoted, or moved from their beats. If the routine reporting of negative news about business from official sources was enraging, the idea of journalists taking the initiative in their own investigation of business, as they do with government, welfare recipients, and organized crime, tended to produce hysteria.

Leonard Matthews, president of the American Association of Advertising Agencies, said that "business and the entire free enterprise system need to be supported by the media" but that this "mutually healthy relationship" had been "impaired in recent years by the overzealous actions of a small but very visible group of investigative reporters who have made a practice of slugging advertisers while their associates in the sales department were accepting an order from the same company."

In the 1980s there are more investigative reporters than ever before. They have their own organization, Investigative Reporters and Editors. But of 1,110 members, only 6 have corporate life as their beat. And the stereotype of the journalist as radical and antibusiness does not match the facts. An authoritative study by Stephen Hess showed that 58 percent of Washington correspondents consider themselves "middle of the road" or "conservative" politically. "In the past," Hess wrote, "the Washington press corps was liberal . . . a stereotype of the news corps that is no longer accurate."

It does not excuse journalists, who should become competent in the subjects they cover, but genuine economic literacy throughout the American population is remarkably low for a society in which economics has become the center of national politics. It is even more remarkable that business people themselves are among the most economically illiterate. A survey of 3,000 persons by the business-oriented Advertising Council showed that "only 8% of all U.S. businessmen can correctly define the functions of these five groups—business, labor, the consumer, the investor, and advertising."

One of the most caustic critics of business reporting has been Walter B. Wriston, chairman of Citibank. He insisted that journalists are interested only in bad news about the economy. "The media, supported by some academic 'liberals,' would have us believe that things are not just going badly, they are growing progressively and rapidly worse," Wriston said in 1975. Wriston's own 1975 prediction was, "I am convinced inflation is going to moderate very, very substantially" and "I don't think there is any question that the price of oil will come down." Five years later, the consumer price index had risen more than 50 percent and the price index for refined petroleum products was up 150 percent. Eventually, inflation and oil prices did fall, but "eventually" is not convincing evidence that a leading banker had any more fore-sight than the "economic illiterates" who happened to be less euphoric than the bankers.

The vigorous corporate campaign against alleged bias in the news contained a large element of cynicism along with whatever genuine anger was involved. Most corporate leaders did not experience criticism by the media. David Finn, leader of a major industrial public relations firm, Ruder and Finn, conducted a survey of the 1,000 largest industries for the American Management Association in 1981. When chief executive officers were asked to describe how the media had treated their companies, their responses were

Poor	6%
Fair	28%
Good	47%
Excellent	19%

Two-thirds of the leading industrial chiefs of the country believe the media treatment of their companies is good or excellent and only 6 percent feel it is poor. Corporations must constitute the best-treated complainers in society.

A few corporate leaders have said that the corporate anti-media campaign is misdirected. J. Peter Grace, president of W. R. Grace Company, says the public's bad image of business originated "because business has countenanced dishonesty in dealing with government employees and purchasing agents on a world-wide basis." William F. May, chairman of American Can Company, said, "There is a tendency for business to stand on tippy toes and communicate only the favorable. We need to present more unvarnished information."

Senator Abraham Ribicoff of Connecticut told a meeting of top business executives in 1979:

> Businessmen are always getting mad and blaming someone else when the blame lies squarely on your shoulders. You let the Japanese beat you in the small-car market. You treat every regulation as an attack when you know very well that some regulation is beneficial to you. You also seem to for-

get that the American people are concerned for their health, life and safety.

Perhaps nowhere is the cynicism more blatant than in the newly energized activity known as "corporate advertising." This constitutes printed and broadcast ads designed not to sell goods and services but to promote the politics and benevolent image of the corporation—and to attack anything that spoils the image. The ideology-image ads as a category of all ads doubled in the 1970s and are now a half-billion-dollar-a-year enterprise.

The head of a large advertising agency described the purpose:

It presents the corporation as hero, a responsible citizen, a force for good, presenting information on the work the company is doing in community relations, assisting the less fortunate, minimizing pollution, controlling drugs, ameliorating poverty.

The publication *Media Decisions* estimated that as much as $3 billion in corporate money goes into all methods of promoting the corporation as hero and into "explanations of the capitalistic system," including massive use of corporate books and teaching materials in the schools, almost all tax deductible.

The energy crises of the 1970s and 1980s intensified the corporate campaign against the media, led this time by the petroleum industry. Extraordinary escalation of consumer prices for energy was accompanied by multiplied profits to the oil companies. The corporate profit announcements were intended, as usual, to impress international investors, and the general public apparently was not supposed to notice. But it did. The public demanded that legislators, civic groups, and the media explain why private citizens were asked to sacrifice but oil companies were not. A survey showed that 25 percent of the American population favored nationalization of the oil industry.

The structure and inner finances of the oil industry are among the most byzantine in the world. Journalists had remained ignorant and for the most part are still ignorant of the realities of energy economics. Journalistic negligence has damaged the public, but it has been to the advantage of oil companies.

In the 1980s the most vigorous promoter of the corporation as hero and the most relentless critic of the news media has been Mobil Oil. In 1981 Mobil and its petroleum allies gave the journalistic world an object lesson in the penalties for journalists who stray from the paths of corporate piety.

Mobil Oil is the third largest industrial corporation in the country (Exxon is second), and it has taken the lead among American corporations in attacking the news media for alleged antibusiness bias. In 1972 it began using some of its $21 million annual public relations budget for advertisements directed against the news media and succeeded in guaranteeing its ads a place on the editorial pages of a dozen major papers (a spot next to editorials that came to be known in the newspaper trade as "the Mobil position"). During the 1973 Arab oil crisis Mobil's editorial ads appeared in hundreds of papers. The company also runs a column called "Observations" in Sunday supplements distributed to thousands of community newspapers. Mobil has an informal network of television stations that carry its political and antimedia commercials. It sponsors books and publishes some books under its own imprint and others by regular trade and university presses. Its book *The Genius of Arab Civilization*, published by New York University Press, is one of a series promoting countries where it has oil interests. Other books and reports it has sponsored have been published by MIT Press and Hudson Institute.

Mobil's own accuracy in advertising has not always been the best model for the journalists it lectures so sternly. In 1980 the company agreed under threat of official penalty to undo the inaccuracy of a Mobil ad that claimed a product would save up to 25 percent in oil consumption when in fact it often increased oil consumption.

Mobil's most noticeable and influential ads against the media have appeared in the editorial space of the *New York Times,* the *Wall Street Journal,* the *Washington Post,* and other major metropolitan newspapers. The ads express anger at error in the media, weariness at media ignorance, and sarcasm at lack of devotion to the true principles of the First Amendment. Unfortunately, Mobil seemed to define one First Amendment for the news media and a different one for the oil company.

One Mobil ad declared, "Any restraint on free discussion is dangerous. Any policy that restricts flow of information or ideas is potentially harmful." It is a noble idea. But shortly afterward, Mobil Oil, a major sponsor of public broadcasting, urged the Public Broadcasting System to suppress the showing of a film that would upset its oil partner, Saudi Arabia.

In 1981 Mobil ran one of its editorial ads in ten major newspapers with a total of seven million circulation. The ad exploited the Benedictine Sisters against their will. The Sisters complained. Only one of the papers, the *Los Angeles Times,* ran the letter of complaint. Mobil's multimillion-dollar editorial ad campaign obviously was more convincing to the other nine papers than grievances of the nonpaying Benedictine Sisters.

Other Mobil editorial ads praised the company itself for sensitive attention to pollution. When a national business group of which it is a member, the Council of Economic Priorities, issued a pollution report that mentioned Mobil's poor record on pollution, Mobil withdrew its support from the council. When Columbia University created a program to give training in economics to business reporters, a project aiming to diminish journalistic "economic illiteracy," Mobil's action may provide a hint at the nature of the "economic literacy" it desired. Mobil was a contributor to the Columbia program but when the university named the director of the program Mobil withdrew its support because the director had once criticized the oil industry.

When a smaller company used a front organization to criticize Mobil, a vice-president of Mobil announced indignantly, "The public has a right to know who is behind any advocacy effect." This prompted the Jack O'Dwyer public relations newsletter to disclose that Mobil is the sponsor of pro-oil, antigovernment cartoons that appear in hundreds of newspapers around the country masquerading as the newspapers' own, with Mobil the unidentified propagandist.

The cynicism of ads focusing on corporate policy is not

always subtle. One Mobil ad said the company needed all its profits for drilling because only 1.7 percent of its wells struck oil. The ad did not explain that this was true for only a small category of drilling and that the average success rate for all drilling is about 60 percent. Even less subtle was the Mobil ad that declared in 1979: "Can oil companies be trusted to put additional revenues into the search for new energy supplies? History says yes."

Sadly, history says no. The top twenty oil companies have used profits to purchase so many firms outside of oil production and distribution that the value of their non-oil properties in 1979, the year the Mobil ad appeared, totaled $35 billion. Mobil itself was investing much of its profits "in search for new energy supplies" by purchasing such assorted non-oil companies as Montgomery Ward, Container Corporation of America, restaurants in Kansas City, condominiums in Hong Kong, and W. F. Hall, of Chicago, one of the largest commercial printing plants in the world. Mobil today indulges its profits "in search for new energy supplies" by printing *Playboy* magazine, *National Geographic,* and Bantam and Random House paperback books.

The quiet power of a large corporation to suppress damaging information and to silence the journalist who brings it to light can be seen in the attack by Mobil and its oil industry allies on an economics reporter for United Press International (UPI), a leading American news agency.

Major oil companies based in the United States pay an extremely low U.S. income tax. The meager percentages are obscured by oil industry finances that are so arcane that even the Securities and Exchange Commission has said that they cannot be dealt with by ordinary accounting methods. But when the complexities of industry finances were expressed in plain language, Mobil and its friends decided to discredit the correspondent who accomplished the task.

The reporter selected for treatment was a poor example of the corporate stereotype of a liberal-radical journalist hostile to business. Edward F. Roby of UPI is a graduate of West Point, was awarded a Silver Star for Vietnam combat, is a devotee of conservative economist Milton Friedman, and personally believes that corporations should pay no income taxes. But he also believes in reporting the news and making it clear.

On June 5, 1981, Roby received a routine government report in the Washington bureau of UPI. It was a study of oil company revenues and taxes prepared by the Financial Reporting System of the United States Department of Energy. He noticed that the effective tax rate for the twenty-six largest energy firms, including Mobil, Exxon, and Gulf, was surprisingly low for their adjusted gross income. The adjusted gross income for the oil companies was the income of the parent firm within the United States after the firm had been forgiven U.S. taxes for any taxes paid in other countries.

The nominal corporate income tax is 46 percent, but in fact the average tax paid by all U.S. corporations in 1979 was 23.7 percent. The twenty-six largest energy companies, according to the report, paid even less—12.4 percent—at a time of record-high oil industry profits. The 12.4 percent income tax rate for the biggest oil companies was, Roby learned from the Internal Revenue Service, the same rate that would be paid by a private citizen who made less than $20,000 a year. He wrote that information in a story that appeared on UPI news wires in June 1981.

Shortly after Roby's story went out on the wires a Mobil ad appeared in "the Mobil position" in eleven influential American newspapers under the headline: WON'T THEY EVER LEARN? "Once again," the ad began, "newspaper readers across the country were recently presented with a massive dose of misinformation on oil industry taxes."

After its usual denunciation of a news article about oil profits being "misleading" and "blatantly incorrect," the Mobil ad concluded, "This is not the first time the oil industry has been falsely accused of underpaying its taxes . . . we hope that UPI will set the record straight so the American public can make judgments based on accurate and reliable data."

The ad told readers that oil company income is

taxed by the country in which it is earned according to the country's corporate tax rate. These foreign income taxes—

and only *income* taxes—are credited by *U.S. law* against
taxes on that foreign income to avoid double taxation on
the same income . . . Despite the fact that we have pointed
it out hundreds of times, reporters still can't seem to get
it right. [Emphasis Mobil's]

But Roby and UPI were correct.

What Mobil had not pointed out hundreds of times—or
ever—was the strange arrangement it had made to define
"income tax" in its foreign tax credits. Mobil is a member of
Aramco, the consortium of four oil companies—Mobil, Exxon,
Socal, and Texaco—that deals with Saudi Arabia for oil. In
1950 the Saudis announced an increase in the price of oil to its
partners. Ordinarily, this would mean that Aramco would pay
higher royalties for the oil and deduct from its revenues as a
cost of doing business this added cost of its raw material, in the
same way that an individual taxpayer can deduct from his or
her total income (not from taxes) some of the amount he or
she pays for doctor bills. But that is not what happened.

In 1977 Representative Benjamin Rosenthal of New York
produced secret Internal Revenue Service documents going back
to 1950. They showed that the tax laws of Saudi Arabia were
drafted with the help of Aramco to call the added price of oil
not a "royalty" or "cost of doing business," as was proper, but
an "income tax." The Saudis did this knowing that income tax
paid to a foreign country is deductible from the income taxes an
oil company pays the United States on all income received in the
United States by the parent firm.

At the time, the U.S. Department of the Treasury called this
"royalty exacted in the guise of income tax" a "sham." But the
power of the oil industry within government is almost unmatched, and the unorthodox provision was accepted by the
Treasury. A 1977 calculation by the House Ways and Means
Committee showed that about 75 percent of what the oil companies paid Saudi Arabia for oil was counted as "income tax,"
reducing their U.S. taxes so much that it cost other U.S. taxpayers more than $2 billion a year. It is such a highly profitable
avoidance of domestic taxes that it has motivated the major oil

companies to emphasize Middle East oil despite its high price and unstable future.

The Mobil ad did not explain the "sham." Instead it denounced accurate news.

(Recently officials in China, which has no income tax, were startled when American oil companies, negotiating for drilling contracts, asked the Chinese to exact an income tax. Presumably this request did not arise so much from a desire to pay taxes to a Marxist regime as from a desire to pay artificially low taxes to the United States.)

A few days after Mobil's attack on the Roby-UPI story, Exxon, possibly in an attempt to help an ally in its offensive, attacked another Roby story and mentioned Roby by name. Roby had reported what was earlier reported by the *Wall Street Journal* and industry trade papers. Secretary of the Interior James Watt, in his philosophy of maximum exploitation of natural resources, had announced that a vast area of the oceanic outer continental shelf was open for drilling bids by oil companies. Roby wrote that some oil companies thought Watt had opened too large an area at that time. It was news that oil companies wanted less, not more, acreage to explore. Roby, in the seventeenth paragraph of his story, had written that Exxon recommended "offering much less acreage in each sale." The Exxon communication to Secretary Watt said precisely that, recommending "offering much less acreage in each sale."

Exxon in teletypes, telegrams, and mailings to editors all over the country simply denounced Roby and UPI as "misrepresenting Exxon's position." Exxon did not tell the editors what Exxon had said to Watt and what Roby had reported. It simply said the company was misrepresented. UPI depends for its existence on the faith newspaper and broadcast clients have in its reports. A major advertiser calling its stories inaccurate could hurt. And Roby, as an individual journalist, was about to be badly damaged by the oil company campaign against his accurate reporting.

Other oil companies had joined Exxon in recommending that less acreage be offered for drilling. These companies included Atlantic Richfield, Union Oil, Sohio, and Marathon.

Their requests for reduced acreage are on record in their own files, in government files, and in their own releases sent to news media. Yet in dutiful support of Exxon in its attack on the media, Charles DiBona, president of the American Petroleum Institute, the oil industry's main lobby, issued his own press release to the news media, saying: "I know of no company which has said that over time it wants less offshore land opened to inventory."

Tony Dinigro, media manager for Mobil Oil, told a meeting sponsored by the right-wing group Accuracy in Media that the "Won't They Ever Learn?" ad was designed to embarrass the wire services. Dinigro said, "We hope this ad will serve to put the reporter, the wire service and other reporters who are writing about this subject—about Mobil—on notice to make sure they take the time to . . . do an accurate piece."

The concerted attack on Roby worked. UPI told him to do no further stories about Mobil and no in-depth stories on oil and taxes, even though his specialty in the UPI Washington bureau was energy and environment and even though his superiors agreed that his stories about the oil companies had been accurate. Shortly afterward, Roby left UPI and became a European correspondent for another major American news organization.

Why did Exxon pick on Roby when the same passage was reported independently by papers like the *Wall Street Journal,* the *Washington Post,* and other news organizations? One possibility is that Roby's story about all oil company income taxes had made him a target.

An object lesson in the Corporate School of Journalism had been given. Corporations have multimillion-dollar budgets to dissect and attack news reports they dislike. But with each passing year they have yet another power: They are not only hostile to independent journalists. They are their employers.

On October 19, 1981, United Press International dutifully reported another attack on American news media. A corporate executive said: "What our country needs worse than anything is freedom from the press . . . The press is absolutely intolerable today."

The speaker was Arthur Temple. Temple at the time was

vice-chairman of Temple-Eastex which was the largest single stockholder in Time, Inc., the largest magazine publisher in the country and employer of hundreds of journalists whom Mr. Temple, still a director at Time, Inc., considered "absolutely intolerable." Among the publications over which Mr. Temple has responsibilities, as a director, is a major reporter on American business, *Fortune* magazine.

* By the late 1970s, Temple-Eastex had increased its shares in Time, Inc. to approximately 15 percent. The next largest bloc of stock was approximately 5 percent, held by the heirs and editors of *Time* founder Henry Luce. Under SEC standards, in a large corporation with widely distributed stock, as is the case with Time, Inc., if the largest single bloc of shares is 15 percent, and the next largest only 5 percent, the largest bloc represents "the power to exercise control, or to be a controlling influence." In the mid-1980s, Temple-Eastex shares in Time, Inc. were reduced.

4
FROM MYTHOLOGY
TO THEOLOGY

NEUHARTH SAYS 1-PAPER TOWNS DON'T EXIST
Headline in trade magazine

No Gannett newspaper has any direct competition.
Allen Neuharth, *chairman of Gannett Co.,*
to Wall Street analysts

HOMER WAS EUROPE'S first epic poet, founder of the Western tradition that celebrates heroism. Scholars argue over the identity of Homer but they agree that he produced enduring works of poetic art. But anthropologists, looking in history for what journalism is supposed to look for daily—the literal truth —know that there is a curious quality to the epic poems. After generations of rewriting, the heroes become wonderfully pure. In real life the dramatic figures in Homer's *Iliad* and *Odyssey* committed more than their share of rape, pillage, and treachery. They tortured prisoners to death and mutilated their bodies. The army that captured Troy was a horde of repulsive savages called the Akhiusha. But as anthropologist Ruth Benedict has observed, it all disappears in the mythology. The mythological men and women are courageous, kind, and faithful. In the rewritten poems the torturers merely conduct unorthodox memorials for the dead. And Troy is conquered by "the godlike Achioi."

Turning life's natural mixture of the noble and ignoble into unrelieved heroism is done by those who, like editors of the *Soviet Encyclopedia,* believe it is their religious duty to mislead the public for its own good or who convince themselves that their heroes' sins are merely misunderstood philanthropy.

Every culture has its official folklore. In ancient times medicine men transformed tribal legends to enhance their own status. The twentieth century is no different, but the high priests who communicate mythic dogmas now do so through great centralized machines of communication—newspaper chains, broadcast networks, magazine groups, conglomerate book publishers, and movie studios. Operators of these systems disseminate their own version of the world. And of all the legends they generate none are so heroic as the myths they propagate about themselves.

The largest and most aggressive newspaper chain in the United States is not so different from other corporate media giants. It is neither the best nor the worst. But Gannett Company, Inc. is an outstanding contemporary performer of the ancient rite of creating self-serving myths, of committing acts of greed and exploitation but describing them through its own machinery as heroic epics. In real life Gannett has violated laws, doctrines of free enterprise, and journalistic ideals of truthfulness. But its official proclamations are a modern exercise, with appropriate Madison Avenue gloss, of the ancient privilege of the storyteller—transforming the shrieks of private sins into hymns of public virtue.

In the beginning there was Frank E. Gannett. He was tall, big-jowled, and genial, he never drank or smoked and only in extremis would utter, "My goodness!" In the mythic tradition, he worked his way through Cornell University and became part owner in 1906 of the tiny *Elmira* (New York) *Star-Gazette.* From this humble beginning came America's largest newspaper chain. (The word *chain,* with its implication of captivity, is shunned by the newspaper industry; the preferred term is *group,* with its appealing connotation of harmony and mutual aid.)

Through his lifetime, Gannett's papers were inflexibly conservative. But Frank Gannett praised the sacred dogma of freedom for his local editors and reporters. He or his foundation might own a local paper but the local editor would work without interference from above. Carl Lindstrom, an editor of the *Hart-*

ford Times, described what happened when a Gannett official addressed the staff after the chain bought the *Hartford Times* in 1928:

> Nobody must ever use the word, "chain," in regard to Gannett newspaper properties. The word must not appear in the paper. It must not be voiced. If outsiders were so indiscreet or ignorant as to utter it they must immediately be apprised that in referring to Gannett newspapers, the word was "group."

Having thus laid down a command from headquarters, the official next declared, "It must be explained . . . that the cardinal principle of Mr. Gannett in operating his papers was local autonomy."

While the Greeks had Homeric poems for their epics, modern corporations have other art forms: executive speeches, press conferences, and publicity releases that are reported in fulsome detail through their own media. Above all else are full-page ads that celebrate the corporations' own spirituality and social service. Gannett has always been a devoted practitioner of the art.

In 1936 a Gannett full-page ad announced transfer of Frank Gannett's nineteen papers to the Frank E. Gannett Newspaper Foundation, whose self-perpetuating directors were all appointed by Frank E. Gannett. The ad did not mention anything as mundane as superior tax benefits. The announced purpose of the reorganization was to provide more service to the community:

> Not newspapers for profit to ownership, but profit to the communities in which they are published. Not newspapers produced with a minimum of expense . . . but rather newspapers that reflect an extravagant hand, yet designed to be commercially successful, but with whatever remaining profits ploughed back into the ground from which they sprung.

One year later, Frank Gannett ploughed back into the ground from which they had sprung two of his papers in Albany, N.Y. Killing these papers removed direct competition for the

Albany papers of William Randolph Hearst. At about the same time, it so happened, Hearst killed his two Rochester, N.Y., papers, giving Gannett a monopoly there. Perhaps it was fitting that Gannett should have no rivals in Rochester, which was to become the seat of his empire. But there were ungenerous souls who regarded this remarkable coincidence—not a rarity among chains with competing papers—as an unconvincing demonstration of free enterprise. It violated the capitalist dogma of uninhibited competition that they proclaimed with religious fervor in their editorials. In the Homeric tradition Hearst and Gannett announced these acts in their papers as enlarged public service.

Only a year later Gannett suffered an irreverent interpretation of his dedication to journalism without fear or favor. It was a period of rapid growth of electric generating systems owned by states and municipalities and of fierce counterattacks by private power company groups, called in those days "trusts." A. R. Graustein, president of International Paper and Power Company, testified before a Senate committee that his company had secretly financed the expansion of the Gannett chain, giving the private power trust influence over Gannett (and other chains for which the power company did the same thing). Senator George W. Norris, who chaired the committee, said this was part of a "campaign going on all over the country by the power trust to get control of the generation and distribution of electrical energy."

It may have been a coincidence that the Gannett papers were enthusiastic supporters of the power trust and scathing attackers of public ownership of generating plants.

Frank Gannett died in 1957 and was succeeded as head of the chain by Paul Miller. Miller, like Gannett, was tall but, unlike Gannett, handsome and imposing. Though patrician in manner, he was born in Diamond, Mo., and grew up in a small town in Oklahoma. It was this rustic background he stressed when he visited owners of local papers, with whom he established father-like relations of friendship and trust. When local owners were confronted with impending estate taxes or heirs fighting over their papers, it seemed natural to turn to Paul Miller for advice and, as it happened, as a buyer for their papers. Under Miller,

Gannett's tradition of growth accelerated. So did the tradition of epic mythology, including, in one instance, Homeric invocation of the dead.

On February 11, 1963, Paul Miller received the William Allen White Award at the University of Kansas. William Allen White had been owner, editor, and publisher of the Kansas *Emporia Gazette,* a small paper he bought in 1895 and turned into a national voice of liberal Republicanism, humanistic ideals, and sensitive prose. His voice, always based in Emporia, carried civilized ideas into the corridors of power. He was a confidant of presidents, including, when it finally came into vogue, a Democratic one. He was one of the few genuine demigods of justified reverence in newspaper publishing. He could even get away with criticizing his fellow publishers for narrowness and greed, or what he called their "unconscious arrogance of conscious wealth." When he died in 1944 he was mourned in solemn resolutions of condolence by publishers who regularly ignored his precepts.

On the occasion of his receiving the William Allen White Award in 1963, Paul Miller asked his audience an interesting question:

> Would William Allen White have approved of chains?
> Would he feel that "chain" newspapers are having good effects or bad on American journalism? Or none at all?
> Could he have reached world eminence as an editor of a so-called "group newspaper"?
> My answers to all . . . of these questions are optimistic and affirmative.

How well William Allen White would have maintained his iconoclastic independence in the Gannett chain may be judged in a moment. In the meantime, it may be worth noting that White hated chains. He hated the idea of all large corporate influence on newspapers. He once wrote:

> As the newspapers' interest has become a mercantile or industrial proposition, the dangers of commercial corruption of the press become greater and greater. The power

trust of course is buying the newspapers in order to control the old vestige of leadership, the remaining fragment of professional status that still remains in the newspaper business.

As a commercial investment the newspaper is yielding good returns for investment. But as a political weapon it is worth to self-seeking corporations hundreds of dollars of undercover influence where it is worth dollars in direct returns.

White's most eloquent view of chains and chain owners was expressed in an obituary he wrote in the *Emporia Gazette* on the death of Frank Munsey, the great newspaper chain operator of his day.

> Frank Munsey, the great publisher, is dead.
> Frank Munsey contributed to the journalism of his day the talent of a meatpacker, the morals of a money changer, and the manners of an undertaker. He and his kind have about succeeded in transforming a once-noble profession into an eight percent security.
> May he rest in trust.

When Plato, that great promoter of the elite, was eliminating unpleasant realities from Homer, he said, "We must beg Homer not to be angry if we delete them." White, safely dead nineteen years when Miller invoked his blessings from the grave, would have had a few choice words about Plato and Paul Miller.

The year 1963 had added importance in Gannett history: Allen Harold Neuharth arrived at Rochester headquarters. Frank Gannett had a limited vision, Miller broadened it, and Neuharth built it into a modern conglomerate empire. Clever, good looking in an impudent way, engagingly frank in love of power and pomp, Neuharth could have starred in dramas of corporate conquest, possibly produced by one of the two television companies he eventually bought. He makes more than $1 million a year, travels in a company jet whose imperial *G* is woven, etched, embossed, and printed on all visible appointments, has a taste for Pouilly-Fuissé and sharkskin suits (of which a friend said, "When Al wears a sharkskin suit, it's hard to tell where the shark stops and he begins"). As Neuharth's mentor, Miller gradually relinquished his titles and Neuharth became company president, chief executive officer, and chairman.

Another crucial year was 1967. That year, Gannett joined large newspaper chains that, beginning in 1963, entered the arena of international finance by listing their shares on Wall Street. In 1967, Gannett had 28 newspapers and $250 million in annual revenues. Under Neuharth's driving energy the corporation, financed by Wall Street, grew to 93 daily papers, 40 weeklies, 15 radio and 8 television stations, 40,000 billboards, Lou Harris Public Opinion Poll, TV productions, a half-interest in McNeil-Lehrer Productions for television and cable, satellite operations in 36 states, and more than $2 billion in annual revenues. It had a spectacular record of ever-increasing quarterly earnings.

More than anyone else in American newspaper publishing, Neuharth reversed the public posture of corporate journalism. In the past, newspaper owners, their private finances known largely to themselves and their local banks, publicly pictured themselves as penniless keepers of freedom of the press. They cried poverty and the First Amendment to fend off antitrust indictments, child labor and wages-and-hours laws, unions, workers' appeals for higher wages, advertisers' complaints of high rates, and politicians' accusations of monopoly bias. Each newspaper failure was reported as proof of the imminent collapse of the industry. In fact, the number of daily papers in the country has remained constant for thirty years; some die and others are born. The failure rate for papers is remarkably low. For decades the newspaper industry has been one of the most profitable in America.

Neuharth recognized that entry of the newspaper business into the New York Stock Exchange changed all this. Big investors are not enamored of small enterprises on the verge of collapse. Like other leading industrialists of the period Neuharth also recognized that it was no longer profitable to conceal the emergence of giantism. Big investors look for giant cash flow. He discarded the mendicant's cup and pitiful whine and began to celebrate power and size as synonymous with efficiency, social responsibility—and profits. He began to use the dread five-letter word *chain* in mixed company. He met regularly, as do all corporate leaders, with Wall Street analysts who question executives so they can then give inside investment advice to important clients. During one meeting, Neuharth was asked whether the corporate name should be pronounced *GAN-nett* or *Gan-NETT*. Neuharth smiled and said the correct pronunciation was *MONEY*.

Gannett (accent on the last syllable) used a great deal of Wall Street money and produced a great deal more. The company went eighteen years, from 1967 to 1985, with each quarterly profit greater than the one before. When all manufacturing return on stockholder equity averaged 15 percent, Gannett's was 21 percent. Even to hard-boiled investors, the profit margin on some Gannett papers was astonishing—30 to 50 percent a year.

But in one respect Neuharth conformed to tradition. Publishers publicly like to insist that there is no such thing as a newspaper monopoly. The word *monopoly* evokes specters of trust busting by the government. It boils the blood of advertisers and of communities in which papers are the only dailies. So publishers created the charming concept of "media voices" that included, when rhetorically necessary, anything and everything printed, uttered, broadcast, seen, or heard in and by a community. Thus, no daily paper is a monopoly. Unfortunately, almost all of them are. By 1986, of all cities with a daily paper, 98 percent had only one newspaper management (in 1910 more than half of all newspaper cities had local daily competition, typically five or six papers).

But if customers and excluded community groups hate monopolies, Wall Street loves them. Otis Chandler, head of another giant newspaper conglomerate, Times Mirror Company, publisher, among other things, of the *Los Angeles Times,* has said: "If a newspaper is noncompetitive, it gives you a franchise to do what you want with profitability. You can engineer your profits. You can control expenses and generate revenues almost arbitrarily."

So Neuharth, like other publishers, insists in public that

there are no monopolies, but in private—with investors—he insists that there are. In 1979, *Editor & Publisher,* the newspaper publishing trade magazine, headlined a story about a Neuharth speech: NEUHARTH SAYS 1-PAPER TOWNS DON'T EXIST. In his speech Neuharth gave as an example his paper in Boise, Idaho. He told his audience (which was in another state) that he had nine local competitors in Boise—"ten choices for the reader." He referred to dispensing boxes around the leading hotel in Boise, but he did not add that these boxes included specialized papers like the *Wall Street Journal,* the *Christian Science Monitor,* and free advertising circulars, none with local news. Nor did he mention that none of the other papers is published in the county where his daily circulates. Not surprisingly, the Gannett paper in Boise has 99.5 percent of all daily sales in the county.

But in private, Neuharth speaks differently. In 1976 he told Wall Street analysts, "No Gannett newspaper has any direct competition . . . in any community in which we published." His appointed publisher in Wilmington, Del., told *Advertising Age* that the chain bought the Delaware papers because "they are the only game in town."

In 1986, Gannett finally bought a big-city paper with competition, the *Detroit News,* close in circulation with Knight-Ridder's *Free Press.* But soon afterward, both papers asked for exemption from antitrust law in order to become business partners. Later the same year, Gannett bought another competing daily, the *Arkansas Gazette,* which had a comfortable 60–40 lead over its rival, the *Democrat.* It was a sign that there are few profitable monopolies left.

As the chain mushroomed in the 1970s, complaints of monopolistic arrogance threatened Gannett's image, so the company turned to the great corporation art form. A series of full-page celebration ads began to appear in major newspapers and magazines seen by journalists, financiers, and prospective sellers of newspapers. The ads used the Gannett slogan: GANNETT— A WORLD OF DIFFERENT VOICES WHERE FREEDOM SPEAKS. A standard ad proclaimed: "Gannett believes in the freedom of the people to know."

From time to time the ads refer to reality. Some of Gannett's thousands of journalists do produce individual pieces of admirable journalism. These become the stuff of the full-page ads. But most of the empire consists of vast silent domains where ruthless demands for ever-increasing profits crush journalistic enterprise and block adequate coverage of the news in their communities.

It does not detract from the positive social benefits of some Gannett policies to note that they were forced on the corporation.

In 1978 Gannett announced its intention to merge with Combined Communications Corporation, at the time the biggest media merger in the country. The merger was crucial to Gannett's leap into the national conglomerate arena. Neuharth said it was a "marriage made in heaven." But some objectors at the wedding were not prepared to forever hold their peace.

A black media group protested that Gannett's history of hiring women and minorities was "worse than the industry average." It said the company had conflicts of interest: In Rochester, for example, its papers had refused to print Urban League reports of supermarket price discrimination in black neighborhoods for fear of offending advertisers. And it said the Gannett papers reported poorly on issues like nuclear power, race, and human relations, perhaps, it said, because Paul Miller was close to Richard Nixon.

The Federal Communications Commission, which had to agree to the merger, said the combined companies would exceed the legal limit of broadcast stations allowed to any business entity. And the FCC had doubts about permitting Gannett to continue to own its Rochester television station in a city where it owned the only daily newspapers.

Gannett resorted to the twentieth-century form of Homeric myth making. It hired the advertising agency Young & Rubicam to produce a $1.5 million public relations campaign to create a heroic image of Gannett. It sold its Rochester television station to black business people (at a record high price). It appointed a black editor for its Oakland, Calif., paper which it had reluctantly acquired as part of the merger (reluctant because

Oakland had too many civic problems and too much adjacent competition for a typical Gannett operation; a few years later, Gannett sold the Oakland newspaper to its black editor, adding to the chain's new program of assisting blacks. It began to promote women aggressively. The FCC approved the merger.

Neuharth stepped up his public speeches. Though the Department of Justice has been comatose on the subject of newspaper mergers, the image of corporation as hero helps maintain government indifference. More immediate was the need to polish the picture of Gannett benevolence for practical corporate reasons. Gannett was in the business of acquiring other firms. Unlike most corporate acquisitions, newspapers are intensely local and highly personal. Advertisers and community groups care about the nature of their local newspaper and who owns it. Staffs work in peculiar operations that require hourly synchronization. If they become demoralized at the prospect of a ruthless owner they can defect and lower the price of the paper asked by the original owner. The local owner often has to remain in the community and face angry peers for selling to an outside exploiter. A bad image is not good for business. Local owners, most of all, like high bidders. But they also like buyers who look nice.

Gannett ads were designed to make any prospective seller feel that selling to Gannett was a patriotic act. The ads and the Neuharth speeches stressed the theme that big corporations can protect freedom of the press better than small corporations can. In 1980, for example, Neuharth said the real danger to freedom of the press came not from networks and big papers but "in Pumpkin Center, South Dakota; or Paducah, Kentucky; or Pocatello, Idaho—the smaller communities across the country—where the resources of the media are more limited and the balance of power shifts to police and sheriffs and lawyers bent on stilling the local voices."

Gannett presumably would never be "bent on stilling local voices." But in Salem, Ore., as in ancient Troy, there was heavy translation between reality and myth.

In 1974 Gannett bought a company that published the morning and evening papers from the owning family in Salem.

It did so with the standard speech with which chain owners bless each new acquisition, telling the new community they admire and respect the existing papers and would never think of telling editors how to operate in this special and wonderful city.

And so it was in Salem. But after the speeches there is, typically, a quiet set of events. If the old owners had two papers, one morning and one afternoon, as they had in Salem, one of them—gradually and with a diplomatic passage of time—is quietly folded into the other. The emerging single paper is more profitable. On the other hand, if they lacked a Sunday edition, produced mostly for its masses of ads, one may be started with no proportional increase in news reporting. If reporters leave or retire they are not replaced, quietly reducing the staff and local news. Outside news services paid for by previous owners are discouraged and the systemwide Gannett service encouraged.

Most important and least visible are the financial expectations most chains impose on their new acquisitions, Gannett with more precision and punishment than most. The local team is given its profit orders. These used to be called "Profit Plan," but as Gannett gained skill in bureaucratic euphemisms the term was changed to "Progress Plan." The local publisher is told precisely how much he or she must produce in profits for each three-month period. Each local quota is carefully orchestrated in Rochester. It is not keyed to the needs of the local community, except as a guess at maximum possible extraction, but is derived for the total system's impact on Wall Street. Every quarter the profits must increase. This maintains the price of stock, big banks are happy to lend the chain money for more expansion, and it entices future sellers of independent papers to sell not for cash but for easy pieces of paper, shares of the ever-rising value of Gannett stock.

Local editors and publishers who meet their profit quotas have considerable freedom. Those who don't are punished. They either lose their jobs or relinquish control to Gannett's regional or national headquarters. When they fail locally they forfeit the goal of most local chain editors and publishers—the chance to be promoted to a larger paper or, ultimately, to the hierarchy of the national organization. In either case, the reward is far from their current local community, their "commitment" to whose future is so often the subject of the full-page ads.

The manager in Salem was shown the list of annual profit increases in other Gannett papers. It was supposed to impress him. It did. For calendar year 1975, one year after the Salem acquisition, some of the figures of increased profit on Gannett papers were hard to believe: 113.6, 90.9, 58.8, 45.3, 32.8 percent. Each "unit"—newspaper, radio station, or television station—had to meet its quota. Salem was told to double its previous profits. Or else. So in Salem, after the echo of the Acquisition Ceremony had faded, changes were made. Former discounts to advertisers were eliminated. In one year ad rates increased 42 percent. The year before Gannett bought the paper, profits were $700,000. In its first year of ownership Gannett raised profits to $1,500,000 and the year after that to $2.1 million—tripled in two years.

Advertisers rebelled at the new high rates of the only paper in town. They called in an outside organization to start a free-circulation paper to carry their ads for less money. The new paper, started by Community Publications, Inc., soon had 20 percent of all ads in Salem.

The Gannett empire struck back. Neuharth appointed a new publisher with orders to "fatally cripple the Community Press." Gannett salespeople were given a bonus for every ad taken away from the other paper. Advertisers were offered cash to abandon the competitor (one was offered $13,000). Hesitant advertisers were taken on expenses-paid trips to Reno and Lake Tahoe. Long-term contracts with attractive terms were offered on condition that all ads would be withdrawn from the competing paper.

When a major advertiser, K-Mart, still balked, national executives of Gannett visited national executives of K-Mart, told them that the other paper was doomed and if K-Mart did not switch soon the Gannett paper, when it returned to being the only paper in town, might not take K-Mart ads on pleasant terms. When the store's executives still wavered, Gannett made intimations about the local K-Mart manager, who said in a sworn deposition that Gannett officials talking to his superiors tried to make him "look absurd from all standpoints, from our decision-making to taking graft and being involved in graft and corruption."

Ultimately, Gannett drove the other paper out of business. The other paper sued. Gannett settled out of court but for a time some of the court documents in the lawsuit were available to the public. When reporters began to look at them Gannett quickly petitioned the court to seal the records. Cassandra Tate, a free-lance writer, asked Allen Neuharth how all his corporate advertising could stress the public's right to know, proclaim the sanctity of open court records, and then make the Gannett court records secret. She cited one Gannett ad that asked: "Can you imagine up to 90 percent of all court cases settled in secret? Gannett could not . . ." Why didn't that apply to Gannett's own court records?

Neuharth answered, "That's business. I don't think it has anything at all to do with the First Amendment."

It was not the first time Gannett had exempted itself from its slogans. In 1974 Gannett supervisors were at the Rochester Institute of Technology (in the Frank E. Gannett Building) being trained to break a possible strike by Gannett's union printers. An alternative paper in Rochester, the *Patriot,* sent a photographer to take a picture of the scene. The photographer was firmly escorted out of the room while some Gannett supervisors yelled, "Confiscate his film!"

When Gannett, notoriously poor at competing, decided to sell the *Hartford Times* in the 1970s because it had local competition, the new owner sued Gannett and won, having charged the chain with fraud. The chain's managers had created a letterhead "survey" company that issued a false report exaggerating the *Times*'s circulation.

In 1979 Neuharth said, "Diversity of news and views and quality of journalism has been greatly enhanced in this decade by growth in newspaper chains." Publicly owned chains, he said, "are providing better news and service to their readers." A large ad in the *New York Times,* obviously aimed at investors and potential sellers, asked, "What happens to a family newspaper when it joins Gannett?" The answer: "It gets better."

How can one know it gets better? Neuharth believed he knew. In a *Los Angeles Times* interview in 1978 he said a locally owned newspaper that gives too much sophisticated news is "out of touch with its community." Chain papers, he said, are realistic, give the readers what they want, and consequently gain circulation.

The Gannett papers fail their own tests. From 1973 to 1978 Gannett papers lost 6 percent in circulation while other dailies of the same circulation size gained circulation.

Neuharth singled out as excessively concerned with quality and quantity of news two papers whose owners had been firm in announcing their rejection of chain ownership, the *Riverside* (California) *Press-Enterprise* and the *St. Petersburg* (Florida) *Independent-Times.* While Gannett was losing circulation during the five years preceding Neuharth's statement, the two independent papers "out of touch" with their communities were gaining more than 8 percent circulation.

Occasional embarrassments like these increased the need for more mythology. The full-page ads increased. Neuharth made even more speeches, which were reported more fully in his papers. In 1977 he said that in the first eight years of the 1970s, "A total of 74 Pulitzer Prizes have been awarded to U.S. newspapers and their staffs. Sixty-one of those 74 went to newspapers of group owners."

His wording was careful. Strictly speaking he was correct, if one counted as "newspapers of group owners" papers like the *New York Times* and the *Washington Post.* These and other large, prestigious papers had in recent years bought other, smaller newspapers. But if one counted papers that were developed independently and only lately had acquired other papers, the independently developed papers won most of the Pulitzer Prizes (the *New York Times* won eight during the period Gannett cited, the *Washington Post* eight, the *Boston Globe* five, the *Chicago Sun-Times* five, the *Chicago Tribune* four, and so on).

Papers that achieved their distinction as the sole papers of their owners won 77 percent of the Pulitzers. Once-independent papers now run by chains won only 23 percent of the prizes, even though they are a majority of all American dailies.

Neuharth himself may have disclosed one cause of the Gannett chain's failure to gain circulation for its monopolies. In a 1978 speech to the American Society of Newspaper Editors, in Washington, D.C., he ridiculed smaller papers that try to be too serious. When it comes to national and international news, he said, "Coffeyville, Kansas, Muskogee, Oklahoma, they don't give a damn; the less they hear about Washington and New York the better they feel about it."

The editor of the *Emporia Gazette,* still owned by heirs of William Allen White, was in the audience. Coffeyville, a site of a recent Gannett acquisition, is near Emporia. The Emporia editor wrote:

> It was my first meeting so I was too shy to go to the microphone and tell Mr. Neuharth that Coffeyville is not a backwoods hillbilly town . . . and that his remarks were an insult to the then newest Gannett property, the *Coffeyville Journal.*

The *Coffeyville Journal,* it turned out, had been greatly respected and its circulation had grown steadily before Gannett bought it. Its former owner, Richard Seaton, and editor, Daniel Hamrick, had won prizes for their fight against attempts by the John Birch Society to take over the city council. After Gannett bought the paper, the amount of news was reduced. When an accurate news story offended an advertiser, the Gannett headquarters told the local editor to make peace. When reactionaries complained about stories the paper had always run, a Gannett regional director supported the complaints and a Gannett senior vice-president said he was grateful for being informed that the local editor was "failing to do a proper news reporting job for its community."

The editor of many years, Daniel Hamrick, quit. A nearby paper, the *Parsons* (Kansas) *Sun,* editorialized: "Its neighbors have watched with dismay the decline of the *Journal* in recent months. Its news content, under chain ownership, had become increasingly small."

The *Emporia Gazette* wrote: "One of the state's best editors quit his job last week because he could not get along with some executives of the Gannett chain that bought the paper . . ."

What happened to news in Salem, in Coffeyville, and in other Gannett cities was not unusual for Gannett local papers or for almost all chain-owned local papers. Profit squeezes and indifference to comprehensive local news is the norm. Systematic studies by researchers over the years make clear that despite grandiloquent rhetoric, chain papers give their communities less serious news than do independent papers.

A study reported in the standard scholarly journalistic publication *Journalism Quarterly* found that papers that were once competitive but were made monopolies by chains produced "higher prices and lower quality." Another study at Brookings Institution showed that chain-owned papers charge 7 percent more for ads than independent papers, but where the chains have competition their rates are 15 percent lower than for counterpart monopoly papers. A 1978 study at George Washington University showed that chain papers give their readers 8 percent less news than independently owned papers. This was confirmed in a separate study by Kristine Keller, who found that of serious current news (as opposed to "soft" features) independent papers printed 23 percent more than did chain dailies.

The most pervasive changes made in independent papers acquired by chains are typically to increase advertising and subscription rates, to introduce cosmetic alterations of page design and makeup to give the impression of modernity, and to quietly reduce the amount of serious news. It is conventional wisdom among publishers that readers are uninterested in "serious" news. As we will see later, this is not true. The real reason publishers shun serious news is that it is more expensive than features. The "serious" papers Neuharth ridiculed gained circulation while his own lost circulation. Detailed and comprehensive news requires experienced reporters who devote substantial time to each story, particularly local stories. The reporters are paid by the local paper, they have fringe benefits, and they often form unions. "Soft" features, in addition to attracting advertising, are inexpensive: they can be bought from a syndicate and delivered by mail or wire from a machine that is cheap, requires no fringe benefits, and never forms unions. It is possible to issue a mediocre paper with a large staff but it is not possible to produce a good paper with too small a staff. Unfortunately, in a monopoly city it is possible even with deficient news to extract excessive advertising revenues.

In 1966, before Gannett began its drive to create its international empire, its twenty-six daily and six Sunday papers averaged approximately forty-five news employees per paper. By 1980, when it had eighty-one daily, fifty-three Sunday, and twenty-three less-than-daily papers (and had added Saturday editions to acquired papers that previously had none), it averaged twenty-six news employees per paper. During this period the average circulation size of its papers remained the same, about 44,000.

Editorial vigor diminishes under chain ownership. A *Journalism Quarterly* study published in 1975 said that more than 85 percent of chain papers have uniform political endorsements. "These data run counter to the insistence of chain spokesmen that their endorsement policies are independent of chain direction," the report said.

The Cox chain, ninth largest in circulation, has ordered all its papers to endorse the same national candidates. Scripps-Howard, the seventh-largest chain, has done the same and annually adopts a uniform stand on major issues. The Panax chain fired editors who refused to put the publisher's propagandistic views on page 1 as news. Copley Newspapers with dailies in Illinois and California, once ran national ads proclaiming its editorial position, "the birth of Jesus Christ, God's only begotten Son," in order to argue against "the defiant polemics of some theologians." Presumably, it was a position that readers of its papers, even if they happened to disbelieve fundamentalist polemics or happened to be Jews, Moslems, and other nonfundamentalists, had to accept from the only paper in their town. Freedom Newspapers, a substantial chain, spent years promoting its founder's libertarian philosophy of dissolving almost all government in favor of private enterprise. When one branch of the family moderated the doctrinaire approach, the papers became far more profitable and popular. But the chain's management was sued by other heirs who feared that the papers were drifting from libertarianism to conventional conservatism.

Chain papers are divided in their political drive. Either they pursue the doctrines of their owners, like Freedom or the chains that impose centralized endorsements, or they become bland to avoid controversy. Editorials that take a stand may offend advertisers or community groups. In general, as all organizations become large and directed from afar, they value predictability and bureaucratic smoothness. Another *Journalism Quarterly* study of editorials over a fifteen-year period found that after an independent paper is bought by a chain the general result "is not helpful to readers who seek guidance on local matters when they turn to the editorial pages of their daily papers."

Chains tend to hire less-qualified journalists. Stephen Hess in a study of Washington correspondents found that although chains have 75 percent of all American daily circulation, they have only 29 percent of the correspondents working for individual papers, and their correspondents have significantly less education than those working for independent papers.

There is seldom daily or detailed interference in the chain papers' news. Given the large number of rapid decisions reached hourly, such interference would be impossible. Instead, there are chain policies. The chain hires and fires its local editors and publishers, the most definitive mechanism of control possible. It controls the budget, another persuasive influence. Gannett has another way of controlling community newspaper money: In 1979 it announced that bank deposits of its local papers, beyond daily operational needs, would be transferred nightly to Rochester—about $4 million a day, not a small loss to the economy of its communities.

There are additional persuasive measures that permit Gannett to publicly declare local independence and private commitment while ruthlessly extracting every possible dollar from the local community. Stock options permit managers to buy Gannett stock at an artificially low price. If, through maximum profit making, they can drive up the price of the stock, they may make a fortune in the future.

In 1981 a Gannett executive told Wall Street analysts that local Gannett managers are offered stock options in the parent company to make certain they will push for profits and, as she expressed it, "to tighten the golden handcuffs." The intriguing title of this executive is Senior Vice-President for Human Resources. The title would have been applauded by the Homeric rewrite artists.

Of all the Homeric incantations of chains, the most resounding is the folklore of Local Autonomy. It is the centerpiece of every speech, press release, and ceremony on the occasion of a chain's purchase of a local paper.

Three themes are mandatory in the ritual speech: The new acquisition is a splendid paper that the outside company has no intention of changing; the chain acquired the paper in order to offer its larger resources for even greater service to the community; and the new owner believes, absolutely, completely, and without mental reservation in Local Autonomy. This is the unholy trinity of newspaper acquisition speeches. And the greatest of these is Local Autonomy.

Gannett's ceremonies are strictly orthodox.

Tucson, Ariz., December 1976: "From long association with the top executives of Gannett I know them to be men of high principle . . . They believe in local autonomy."

Three weeks later, in Reno, Nev., on the occasion of another Gannett takeover: "Both companies have long had policies of local autonomy. This approach guarantees that all news and editorial decisions will continue to be made by local editors and publishers."

Nashville, Tenn., July 1979: "In keeping with Gannett's policy of local autonomy [the present editor] will have full responsibility for all news and editorial matters."

Allen Neuharth, in 1978, about all his papers: "We believe completely in the concept of local autonomy."

But alas, periodically the golden handcuffs come apart and the hymns of local service turn sour.

On the morning of February 27, 1976, journalistic hierarchs conducted the Local Autonomy rite in Santa Fe, N.Mex. Gannett had bought the local monopoly daily, the *New Mexican,* founded in 1849 and owned since 1949 by Robert McKinney. McKinney was a tough, irascible man who sold to Gannett with an ironclad contract for Local Autonomy. The contract gave McKinney continued total control of his paper for several years, during which he would be chairman, chief executive officer, publisher, and editor-in-chief. The contract specified that McKinney, suffering from heart trouble, would necessarily be out of Santa Fe, with its 7,000-foot altitude, much of the time. But he would still be boss and his deputy, Stephen E. Watkins, would, as in the past, run the paper as president and chief operating officer.

On that February morning in Santa Fe, Paul Miller, then chairman of Gannett, conducted the ceremonies: "The *New Mexican* will add to our group one of the nation's distinguished newspapers and the West's oldest . . . It is generally regarded as one of the best studied, best printed and best managed in the country."

Allen Neuharth uttered the benediction: "Mr. McKinney has developed a splendid newspaper that exercises a positive, useful influence throughout its area. He has laid the groundwork for continuing growth and we look forward to his further leadership."

Once the ceremonies were concluded and the sacred words had their obligatory reproduction on page 1 of the purchased paper, the curtain was drawn on the stage. Behind the curtain all was not peace. Watkins was given his marching orders from Rochester, including his profit quota. He was stunned when he saw the profits other Gannett papers were making but he tried his best to meet the quota. One year after Gannett took over, Watkins had produced the sixteenth-highest increase in profit in the chain. Local news was cut, as it usually is, and replaced by inexpensive syndicated matter from afar. Hispanic news, important for New Mexico, was sharply curtailed. Cartoonist Bill Mauldin, who has lived in Santa Fe for years, said of the Gannett-style *New Mexican,* "It could be printed in Hutchinson, Kansas, or Amarillo, or Pecos, Texas. Essentially it lacks character. It particularly lacks the character of the place it's being printed in."

Inside the chain, memorandums circulated and meetings were called as executives planned how to circumvent the tough McKinney contract to produce a standard Gannett paper. Gannett's western regional vice-president proposed one option to a Gannett operative on the scene: "Look, this is the way the contract reads, so be nice to the old coot and tell him what you've done after you've done it and be sure that his empty office is kept dusted in case he ever drops in."

When McKinney ordered an editorial endorsing Democratic candidate Bruce King for governor in June of 1978, the Gannett appointee did it reluctantly and, against McKinney's orders, criticized King in the endorsing editorial.

A little later, Gannett fired Watkins, McKinney's chief in Santa Fe. Watkins's replacement was referred to as "Quinn's spy on the scene." John C. Quinn is Gannett senior vice-president for news.

Finally, McKinney sued for fraud and breach of contract. The trial lasted fourteen weeks, the longest in New Mexico history. A jury in U.S. District Court found Gannett guilty of breach of contract. Judge Santiago E. Campos ordered the paper returned to McKinney. The judge's official order was not kind. He noted that Watkins had pushed for the big profits Gannett demanded to match its other papers. He cited one paper, in Bellingham, Wash., with 50 percent annual profit and another in Olympia, Wash., with 36 percent profit. The judge wrote:

> This worried Watkins. A precipitous rise in profits, he felt, would damage the quality of the newspaper and lead to its eventual demise. Watkins became defensive toward the profit push. This convinced Gannett officials that he was standing in the way of progress . . .

Gannett has already wrought, and daily continues, an unconscionable and malicious deprivation of precious rights belonging to McKinney ... the right to control editorial policy of the only newspaper published in the capital city of the state of New Mexico ...

One of the greatest sources of wonder to me at trial was the attitude of some of the Gannett men when they addressed McKinney's right of "complete charge" and "complete authority" ... They attempted to project sincere impressions that these contractual provisions did not really mean what they clearly state ... The effort failed. Neuharth, for example, cavalierly characterized McKinney's solid and substantial contract rights of "complete charge" and "complete authority" as "window dressing" ... McKinney would not have entered into the bargain if he had contemplated that Gannett would not keep its word . ... He was attracted to Gannett because of its policy of "local autonomy."

On June 27, 1980, the jury in New Mexico found that Gannett had violated its contract that granted McKinney autonomy. Four months later, Gannett, in the tradition of Homeric revisionists, ran full-page ads. They depicted two stern and determined men, marching to their own drumbeats, on the keys of massive typewriters, giants of integrity. The headline read: DIFFERENT VOICES OF FREEDOM. The text was inspiring:

Each Gannett newspaper forms its own editorial opinions. Nobody tells local editors what to think.

Each Gannett editor marches to his or her own beat, and these are as different as the pulses of each editor's community. That is why Gannett newspapers, broadcast stations and other media are "A World of Different Voices Where Freedom Speaks."

The Homeric rewrite artists would have been envious.

5

"DEAR MR. PRESIDENT . . ."

*More people are bribed by their own money than anybody
else's.*

Jonathan Daniels

"DEAR MR. PRESIDENT," the letter began, nothing extraordinary in a country where every day hundreds of citizens write
to the president of the United States. But this was not an ordinary letter. The recipient on this July day in 1969 was President
Richard M. Nixon. The writer was Richard E. Berlin. The name
of Berlin and six other men whose cause he invoked meant nothing to the general public but they meant a great deal to Richard
Nixon. And in the symbiotic equation of power, Richard Nixon
meant a great deal to them.

Berlin was asking the president to use his influence to exempt him and his friends from a federal law that in previous
years had sent other corporate executives to jail. That is why
they needed the president. The reason President Nixon needed
them was nearly as obvious.

Richard Berlin, as noted on his stationery, was president
and chief executive officer of the Hearst Corporation in New
York. The Hearst Corporation owned nine newspapers, ten
broadcasting stations, twenty-six magazines, and a book publishing house. Berlin spoke for his corporation and for six others,
so his letter represented a massive complex of popular communications—dozens of newspapers, national magazines, cable
systems, radio and television stations, book publishers, and the

country's second-largest news service. These media produced news and information that helped create the country's perception of the world in general and of Richard Nixon in particular.

No politician likes to lose the sympathy of even a single newspaper or radio station. For a national leader to lose the support of a major portion of all American media can be a political disaster. Richard Nixon needed no education on the subject, but Berlin was not famous for subtlety. In the unlikely event that the president missed the point, Berlin took pains to hint that if Nixon did not come across with the favor Berlin requested, the media chiefs would remember this when Nixon ran for reelection in 1972.

The Hearst executive and his fellow publishers were not conducting a novel experiment. By the nature of their positions they were all familiar with power: Many corporations lobby for favorable government treatment, but only media corporations control access to the American mind. The more media power possessed by a media corporation, the more a government leader has reason to feel its displeasure.

Few media corporations deny that they have power. They usually assert that they would never use their power for selfish purposes. But no corporation, media or otherwise, will fail to use its power if it feels a threat to its future or to its profits. The threat could be a national political movement it dislikes, as the New Deal seemed to most newspaper publishers during the Great Depression. Or it could be a threat to profits that makes them urge creation of loopholes in the law, like the Newspaper Preservation Act.

Whatever the provocation, when a media corporation executive approaches a politician for a favor or to deliver a threat, there is no doubt in the mind of either party what is at stake.

Lionel Van Deerlin, an ex-journalist, is former chairman of the House Subcommittee on Communications. He says that every member of Congress is familiar with the special power of broadcasters and publishers. Van Deerlin describes it simply: "They can make or break you."

Frank Leeming, when publisher of the *Kingsport* (Tennessee) *Times-News,* said that on the occasions when he asked his delegation in Congress for favorable action, "When they look at Kingsport they would see me both as a businessman and as the person who controls the editorial policy of the paper."

Katharine Graham, head of the Washington Post media empire, as president of the American Newspaper Publishers Association lobbied personally for legal restrictions to prevent AT&T from competing with newspapers. That is a normal activity for the head of any trade organization. She also spoke to the editorial writers and reporters covering the issue for the *Washington Post*. That, too, is normal for trade associations seeking public support. It is not normal that the lobbyist looking for media support is also the employer of the journalists being lobbied.

Joseph Costello owned five radio stations in Louisville. When he went to Washington to lobby for deregulation of radio, he said of each of the members of Congress in the various districts covered by his stations: "He knows he's got to buy time on my radio station, so he's going to lend me an ear. We're keeping them alive back home and that's why the newspaper and radio and TV people are more effective lobbyists."

The National Association of Broadcasters, with a $7 million budget and 6,000 members, lobbies in Washington for broadcasters and presents large speaking fees to members of Congress who, through their committees, have influence over broadcast legislation. It uses a special network to mobilize individual stations to bring pressure on their local members of the Senate and House. It says that it uses this lobbying power to "preserve the American way of broadcasting," which Jonathan Miller of *TV Guide* said really means "preserving their hegemony over the eyeballs of America."

The results over the years have been impressive. Newspapers have obtained special favors to exempt them from child labor laws and to obtain favorable postal rates, tariffs on imported newsprint, and media taxes. Broadcasters were able to hold back cable broadcasting for more than ten years, obtained the deregulation of radio, and moved toward deregulation in television.

Important issues can be promoted by the media, but at strategic times they can also be ignored. On March 29, 1979,

Van Deerlin made a historic announcement: a bill for the first basic alteration of communications law in forty-five years. It would give commercial broadcasters what they had lobbied for —semipermanent possession of their station licenses, cancellation of the requirement to provide equal access for political candidates, and no further need to present community issues or to do it fairly. It proposed a fundamental change in the law controlling the most pervasive common experience in American life, the seven and a half hours a day that the average household uses its TV set. When Van Deerlin made the announcement of the proposed change there were 200 persons present at the press conference, including representatives of the television networks. That night no television network in the country mentioned the event.

A fair report on the Van Deerlin proposal might have said that the station the viewers were watching and all other stations would, under the proposal, no longer be required to operate in the public interest, to be fair in their presentation of issues and candidates, or to give equal time for rebuttals. It was important news, but it was not broadcast.

Huge umbrella corporations with control over a variety of media can use one medium they control to enhance another, and at times the leverage is used to change the news in order to woo governments. United Press (now United Press International), like the Associated Press, not only reports the news but sells its services to news systems which, in many countries, means selling it to governments. Colin Miller is the syndicate consultant who helped create what was once the most popular political column on the continent, "Washington Merry-Go-Round," by Drew Pearson and Robert Allen. Miller, Pearson, and Allen planned a special column that would do for Latin American papers what they did for American ones—expose political malpractices in each country. The column was distributed by United Features, which was corporately controlled by United Press International. Miller testified before a Senate committee:

> When word of this reached the front office of United Press, we were ordered to drop the idea. They were afraid that

what Pearson and Allen might expose in Lima, Peru, or Asunción, Paraguay, or Rio de Janeiro, might evolve to become a negative factor insofar as the governments were concerned and, through the governments, upon the papers to which the United Press sold its service.

In 1981 two editors of the national news agency of Canada, Canadian Press, told a Canadian government commission that the news service edited its news about the media in ways to please major media owners. The press service is bought by 110 newspapers, forty of which are owned by the Thomson chain. The two editors said that a news account of a Thomson paper strike was deliberately reduced to three paragraphs and that a speech by the president of the Ontario Federation of Labor criticizing the Thomson organization was killed. When a branch of Canadian government investigated to see if a series of birth defects in women employees of Thomson was caused by electronic terminals used in the newspaper's plants, the wire service delayed the story for twelve hours until they saw what the Thomson paper would report about itself.

Time, Inc. owns book publishing houses, national news magazines, and book clubs, among other media properties. *Time* magazine has been a steady supporter of the policies of Henry Kissinger. The Time, Inc. book house, Little, Brown, published both volumes of Kissinger's memoirs and his ideas on foreign policy. *Time* magazine excerpted large sections of the books and ran Kissinger's picture on the magazine's cover. Kissinger's books were also selections of the biggest book club in the country, Book-of-the-Month Club, owned by Time, Inc. These coordinated promotions of Kissinger's books could have been coincidental but it is a coincidence experienced by few authors and publishers who lack control of so many media.

Large media corporations have their own political action committees to give money to favored candidates or, in the growing fashion, to defeat unfavored ones. Some media corporations also own other industries that will benefit from the right candidates.

Time, Inc., which owns and operates *Time, Life, Fortune,*

Sports Illustrated, People, and *Money* magazines, has a political action committee in its own name. Candidates receiving contributions from a Time, Inc. political committee are quite aware that they have become special beneficiaries of the media empire, whose reporting can affect their political careers. In 1986, after General Electric acquired the National Broadcasting Company, it installed a GE president who informed employees of its new radio and television unit that they were expected to support General Electric's political goals, including a political action committee to influence legislation. The head of the news staffs said that those employees would be exempted. The rest of NBC presumably will be expected to support the corporate politics.

It is not every American business person who easily makes appointments with the president of the United States or, like Richard Berlin, is certain to have his or her letters read and acted upon by the president. Berlin's letter created serious change within the Nixon administration even though the favor Berlin asked affected only one Hearst newspaper, the *San Francisco Examiner.* The other publishers whose names he invoked were not much more involved. Cox had only one paper affected, Knight had only one, Worrell one, Block one, Newhouse two, and Scripps-Howard seven (while Berlin mentioned all of the chains, there is nothing to indicate that the others participated in his letter to the president, though they, too, were actively pressing for the change Berlin pursued). But Berlin and his fellow publishers were speaking not with the power of fourteen papers, but with the power of seventy-four. In addition to their total newspaper holdings, they spoke with the media power and influence over public attitudes that flowed from their magazines, books, and broadcasting stations. Most of the publishers' properties would be unaffected by the requested law, but all of their media properties could be used to influence the president.

Berlin wanted President Nixon's influence to exempt a group of newspapers from antimonopoly law, which forbids competing firms to perform the act usually described in headlines as "rigging prices"—quietly agreeing on prices among themselves while appearing to compete. Fixing prices is also contrary to the rhetoric of free enterprise with which the same media flood the public. Only occasionally does unpleasant reality puncture the surface appearance, as in 1961 when executives of some of the country's best-known corporations were jailed for conspiring to fix the prices of electrical equipment. Now a few newspapers had somewhat the same problem.

In twenty-two cities of the country, ostensibly competing local papers had, over the years, agreed to become business partners, fixing prices and sharing profits while maintaining separate newsrooms. In 1965 a U.S. district court found this a violation of the antitrust law. The newspapers appealed that decision and began lobbying for special exemption from the law for any competitive newspaper that felt it might be failing financially. The effort was rejected by Lyndon Johnson's Democratic and Richard Nixon's Republican administrations in 1967, 1968, and the summer of 1969, on grounds that it was harmful social policy. If newspaper companies were permitted to ignore antitrust laws, other kinds of firms would demand the same exemption.

In 1969 the United States Supreme Court upheld the finding that the forty-four papers were in violation of the law. The publishers felt an impending crisis. Faced with the terrifying prospect of competing in the open market, they became desperate. Richard Berlin, speaking for the most powerful operators, became a crucial operative.

Berlin shrewdly sent two letters. The one to the president was partly Uriah Heep proclaiming loyalty before the majesty of the president. The letter ends with a conventionally typed "Sincerely." But Berlin, who presumably had no hesitation in asking secretaries to retype letters to the president of the United States, used his pen to scratch out the "Sincerely" and in a heavy hand wrote in large letters, "Faithfully, Dick."

Even in the Nixon letter, Berlin permitted the scent of power to escape.

> ... I am taking the liberty of addressing myself to a matter
> of common interest to both you and me . . . Many other im-

portant publishers and friends of your administration (including Scripps-Howard who are involved in seven of these arrangements) are similarly situated. All of us look to you for assistance.

But at the same time Berlin wrote a different kind of letter to Nixon's assistant attorney general in charge of antitrust, Richard W. McLaren. There was no Uriah Heep in the McLaren letter. It was a tough demand with a clear threat:

> Those of us who strongly supported the present administration in the last election are the ones most seriously concerned and endangered by failure to adopt the Newspaper Preservation Act . . . the fact remains that there was almost unanimous support of the Administration by the newspapers who are proponents of the Newspaper Preservation Act. It therefore seems to me that those newspapers should, at the very least, receive a most friendly consideration.

Berlin again made certain that his threat to Nixon and the Republican party could not be misunderstood:

> Those of us . . . now find that, by supporting that person and that party which we thought best exemplified those very ideals, we have become the victims and the targets of a narrow and tortured economic concept advanced and implemented by those in whom we placed the highest confidence.

Berlin sent a copy of this letter to President Nixon.

The "narrow and tortured economic concept" was the Sherman Act, a law in effect since 1890, which simply codified the supposedly sacred catechism of capitalism that is endlessly enunciated by most newspapers, magazines, broadcasters, and movie studios—that competition is the life of trade and that free enterprise requires the marketplace to decide who shall survive.

There followed a strange minuet by the Nixon administration.

In June, before the Berlin letters, Assistant Attorney General McLaren, speaking for the administration, testified against the publishers' bill. The chairman of the committee handling the bill, the late Senator Philip A. Hart of Michigan, responded:

> I want to congratulate you and the Nixon Administration for the position you have taken ... I know it would be easier for all of us in public office to grant newspapers special favors because they deal with us intimately every day.

But Senator Hart's congratulations were premature. Several weeks later, after the Berlin letters, the Nixon administration reversed itself and announced that it was now in favor of the bill. The publishers obtained their Newspaper Preservation Act and President Nixon was given his political reward, the support of the large media organizations.

In his letter to the president, Berlin had referred to "many important publishers" who wanted the bill. He meant seven chains, a few of whose dailies were in quiet business partnership with their local competitors. The chains owned only fourteen of the forty-four newspapers involved in the Newspaper Preservation Act. But it did not take an angel from heaven to inform Richard Nixon that when the Hearst executive issued a threat he was not speaking merely with the power of the one Hearst paper needing the favor. Nixon knew he was dealing with seven chains that owned seventy-four daily newspapers with forty million circulation—at least eighty million readers—in twenty-six states, including the major states without whose electoral votes no presidential candidate can win an election. When Berlin raised the issue of political support for Richard Nixon he was talking about papers read by more people than would vote in the next election.

These same corporations had additional ways to influence the public. Hearst was a major owner of magazines, broadcasting stations, and book publishing. Scripps-Howard owned sixteen newspapers, and its parent corporation operated broadcasting stations, United Press International, and United Features, a leading syndicator of feature and political commentary. Cox, in addition to owning a major chain of newspapers, was in book publishing and film distribution.

Some newspapers were opposed to the special exemption,

frightened—justifiably, as events proved—that it would permit controlled prices that would make life difficult for independent competitors. But forty million combined circulation and other media power is more politically persuasive than the 35,000 circulation of the average single daily paper.

The performance of American daily papers in the 1972 presidential election was bizarre. For four years the Nixon administration had attacked not only the news media but their constitutional rights. Nixon had sent his vice-president on a crusade attacking newspapers that criticized the White House or ran news of negative events that were normal fare in ordinary reportage. In the Pentagon Papers case the Nixon administration obtained the first court-ordered cessation of publication in the country's history. In the summer of 1972, months before the election, the first Watergate stories began to disclose the profound corruption permeating the White House. But in early October, directors of the American Newspaper Publishers Association were reported "chary of taking any action that implied criticism of the President's policies." At a time when the first Watergate stories should have been of greatest value to voters, the response outside a minority of papers was strange. A study of major papers around the country—dailies with a quarter of all national circulation, including papers in the Hearst, Scripps-Howard, and Cox chains—showed that in the months before the election "pro-Nixon papers had a much higher tendency to suppress damaging Watergate stories than papers making no endorsements." These included the papers who had obtained their antitrust favor from Nixon.

In 1972 Richard Nixon received the highest percentage of newspaper endorsements of any candidate in modern times.

Prominent in this massive support of the man who most threatened their journalistic freedom were chains whose names Berlin invoked in his letters. In the previous three presidential elections—contrary to Berlin's assertion that there was "almost unanimous support of the Administration"—a third of all Hearst papers had endorsed the Democratic candidate, as had a third of the Cox papers and half of the Scripps-Howard papers. In 1972, after passage of the Newspaper Preservation Act, every Hearst paper, every Cox paper, and every Scripps-Howard paper endorsed Nixon. Scripps-Howard ordered a standard pro-Nixon editorial into all its dailies. Cox ordered all its editors to endorse Nixon (causing one editor to resign in protest).

It is likely that Nixon might have won the 1972 election without this wholesale shift to his support and the sympathetic reluctance to print Watergate disclosures before the election. But it was not long after the election, when Watergate stories finally broke through the barriers of publishers' protection, that the president's power began to crumble. Studies throughout the years have shown that any bias in the news tends to follow a paper's editorial opinions.

Without the chains whose local papers benefited from the White House reversal on the Newspaper Preservation Act, Richard Nixon would have had, with the exception of Barry Goldwater in 1964, the lowest newspaper support of any Republican candidate since World War II. Instead, he had the highest newspaper support of any candidate in U.S. history. Without this massive support from the press, much of it implicitly sealed in 1969 by the mutual exchange of favors, Richard Nixon and his aides might have been less confident in their illegal activities.

The rhetoric of media corporations is consistent: They do not interfere with the professional selection of content for their newspapers, magazines, broadcast stations, book houses, and movie studios. This book shows that this is technically true for most operators in day-to-day, hour-by-hour operations, but it is not true for larger issues in which the media corporations have a strong self-interest. In the case of the Newspaper Preservation Act, three media operators, with a stroke of a pen, ordered their professionals to endorse for president a man who had previously attacked their constitutional freedoms but who had recently granted them a corporate favor. And because of the high degree of concentrated control over the mass media, the seven chains that benefited from Richard Nixon's change of mind owned papers read by most of the voters.

Protection of independence in the gathering and disseminating of news and other public information depends on something more than rhetorical declarations of freedom of expression.

Richard Nixon's depredations on freedom of the press were the gravest since the Alien and Sedition Acts of 1798. Ten years after his departure from office in disgrace, the momentum he initiated has become a continuing crisis. But the dominant newspaper publishers were willing to support the suppressor of freedoms of the press in return for a corporate favor. Nixon's favor was not crucial in the life of the three corporations that ordered their papers to endorse Nixon. Their nine local newspapers were saved not from extinction but merely from competition. The Hearst, Cox, and Scripps-Howard chains had sixty-five other, unaffected newspapers plus a large body of profitable properties in other media. Yet in exchange for so small a prize they were willing to order all their papers—not just the nine—to support a corrupt administration hostile to an independent press. It is not reassuring to consider what might happen to the integrity of national news if dominant media corporations felt their basic power threatened.

Part II

THE HIGH COST OF FREE ADVERTISING

6

ONLY THE AFFLUENT
NEED APPLY

We make no effort to sell to the mob.
Donald Nizen, senior vice-president,
New York Times

NOTHING IN American publishing approaches the profitable heresies of *The New Yorker* magazine. In an era when magazine editors regard covers with eye-catching headlines and striking graphics as imperative for survival, *New Yorker* covers typically are subdued watercolors of idyllic scenes. While other magazines assume that modern Americans don't read, *New Yorker* articles are incredibly long and weighted with detail. The magazine's cartoons ridicule many of its readers, the fashionably affluent who are portrayed in their Upper East Side penthouses speaking Ivy League patois. Editorial doctrine on other leading magazines calls for short, punchy sentences, but *The New Yorker* is almost the last repository of the style and tone of Henry David Thoreau and Matthew Arnold, its chaste, old-fashioned columns breathing the quietude of nineteenth-century essays.

New Yorker advertisements are in a different world. They celebrate the ostentatious jet set. Christmas ads offer gold, diamond-encrusted wristwatches without prices, the implied message being that if you have to ask you have no business looking. A display of Jaeger–Le Coulture advises that the wristwatch "can be pivoted to reveal . . . your coat of arms." One ad for Audeman Piquet watches suggests giving three to impress a woman while another ad does suggest a price, murmuring in fine print, "From $10,500."

There are some homely products, like a Jeep station wagon. But it is displayed with a polo field in the background and is redeemed by other ads like the one that shows a couple in evening clothes embracing in the cockpit of an executive jet. Even in advertisements for products that cost less than $5,000 the characters seem to come from adjacent ads where cuff links are offered at $675, earrings at $3,500, a bracelet at $6,000, a brooch at $14,000. A Jean Patou perfume ad has no vulgar listing of price but says in bold letters what the spirit of all *New Yorker* ads seems to proclaim: "So rare . . . and available to so few."

Despite its violation of the most commanding conventions of what makes a magazine sell, *The New Yorker* for decades has been a leader in making money.

Over the years the magazine was the envy of the periodical industry in the standard measure of financial success—the number of advertising pages sold annually. Year after year, *The New Yorker* was first or second, so fixed in its reputation that other magazines promoting their effectiveness would tell prospective advertisers they were first or second "after *The New Yorker*," the implication being that, like 1950s baseball and the New York Yankees, first place was unassailable.

That was true until 1967. The year before was a record one for *The New Yorker*. Most people in the industry believe that in 1966 the magazine attained the largest number of ad pages sold in a year by any magazine of general circulation in the history of publishing. In 1966 *The New Yorker* sold 6,100 pages of ads. Its circulation was at its usual level, around 448,000.

In 1967 a strange disease struck. *The New Yorker*'s circulation remained the same but the number of ad pages dropped disastrously. In a few years 2,500 pages of ads disappeared, a loss of 40 percent. The magazine's net profits shrank from the 1966 level of $3 million to less than $1 million. Dividends per share, $10.93 in 1966, were down to $3.69 by 1970.

The disastrous loss of advertising occurred despite a continued high level of circulation which, to lay observers, would seem the only statistic needed for a magazine's success. The popular assumption is that if enough people care enough about a publication or a television program to buy it or to turn to it, advertisers will beat a path to their doorway. That clearly was not happening at *The New Yorker*.

The onset of *The New Yorker*'s malady can be traced to July 15, 1967. That issue of the magazine carried a typically long report under the typically ambiguous title "Reporter at Large." This is the standing head for *New Yorker* articles dealing in depth with subjects as diverse as the history of oranges, the socialization of rats, and the culture of an Irish saloon. This time the subject was a report from the village of Ben Suc in Vietnam.

The author was Jonathan Schell, a recent Harvard graduate who, after commencement, visited his brother, Orville, in Taiwan, where Orville was doing Chinese studies. Once in Taiwan, Jonathan decided to take a trip to Vietnam, where, according to the standard press, the American war against the Vietcong was going well. In Saigon, Schell was liked and "adopted" by the colonels, perhaps because he had proper establishment connections: He carried an expired *Harvard Crimson* press pass and his father was a successful Manhattan lawyer. The military gave him treatment ordinarily reserved for famous correspondents sympathetic to the war. In addition to attending the daily military briefing sessions in Saigon, the basis for most reports back to the United States, Schell was also taken on helicopter assaults and bombing and strafing missions and given ground transportation to battle scenes.

The assumption of his hosts was that the nice kid from Harvard would be impressed with the power and the purpose of the American mission. But Schell was appalled. The war, it seemed to him, was not the neat containment of Soviet-Chinese aggression that had been advertised at home or the attempt of humane Americans to save democracy-loving natives from the barbaric Vietcong. Like all wars, this one was mutually brutal. Americans shot, bombed, and uprooted civilians in massive campaigns that resulted in the disintegration of Vietnamese social structures. And the Americans were not winning the war.

Schell returned to the United States disturbed by his find-ings. He visited a family friend, William Shawn, the quiet, ec-centric editor of *The New Yorker,* who had known the Schell children since childhood. Shawn listened to Schell's story and asked him to try writing about his experiences. Schell produced what Shawn called "a perfect piece of *New Yorker* reporting." The story, which ran in the July 15, 1967, issue, told in clear, quiet detail what the assault on one village meant to the villagers and to the American soldiers.

Shawn said he had serious doubts about the war before Schell appeared, "but certainly I saw it differently talking to him and reading what he wrote. That was when I became convinced that we shouldn't be there and the war was a mistake."

Thereafter *The New Yorker* in issue after issue spoke simply and clearly against the war. It was not the first publication to do so, but at the time most important media followed the gen-eral line that the war was needed to stop international com-munism and to save the Vietnamese and that the United States was on the verge of victory. Most newspapers, including the two most influential dailies in the country, the *New York Times* and the *Washington Post,* editorially supported the war. There were growing popular protests but the mass marches were yet to come. Neither the My Lai massacre nor the Tet offensive had occurred, and the exposure of the Pentagon Papers detailing a long history of government lying about Indochina was still four years away.

The New Yorker was the voice of the elite, the repository of advertisements for the hedonistic rich, of genteel essays on the first day of spring, of temperate profiles of aesthetes, of humor so sophisticated that it seemed designed solely for intelligent graduates of the best schools. The *Wall Street Journal* once labeled it "Urbanity, Inc." When the magazine spoke clearly against the war, it was a significant event in the course of public attitude toward the American enterprise in Vietnam. If this apolitical organ of the elite said the war was morally wrong, it was saying it to the country's establishment.

At the same time, the magazine was giving the message to a quite different constituency. A *New Yorker* staff member recalled that in 1967, "Our writers would come back from speaking on campuses and say that the kids are reading *The New Yorker* out loud in the dormitories."

Ordinarily this is a happy event in the life of a magazine. There is always a need for some younger readers so that when older subscribers die the magazine will not die with them. But advertisers live in the present. Throughout its crisis years after 1966, *The New Yorker* audience actually grew in numbers. But while the median age of readers in 1966 was 48.7—the age when executives would be at the peak of their spending power—by 1974 *New Yorker* subscribers' median age was 34, a number brought down by the infusion of college students in their late teens and early twenties. Many college students will form the affluent elite of the future, but at the moment they are not buying $10,500 wristwatches and $14,000 brooches. They were buying the magazine because of its clear and moral stand against the war and its quiet, detailed reporting from the scene.

It was then that ad pages began their drastic disappearance. An easy explanation would be that conservative corporations withdrew their ads in political protest. Some did. But the majority of the losses came from a more impersonal process, one of profound significance to the character of contemporary American mass media. *The New Yorker* had begun to attract "the wrong kind" of reader. Circulation remained the same, but the magazine had become the victim, as it had formerly been the beneficiary, of an iron rule of advertising-supported media: It is less important that people buy your publication (or listen to your program) than that they be "the right kind" of people.

The "right kind" usually means affluent consumers eighteen to forty-nine years of age, the heavy buying years, with above-median family income. Newspapers, magazines, and radio and television operators publicly boast of their audience size, which is a significant factor. But when they sit down at conferences with big advertisers, they do not present simple numbers but reams of computer printouts that show the characteristics of their audience in income, age, sex, marital status, ethnic background, social habits, residence, family structure, occupation, and buying patterns. These are the compelling components of that crucial element in modern media—demographics, the study of characteristics of the human population.

The standard cure for "bad demographics" in newspapers, magazines, radio, and television is simple: Change the content. Fill the publication or the programs with material that will attract the kind of people the advertisers want. The general manager of *Rolling Stone* expressed it when that magazine wanted to attract a higher level of advertiser: "We had to deliver a more high-quality reader. The only way to deliver a different kind of reader is to change editorial." If an editor refuses or fails to change, the editor is fired.

The New Yorker faced this problem but it did not fire the editor; nor did the editor "change editorial." It is almost certain that for conventional corporate ownership the "cure" would be quick and decisive. William Shawn would have "changed editorial," which would have meant dropping the insistent line on the war in Vietnam, or he would have been fired. In the place of the Vietnam reporting and commentary there would have been less controversial material that would adjust demographics back to the affluent population of buying age and assuage the anger of those corporations that disliked the magazine's position on the war.

But at the time, *The New Yorker* was not the property of a conglomerate. Later, in 1986, it would be sold to the Newhouse publishing group. The new owner altered advertising and promotion policies but left editorial content the same. After a year, however, the new owner replaced the editor, William Shawn.

Shawn, a Dickensian man, modest in manner and speech, reddens in indignation when asked whether, during the critical 1967–1974 period, the business leaders of the magazine informed him that his editorial content was attracting the wrong kind of reader.

> It would be unthinkable for the advertising and business people to tell me that . . . I didn't hear about it until the early 1970s . . . It gradually sank in on me that *The New*

Yorker was being read by younger people. I didn't know it in any formal way. Who the readers are I really don't want to know. I don't want to know because we edit the magazine for ourselves and hope there will be people like ourselves and people like our writers who will find it interesting and worthwhile.

Shawn's words are standard rhetoric of publishers and editors when they are asked about separation of editorial independence and advertising. The rhetoric usually has little relation to reality. Increasingly, editorial content of publications and broadcasting is dictated by the computer printouts on advertising agency desks, not the other way around. When there is a conflict between the printouts and an independent editor, the printouts win. Were it not for the incontrovertible behavior of *The New Yorker* during the Vietnam War, it would be difficult not to regard Shawn's words as the standard mythic rhetoric.

"We never talk about 'the readers,' " Shawn said. "I won't permit that—if I may put it so arrogantly. I don't want to speak about our readers as a 'market.' I don't want them to feel that they are just consumers to us. I find that obnoxious."

The full-page ads of other newspapers, magazines, and broadcast networks in the *New York Times* and the *Wall Street Journal* are often puzzling to the lay reader. They do not urge people to read and listen. They seem to be filled with statistics of little interest to potential subscribers or viewers. They are intended to show the advertising industry that the demographics of the publication or station are "correct," that their audience is made up not of a cross-section of the population but of people in the "right" age and income brackets.

Eventually during the 1967–1974 period Shawn did hear what he called "murmurings":

There were murmurings in the background about three things: The magazine was getting too serious, the magazine was getting too much into politics, and the pieces were getting too long. My reaction was that we should do nothing about it. Whatever change took place did so gradually and

spontaneously as we saw the world . . . There's only one
way to do it: Did we think it was the right thing to do? Did
we take the right editorial stand? . . . To be silent when
something is going on that shouldn't be going on would be
cowardly . . . We published information we believed the
public should have and we said what we believed. If the
magazine was serious it was no more serious than we were.
If there was too much politics, it was because politics became more important and it was on our minds . . . I wish
we could remain out of politics but we can't . . . I could enjoy life more if we could do nothing but be funny, which I
love . . . but *The New Yorker* has gradually changed as the
world changed.

Shawn noted that the Time-Life and Reader's Digest empires succeeded because they were started by men who expressed
their own values regardless of the market and thereby established
an identity that made for long-range success.

Now the whole idea is that you edit for a market and
if possible design a magazine with that in mind. Now magazines aren't started with the desire for someone to express
what he believes. I think the whole trend is so destructive
and so unpromising so far as journalism is concerned that it
is very worrisome. Younger editors and writers are growing
up in that atmosphere. "We want to edit the magazine to
give the audience what they want. What do we give them?"
There is a fallacy in that calculation . . . The fallacy is
if you edit that way, to give back to the readers only what
they think they want, you'll never give them something new
they didn't know about. You stagnate. It's just this back-
and-forth and you end up with the networks, TV and the
movies. The whole thing begins to be circular. Creativity
and originality and spontaneity goes out of it. The new
tendency is to discourage this creative process and kill
originality.
We sometimes publish a piece that I'm afraid not more
than one hundred readers will want. Perhaps it's too difficult, too obscure. But it's important to have. That's how
people learn and grow. This other way is bad for our entire

society and we're suffering from it in almost all forms of communications.

I don't know if you tried to start up a *New Yorker* today if you could get anybody to back you.

A magazine industry executive was asked if a magazine owned by a conventional corporation would have supported Shawn during the lean years. He answered: "Are you kidding? One bad year like the one *New Yorker* had in 1967 and either the editorial formula would change or the editor would be out on his ear. It happens regularly."

By the 1980s *The New Yorker* was economically healthy again. Its circulation in 1980 was over 500,000, it was running 4,220 pages of ads a year, fourth among all American magazines, and its profits were back above $3 million. That seems to be a heartwarming morality lesson in the rewards of integrity. But a few years later, even *The New Yorker* would become another conglomerate property. Newspapers and magazines in the main do not want merely readers; they want affluent readers. Broadcasters do not want just any listeners; they want rich ones. Those who are not going to buy are not invited to read, hear, or watch.

Media executives don't tell the general public that only the affluent are wanted. But just as there is sometimes unguarded truth in wine, there is sometimes unguarded truth in the heat of competition. When individual media companies fight for business, or one medium tries to lure advertisers from another medium, the unvarnished truth escapes from behind high-sounding rhetoric. In 1978 the American Broadcasting Company emerged as the leading television network in size of audience; other networks fought to maintain their advertising revenues by deprecating the "quality" of ABC's audience. Paul Klein, then program director of NBC-TV, said ABC's audience might be the largest but it is "kids and dummies."

Reminded that ABC had large ratings "in homes making $20,000 and over," Klein said:

Well, that is the kids watching in those homes, and sometimes the adults . . . We would like to pull away those adults, and leave ABC with the children . . . [ABC] may still have a very big audience but their audience will be worthless.

Broadcasting Magazine reported:

More specifically, Mr. Klein defined as his target audience 18-to-49-year-old women who are in reasonably secure financial situations—"the women with some money to buy a product and the necessity to buy it." Since the cardinal rule of program demographics is that people like to watch people like themselves, Mr. Klein is pouring females into his prime-time programs . . . Sexually oriented plots also are becoming increasingly prominent.

In counterattack, ABC issued a booklet to impress potential advertisers. One section of the booklet was entitled "Some people are more valuable than others." When word of this title reached the nonadvertising world, ABC, not wishing to appear nonegalitarian in public, withdrew the booklet—but retained the demographic boast.

Broadcasters can safely be blunt in trade publications seen by advertising agencies. *Broadcasting Magazine,* for example, carries a great deal of corporate promotion aimed at advertisers. One ad announces in heavy type over a photograph of Mike Douglas, the talk show host:

WOMEN 18–49: MIKE'S GOT YOUR NUMBER!
The Mike Douglas Show today delivers more women in its audience 18–49 . . . a higher percentage of women 18–49 in its audience than the John Davidson Show.

Such advertising is also crucial for magazines in closed business circles. An issue of *Public Relations Journal* carried the following full-page ad:

WANTED: 77,000,000 MOVERS AND SHAKERS
Did they go to college? Are they professionals or managers? Are their household incomes $20,000 plus? Are their homes $40,000 plus? Are their corporate securities $20,000 plus? Have they played active roles in local civic issues? Have they written any elected officials or editors lately?

Have they written any books or articles? Have they addressed any public meetings or worked for any political parties?

Only 77,136,000 adults can answer yes to one or more of those questions . . . they're big on magazines and not so big on television . . . Make this your year to re-evaluate the balance of power between television and magazines in your media planning . . .

MAGAZINES. THE BALANCE OF POWER.

The original mass medium, newspapers, in its early period carried ads that were marginal in the medium's economics. But in the late 1800s mass production of consumer goods expanded beyond normal consumption. At the time advertisers spent an average of $28.39 a year per household urging people to buy goods and services. By 1980 they were spending $691 per household, an increase far greater than the rate of inflation, with 29 percent of ad money going to newspapers, 21 percent to television, 7 percent to radio, and 6 percent to magazines. By now newspapers get 75 percent of their revenues from ads, general-circulation magazines 50 percent, and broadcasting almost 100 percent.

With more than $30 billion spent on those media each year, advertisers do not leave to chance who will see their ads. Surveys and computers make it possible now to describe with some precision the income, education, occupation, and spending habits of newspaper and magazine subscribers and broadcast audiences, though each medium tends to exaggerate the "quality" of its audience. Media operators fear "the wrong kind" of audience—too young or too old, or not affluent enough. The greater the pressure on newspapers, magazines, and broadcasters to increase their profits, the more they push not just for larger audiences but for higher-quality audiences, as each newspaper, each magazine, each broadcast station insists to the major advertisers that it has the highest-quality audience.

With billions in ads and more billions in product sales at stake, advertisers no longer leave the demographics of their ad carriers to rhetoric and speculation. They now insist on carefully audited subscription statistics and scientifically gathered audience data, with sophisticated computer analysis of exactly the kind of individual that is exposed to a particular kind of advertisement in a newspaper, magazine, or broadcast. And they are increasingly interested in the context of their ads in the medium—the surrounding articles in newspapers and magazines and the type of broadcast program in which their commercials are inserted. An ad for a sable fur coat next to an article on world starvation is not the most effective association for making a sale.

Thus, both the "quality" of an audience and the nonadvertising content around the ads have become dominant in the thinking of major advertisers. Not surprisingly, those factors have consequently become dominant in the thinking of owners of newspapers, magazines, and broadcast stations.

The president of Harte-Hanks Century Newspaper Group, owner of twenty-eight daily papers in the United States, said in 1980 that the company's editors are losing what he called their "prejudices" about separating news content from the desire to reach advertisers' model audience. "The traditional view has been for editors to focus only on the total circulation figures. Today we are seeing more editor emphasis on the quality of circulation."

The largest newspaper chain in the country, Gannett, owns ninety-three daily papers. A study of the Gannett chain by William B. Blankenburg of the University of Wisconsin concluded that the chain aims at fewer subscribers who are richer: "The lost subscribers, if less wealthy . . . may not have fitted into their marketing scheme."

Otis Chandler, head of the Times Mirror empire, owner of the *Los Angeles Times* and the fourth-largest newspaper chain, said, "The target audience of the *Times* is . . . in the middle class and . . . the upper class . . . We are not trying to get mass circulation, but quality circulation." On another occasion, he said, "We arbitrarily cut back some of our low-income circulation . . . The economics of American newspaper publishing is based on an advertising base, not a circulation base."

Years after the near-fatal disease struck *The New Yorker*, when recovery had set in, the magazine's Market Research Department commissioned a professional survey to analyze its subscribers. For the edification of prospective advertisers in *The New Yorker*, its salespeople could display 134 pages of statistical tables that showed that the magazine's readers were 58.5 percent male, 63.8 percent married (6.6 percent widowed, 8.1 percent separated or divorced); 94.0 percent had attended college or had degrees (21.8 percent had Ph.D.'s); 71.0 percent were in business, industry, or professions; 19.3 percent were in top management; 16.6 percent were members of corporate boards of directors; 40.1 percent collected original paintings and sculptures; 26.1 percent bought wine by the case; 59.3 percent owned corporate stock, which had an average value of $70,500 (though a scrupulous footnote to this datum says, "In order not to distort the average . . . one respondent reporting $25,000,000 was omitted from the calculation"); and the median age was 48.4. In other words, the elite audience was "the right kind" for advertising expensive merchandise.

By 1981 *The New Yorker* had recovered enough of its high-quality demographics to make it a desirable carrier for a full-page ad by the Magazine Publishers Association. The ad pursued the theme that magazines are superior for advertising because they don't want readers who aren't going to buy. The headline on the ad read: A MAGAZINE DOESN'T WASTE WORDS ON WINDOW SHOPPERS.

Neither does any newspaper or broadcast station that makes most of its money from advertising.

7

MONOPOLY

Newspapers are read at the breakfast and dinner tables.
God's great gift to man is appetite. Put nothing in the pa-
per that will destroy it.

W. R. Nelson, publisher of the
Kansas City Star, 1915

THE FIRST SHOCK of the year was in August 1981 when the
Washington Star, landmark in the nation's capital for almost
140 years, with a third of a million copies sold every day, owned
by a $3-billion-a-year corporation, went out of business. Three
weeks later in New York the evening sister of the country's biggest newspaper, the *New York Daily News,* collapsed. Four
months after that the *Philadelphia Bulletin,* born before the Civil
War, died despite a circulation of more than 400,000. Two
months later the *Minneapolis Star,* more than 100 years old,
folded. Then death came to the *Cleveland Press,* born in 1878,
selling 300,000 copies daily. The *New York Daily News,* the
country's largest general-circulation daily, with more than
1,500,000 customers every morning, said it was thinking of going
out of business because it was losing money.

Within one year the American newspaper industry had lost
some of its biggest and most established publications. Washington, D.C., with only one paper, was unique among capitals of
major nations: London has fourteen dailies, Paris fourteen, Rome
eighteen, Tokyo seventeen, and Moscow nine. No city in the
United States had as many papers as New York, with only three.

Ninety-eight percent of all cities with a daily paper had only one. Most of the public and most journalists assumed that the newspaper industry was on its deathbed. They were wrong.

The American newspaper industry is fabulously profitable, its earnings resistant even to recessions. It is the third-largest industry in the country and for years has remained among the ten most profitable. On the stock market its shares outperform other blue-chip corporations.

If the newspaper industry was not in trouble, why had so many large newspapers succumbed? The dead papers are the latest victims of an epidemic, but not a new one. They are merely the most recent statistics in a process that started almost a century ago.

Published accounts of this epidemic are curious. Despite tons of newsprint expended over the decades on the death of individual newspapers, the origins of the epidemic, like dreaded words among superstitious tribes, remain unspoken.

When a newspaper dies an almost standard ritual occurs, with all the passion of terrorized villages during medieval plagues. Owners almost invariably attribute death to the evil spirit of labor unions. Workers have a different devil—owners' mismanagement and greed. Or they both accuse the public of being too fickle and illiterate. The accusing finger is sometimes pointed at television, or at economically sick communities or changing American lifestyles.

At one time or another, in one place or another, some of these indictments have been valid. But for most failed newspapers these were only contributing factors that determined the particular date on which the epidemic would strike, regardless of owners, unions, television, and all the rest.

The fatal affliction, let its name be whispered, is mass advertising.

In its quiet way, mass advertising has been deadly and inexorable. It has been selective, aiming not at newspapers indiscriminately but at competitive papers.

The history of the epidemic is ironic. Despite its unbroken record of victims, it is not feared but is actively pursued. As publishers compete for mass advertising they guarantee that in the race there will be not just one winner but death for all the others. Mass advertising has ordained that each city in the United States that has a daily paper will have only one and that most cities will have none.

The main problem is not that there is a multitude of small advertisers, like corner grocery stores aiming at particular neighborhoods or communities. That kind of small, localized ad has been resident in newspapers since the first American paper began in 1690, and it has never brought death to the carrier. Death to newspaper competition comes from large regional and national merchants aiming at an audience over wide geographic areas.

Mass advertisers do not intend or even desire media monopoly. At times they complain bitterly that absence of newspaper competition robs them of sufficient bargaining power over advertising rates. Nonetheless, they have been the basic cause of monopoly newspapers in the United States, not out of bad intentions or conspiracy but by rational choices they make in the modern pattern of media economics. Unwittingly, they have eliminated second place. The prize in money and power for the winning merchants and the surviving media has been stunning.

In the last two generations, during the rise of mass advertising, the merchants have wiped out much of their former competition, the small enterprises like corner grocery stores and locally owned department stores. The big advertisers doubled their share of national retail sales during this period of growth of advertising in the United States. Instead of thousands of individual local retail entrepreneurs there are now national and multinational corporations with outlets spread over every major metropolitan area. The giant survivors ideally need only one ad covering thousands of square miles in each urban center—too wide an area and too expensive for the small, local merchant. For the chain store, a large single ad, requiring a large initial outlay that by itself eliminates the small competitor, is ultimately cheaper per customer than smaller, localized ads.

Large advertisers stimulate large cash flows that finance heavy investment for still more expansion. This has given a relatively small number of corporations in each retail field such a large portion of the total national business that they exercise a degree of control over prices that contradicts the traditional image of supply and demand. If local competition should attempt to take away some of the business, the national corporation need not reduce prices in the "classical" economics maneuver but simply increase advertising pressure. In extremis, there might be a momentary drop in prices combined with the added advertising; after defeat of the new competitor, the prices can rise again.

The magnitude of money handled by national retail organizations gives them disproportionate political power, as all economic concentration does. They can afford to hire large, centralized legal firms and lobbyists to influence, and sometimes to write, national, state, and local legislation that affects their business operations and taxes, never to the advantage of their smaller competitors.

Thus, mass advertising has been a major contributor to the drastic shrinkage in shares of sales by small, local businesses and has helped large national and multinational corporations achieve market control and political power.

The prize for media winners has been similarly impressive. Newspapers, magazines, and broadcasters in 1981 collected $33 billion a year from advertisers and only $7 billion from their audiences. The almost 5-to-1 dependence on advertisers has insulated these media from the wishes of their audiences. It has given media victors their own monopoly and with that the power to control their markets. It has made them large so that, like their large advertisers, they are relatively free from the fear of new competitors entering their field. The process has let giant media firms join their giant advertising clients in the arena of national and multinational economics and politics (an incestuous giantism that has led to the phenomenon that some of the largest media corporations, sellers of ads, are among the largest buyers of ads).

There have been some benefits for consumers in the growth of national merchants and media. Large retailers can produce more quality control and greater variety. Monopolylike media can reduce sensationalism and hasty publication. Some of these gains come not from giantism but from the evolution of technology in production, of professionalism in journalism, and of sophistication in audiences. But advantages from large size have to be weighed against the growth of bureaucracy, impersonality, and excessive prices permitted by market control and loss of diversity in media.

The process by which mass advertising has produced monopoly and monopolylike media is not a mystery except in the silence with which the subject is treated in the media. One typical example is the way mass advertising left only one paper in the nation's capital.

When the *Washington Post* was founded in 1877 the city had a population of 130,000 and five daily newspapers. By 1970 attrition in competitive papers had left only three dailies, even though the metropolitan population was then 2.8 million. The *Post* had 500,000 circulation, the *Star* about 300,000, and the *Daily News* about 200,000.

The *Star* and the *News* were losing revenues; the *News* was actually in the red and the *Star*'s profit margin was shrinking ominously. Yet all over the country there were papers with much smaller circulations making comfortable and even spectacular profits. If a paper in Peoria, Ill., for example, with only 100,000 circulation, could make a handsome, stable profit, why couldn't the *Star* with three times the circulation and the *News* with twice the circulation, and in a market far more affluent (Washington has $16 billion in retail sales a year, Peoria has $2 billion)? The answer is that the *Peoria Journal Star* has no local competition.

The cost to all three papers was roughly the same for preparing each day's editions—gathering and processing news and advertising, printing and distribution (actually for the smaller *Star* and *News* the costs were less, but for this description that is not important). In 1970 the *News* was stopping its presses at 200,000 copies, the *Star* at 300,000, and the *Post* at 500,000. Thus, their costs for each copy of the paper were divided by vastly different numbers (more than overcoming the smaller preparation costs of the two smaller papers). So the *Post*, thanks to mass production savings per copy, could deliver each of its half-million papers more inexpensively than the smaller *News* and *Star*.

The price each firm charges its advertisers and subscribers is a reflection of its cost of producing each individual copy of the paper, adjusted by its desire to attract as many advertisers as possible while maximizing profits (or minimizing losses).

A look at the actual ad rates of the three papers will demonstrate the process by which advertising can eliminate competitive newspapers. In 1970 the same large ad for which the *News* charged $9,676 would cost the *Star*'s advertisers $12,634 and the *Post*'s $16,676. The *News* charged the least, the *Post* the most, but the *News* ad was seen in only 200,000 households, the *Post* ad in 500,000. So if an advertiser could afford the larger investment in a *Post* ad and could use the ad for the whole geographic area covered by the *Post,* the *Post* ad cost only 3.34 cents per household and the *News* ad 4.84 cents per household. For a big advertiser, wanting to reach the larger audience and greater reach, with plenty of money for the *Post*'s larger paper, the *Post* was the most economical per household. The *Post,* with ever-increasing revenues and profits, could spend more on salespeople, on editorial vigor, and on circulation promotion. The *Star* and the *News,* their revenues and profits shrinking, had less to spend, while they were under growing pressure from the *Post*.

That is the process by which competitive papers have been eliminated in the United States for the last three generations. The *Washington Daily News* suspended operations on July 12, 1972, the *Star* on August 7, 1981.

Shortly after the failure of the *Star* left the *Post* the only daily paper in Washington, the *Post*'s circulation rose to 700,000, reducing even more its production costs per paper. And its advertising rate had been raised, as every monopoly's ad rate is raised. Two years after the *Star* folded, the *Post*'s ad rate had risen 58 percent (and was four times higher than the year before the *News* dropped out of the race). For the winner, victory is sweet. But there is only one survivor.

Thus, the mass advertising process helps kill off small retail businesses who cannot afford mass circulation rates in favor of large businesses, and it leads to monopoly in daily newspapers.

Exceptions to monopoly newspaper cities are more rare each year. In 1920 there were 700 cities with competing dailies. In 1986, though the country's population had more than doubled, there were only a dozen cities with competing dailies (another two dozen cities had papers editorially separate that were business partners). In almost every city where there are still truly competing papers, either the second paper is losing money and leading a precarious existence or the two papers are so close in circulation that the shift of ads to the leading paper has not yet started. (In 1982, for example, a majority of the competing papers in the country had closer ratios of circulation than 40-60 and in four cities—Detroit, Trenton, Wilkes-Barre, and Seattle—they were divided 50-50.) For 98 percent of American cities with daily papers, the major advertisers had already made their rational business decisions and there is now a newspaper monopoly.

The monopoly process is clear when one paper pulls ahead decisively. But what causes one paper to pull ahead?

Newspapers attract subscribers for many reasons—serious news, sports, features, comics, advertising. And they succeed for external reasons as well, such as the growth and affluence of their community, or managerial ones like the shrewdness of owners and editors. The total explanation of a newspaper's editorial success is a complex of factors, but it is remarkable how long such a crucial question has remained largely mythological or debatable in an industry that prides itself on factuality.

A favorite argument is that competition in the past made sex-and-sensation coverage inevitable as rival papers did anything they could to catch every passing eye. The result, this argument insists, is a Gresham's law by which bad papers drive out good ones and only monopoly has brought serious journalism to the average community.

Some history seems to support this notion. In the nineteenth century and part of the twentieth, newsboys waved blaring headlines and screeched fragments of alarming news to passers-by. Any fire, crime, or scandal was used as a selling point. Scurrilous and self-serving propaganda often masqueraded as news.

But history also supports the opposite point. Some sensationalism did come from intense competition, but it merely reflects a stage in the evolution of American journalism. There were no professional reporters until the early decades of the twentieth century. Formerly, reporters were boys who came off the streets and learned to imitate their predecessors. Training and professional standards were almost nonexistent. Most sales were made on the street, so blaring headlines and exaggerated drama affected pedestrians. Training and professionalism in journalism, as in many other lines of work, became the standard after World War II. And the shift to home delivery of newspapers, now 80 percent of all daily circulation, removed the advantage of sensationalized news.

An important element is missing in the standard newspaper histories of the late nineteenth century. Most stories of "yellow journalism" and the wild circulation wars of Hearst and Pulitzer in New York and the newspaper gangs in Chicago are true. But they are mistakenly presented as the main reason newspapers became popular with ordinary citizens. Before mass advertising, however, papers succeeded solely because they pleased their readers. Readers were clustered in terms of their serious political and social ideas—some were conservative, some liberal, some radical—and they had religious or regional loyalties. Each paper tended to focus a great deal of its information on the preferences of its readers. Because papers were physically smaller, lacking mass advertising, they were cheaper to print. And because they appealed to the strong interests of their readers, subscribers paid more for newspapers as a percentage of average wages than they otherwise might have done. Because newspapers were cheaper to print, newspaper businesses could be started more easily, either when new communities arose or when existing papers did not satisfy the interests of some significant group in the community. The result was a wider spectrum of political and social ideas than the public gets from contemporary newspapers. The frequent excess among adversarial papers of the past is a normal social cost of rigorous debate in a democracy.

Most standard journalistic histories omit the nonsensationalist reason for success of the three most powerful publishers of the past—Hearst, Joseph Pulitzer, and E. W. Scripps. Hearst and Pulitzer often acted irresponsibly; in fact, their irresponsible activities culminated in Hearst's campaign that pushed the United States into the Spanish-American War. But Hearst, Pulitzer, and Scripps extended the newspaper into every corner of national life through a technique uncelebrated in history: serious social and political content. They secured deep loyalties among readers because their papers crusaded in direct and unmistakable terms for reforms most needed by the powerless majority of the times.

Edward Wyllis Scripps, at the turn of the century, for example, founded the first modern newspaper chain, thirty-four papers in fifteen states. He did it in ways that would chill the blood (and shock the shareholders) of a contemporary chain operator. Everything he did violated the operating principles of newspaper publishers today: Scripps created new papers, sometimes in competition with existing papers, rather than acquiring established papers. He charged as little as possible for his papers. He took as few ads as possible and in some papers took none. He was a socialist and pressed for socialistic reforms of abuses against working people. In twenty years, Scripps was a major newspaper proprietor with a fortune of $50 million.

Hearst, in his beginning years as a publisher, also called himself a socialist and defended the poor and the working population. Pulitzer's papers were filled with much the same values, though Pulitzer rejected socialism in favor of the progressive movement.

The descendants of Scripps, Hearst, and Pulitzer are still prominent names in the American daily newspaper scene and still editorialize their own preferred politics. But the descendant papers in content and philosophy are like other papers today. Neither they nor any other publisher of a standard newspaper, magazine, or broadcasting station would send to their local editorial executives a memorandum in the spirit of one sent by E. W. Scripps to his editors:

A newspaper ... must at all times antagonize the selfish interests of that very class which furnishes the larger part of a newspaper's income ... The press in this country is now and always has been so thoroughly dominated by the wealthy few of the country that it cannot be depended upon to give the great mass of the people that correct information concerning political, economical and social subjects which it is necessary that the mass of people shall have in order that they shall vote and in all ways act in the best way to protect themselves from the brutal force and chicanery of the ruling and employing classes ... I HAVE ONLY ONE PRINCIPLE AND THAT IS REPRESENTED BY AN EFFORT TO MAKE IT HARDER FOR THE RICH TO GROW RICHER AND EASIER FOR THE POOR TO KEEP FROM GROWING POORER.

Or Pulitzer's editorial position:

Tax luxuries, inheritances, monopolies ... the privileged corporation.

Or Hearst's editorials from that era:

Which would be better for America: to let one man have five millions a year, and keep ten thousand men on the edge of want; or let the one ... man have one million a year and divide the four millions among ten thousand families? ...

This newspaper hopes for labor union victory and means to help it along, because the public welfare demands it ...

Shall organized capital control the people, or shall the people control capital and limit its power? ... The trusts ... are teaching us that it is feasible and necessary for the nation eventually to take possession of and manage its own properties, industrial as well as others.

In the late nineteenth century, before mass advertising, a daily paper did not have to be socialist or progressive to succeed. Most papers were moderate or conservative in the philosophy of their news selection and editorial values. But radical and reformist papers appealed to those in the population who were not affluent, who were dissatisfied with the impact of the economy and politics of the time, or who had strong preferences for something other than conservative and established politics— a combination that always makes up a significant part of every generation.

Before mass advertising, a paper had to appeal to the personal wishes of a significant portion of the community or it had to have vigorous and unstinted news coverage. Hearst, Pulitzer, and Scripps succeeded with their political points of view. Men like Adolph Ochs in New York, Harry Chandler in Los Angeles, Robert McCormick in Chicago, and William Loeb in New Hampshire succeeded with conservative papers. Both approaches were good for profits and, were it not for monopoly, good for democracy.

If political intensity and vigor in news made for success before mass advertising, what led one paper to pull ahead of another in circulation once mass advertising began its selection process? In city after city where papers fought to pull ahead in order to survive in the long run, the papers that chose to emphasize the primacy of news over the primacy of advertising revenues developed the strongest reader loyalty, and they were the papers that survived.

The most dramatic example of the long-run importance of reader loyalty is the post–World War II history of the *New York Times* and its morning competitor, the *New York Herald-Tribune*. Both were among the best papers in the country. But the battle is won or lost not in the outer world but on the battlefield of the home city. Both papers entered World War II with viable circulations. When the war brought newsprint rationing and at the same time more advertising and more news than would fit in the fixed size of the papers, each had to decide which to emphasize. The *Times* decided to emphasize news, the *Herald-Tribune* advertising. The *Herald-Tribune* died in 1966. Orvil Dryfoos, the publisher of the *Times* when the *Herald-Tribune* folded, said that the single most important factor in the *Times*'s triumph was its decision to favor news over advertising during World War II, giving it reader loyalty on which to build for years afterward.

The publisher of the *Miami Herald* also said that its decision to make the news more important during World War II was decisive in its eventual victory over its rival, the *Miami News*.

In 1975, under a grant from the Markle Foundation, I

studied success and failure factors in daily newspapers, using as a base the 164 dailies that failed in the 1960s. One part of the study looked at dozens of demographic characteristics of the communities of the failed papers, most of them monopolies, and another looked at the quantities of each kind of editorial content in the failed papers. Using successful papers whose communities had similar characteristics to those in which papers failed, I compared the quantities of different kinds of editorial content in both the failed and the successful papers. In addition, respected editors and researchers in newspapers were asked to analyze the coverage of three full days of twenty-five of the failed papers and twenty-five successful ones of matched size and community circumstances.

The results were clear. Papers that failed had 23 percent less serious news and less news of all kinds than their successful counterparts. Successful papers had 21 percent more local and 18 percent more national news. The panel of experts that looked at overall quality (without knowing the results of the quantitative study) judged the successful papers as twice as high in general quality of news.

In every case, competitive papers were superior to monopoly ones. These findings were later supported by studies of the Newspaper Advertising Bureau, which found, similarly, that papers in competitive markets contain more serious news and gain circulation more readily. The director of those studies, Leo Bogart, concluded: "With the best of intentions in the world, it is difficult for a monopoly daily to avoid complacency and establishmentarianism."

As mass advertising grew, the liberal and radical ideas— in editorials, in selection of news, and in investigative initiatives —became a problem. If a paper wished to attract maximum advertising, its explicit politics might create a disadvantage. To obtain more advertising it needed readers of all political persuasions. So it found it advantageous to tone down or make less obvious strong political statements. Such editorial policy, in turn, appealed to large advertisers, who disliked liberal and radical-left views that might raise questions about the role of big business. This explains the retreat of explicit political statements to the editorial pages, and why these pages might remain radically conservative and still succeed—like Colonel Robert McCormick's *Chicago Tribune* in the years 1914–1955—and why liberal or left-radical editorial opinions in standard newspapers virtually disappeared. The news column, to which the average reader paid the most attention, could not be so explicit and still attract a wide spectrum of readers and please advertisers. The answer in the news was a technique called "objectivity."

The doctrine of objectivity sounded splendid. Reporters should not express their own values in their stories. As much as possible, newspaper stories should stick to the facts and each fact should be certified by some authority. In fact, the doctrine did much to stimulate discipline and ethics in reporting and to diminish wild and fictionalized stories.

But it had other, more dubious effects as well. News, like all human observations, is not truly objective, in the scientific sense in which, for example, every competent mathematician will get the same sum in adding a column of figures. Human scenes described by different individuals are seen with differences. Since the doctrine of objectivity called for the meticulous certification of almost every phenomenon by an authority with a title, the news came increasingly to be presented by the authorities. In fact, American news, under that doctrine, has become increasingly conservative, not truly neutral, and too often devoid of meaning. The doctrine led journalists in the standard media to "safe," politically neutral subjects like crime and natural disasters, and it delayed for decades intelligent examinations into the causes of events. The doctrine of objectivity, despite its positive accomplishments of strict rules of observation and verification of simple, physical events, has led to some of the most damaging failures of reporting—in wars, social explosions, and episodes like that of Senator Joseph McCarthy, whose fantasies were accepted because he was a certifying authority under the rules of objectivity. It has given American standard news a profoundly establishmentarian cast under the guise of a press independent of established authority.

In recent years, journalism has moved beyond the most unintelligent strictures of objectivity, substituting instead the ideas of fairness and balance. A competent journalist is no longer expected to remain passive when an authority figure utters a "fact" for which there is documented contrary evidence. But there persists the illusion throughout American journalism that it operates as a value-free discipline.

The impact of mass advertising on magazines was in some ways more dramatic than on newspapers. Mass advertising produced monopoly in newspapers. At first it brought national magazines unparalleled prosperity. Then it killed them.

Magazines first attracted national advertisers because for more than one hundred years after the first major venture magazines were the only national medium. In addition, graphic reproduction of the magazines was superior to that of newspapers. Because the early magazines depended almost entirely on subscriptions, they represented a medium subscribers believed in. After 1900 the biggest magazines also were printed in full color, always a powerful plus for advertising. They had the inherent advantage of all printed matter—they were stable and remained in households for extended exposure.

Magazines like the *Saturday Evening Post, Collier's,* and *Liberty* had been household fixtures for decades, read religiously in every city and town. In 1936 Henry Luce started *Life,* which was so suddenly successful it almost failed when its growing printing bills were not covered by its underestimated initial advertising rates. *Look* magazine, created by Gardner Cowles, Jr., followed in 1937. With circulations in the millions, with full color and precise graphics, magazines were a natural carrier of national ads. They diminished the ratio of national ads carried by newspapers, which then emphasized regional and local advertisers. Magazines increased the percentage of their ad revenues to 60 percent.

Then came television. Television did not deliver a fixed image to be looked at in leisure over a period of time. It was ephemeral; something was on the tube for seconds then gone forever. Magazines, struggling to keep their advertisers, stressed that a magazine ad could be studied over time, whereas a television ad could not. But it was a double-edged argument. The speed with which a television image disappeared turned out to be an advantage for large classes of ads—the less time for reflection, the easier to imbed an emotional association into the viewer's unconscious. The big national magazines began to sink. Ironically, perhaps in desperation, they turned again to primary reader interests and became more socially conscious than in the past. *Life* and *Look* published photojournalism on important issues and the *Saturday Evening Post* in the 1960s left its old philosophy of small-town nostalgia to become reformist. They gained circulation. But the introduction of color to television was the fatal blow. The national, general-circulation magazines died at the height of their popularity. The *Saturday Evening Post* folded in 1969 with seven million circulation, *Look* in 1971, and *Life* in 1972, each with more than seven million circulation. (Sold and resold, the *Saturday Evening Post* later reemerged with much the same character of its initial nostalgic appeal. *Life* also reappeared but in a new approach.)

Surviving magazines are increasingly special-interest ones, often created solely to carry ads to a target audience. Such magazines are read by runners, tennis players, antique collectors, weight watchers, and so on. The magazine industry's dependence on ads for revenue has changed from 60 percent to a figure approaching 50 percent.

Mass advertising made television a profitable spectacle called "a license to print money." And it produced extraordinary uniformity. There are 1,000 television stations in the country and three national networks, but a person unacquainted with the personalities involved would have trouble distinguishing anything individual about any one station, either in its entertainment, which is literally interchangeable, among stations and networks, or in its news. The three networks, it has been observed, are one network in triplicate.

The sameness that pervades this most powerful of national media is the result of the dynamics of advertising. Designed to reach as many people as possible, advertising is uniquely suited to television because the signal, once sent to the antenna, costs the station nothing, no matter how many people listen or watch. And since the picture is seen, typically, over thousands of square miles, it has maximum advertising power as long as it offends or bores as few viewers as possible. So with few exceptions—which ironically usually have large audiences—programming is carefully noncontroversial, light, and nonpolitical in order to create a "buying mood." And because television is so effective a selling agent and the profits for using it to merchandise goods are so high, the costs of commercials are high. If an advertiser is large enough to make the initial payment, each household is reached at a relatively low cost. In the familiar dynamics, this in itself favors the big operator over the small, a contributing factor to the emergence of giantism in the American economy.

The desire to keep the attention of everyone to sell them advertised goods is a natural motivation of media operators who are in business for a profit. Advertising has produced remarkable profits for large operators in industry and in the media, but it has had profound social costs. Among the social costs is loss of diversity of information and ideas. Blandness in printed and broadcast content is intensified by the illusion that media operators are engaged in a value-free enterprise. Neither news nor advertising is value-free, of course. But the bleaching of controversy and the blunting of distinctions in points of view have damaged the country's political process.

If all things are projected as value-free and as equally important, they all appear to have equal significance. This obliterates the process of choosing from clear alternatives by which individuals make social and political decisions. Unless information in their media has clarity and sharply delineated differences in values and importance, citizens lose the ability to discriminate what is best for each of them. Collectively they lose their influence over the truly conflicting forces in the real world.

8

THE HIGH COST OF
FREE LUNCHES

*With no ads, who would pay for the media? The good
fairy?*

Samuel Thurm, senior vice-president,
Association of National Advertisers

NEWSPAPER PUBLISHERS buy boiled pine trees at wholesale and sell them at retail. Their newsprint, manufactured from
cooked wood chips and spread on moving screens to make paper, is trucked into one end of their plants in huge rolls of plain
white sheets and leaves at the other end as printed and folded
newspapers. In between, of course, something is done to the paper: news, features, and advertisements are printed on it.

But for business people, publishers are engaged in a strange
act. They sell their boiled pine trees for about one-third less
than they pay for them. It seems part of a magical performance:
Publishers sell their raw material for less than they pay for it
and they make billions of dollars in profits. Advertisers eagerly
pour billions into this seemingly uncapitalistic transaction and
they, also, make billions in profits. And the whole act is for the
ultimate benefit of the readers, who get something for nothing.

This has all the appearance of a cosmic free lunch. Media
owners regularly preach to working people the Spartan message
that there is no such thing as a free lunch, but when it comes to
media economics they suspend the doctrine. They insist that the
public is granted the gift of newspapers and magazines at less
than cost and that broadcasting is completely free.

134

But in the theater of the media there are economic sleights of hand. Americans do not get their newspapers and magazines at less than cost. They do not get their radio and television free. They pay for everything. They pay for their "free" television, they pay extra for their "subsidized" newspapers, they pay for the advertising. And then they pay extra for most of the goods promoted in the advertising. All of this is never made clear to them in the communications they most depend on—the advertising-supported newspapers, magazines, and commercial broadcasting. The "magic" in newspaper economics helps explain the illusion.

In 1940 daily newspapers averaged thirty-one pages, of which advertisers occupied 40 percent, or twelve and a half pages. Consumers paid 2 cents for the whole paper and got eighteen and a half pages of editorial matter for it. In 1980, papers averaged sixty-six pages, of which 65 percent or forty-three pages, was advertising. By this time readers were paying 20 cents for the whole paper, out of which they got twenty-three pages of editorial matter. Applying price indices from 1940 to 1980 brings the cost of a 1940-size paper to 5.7 cents in 1980. The reader got 24 percent more editorial matter in 1980, which brings the price to 7 cents. If another cent were added to give the publisher an extravagant profit beyond the 1940 margin, the price would be 8 cents, four times the 1940 price. But the price in 1980 was 20 cents, ten times the 1940 price. The difference is mainly the money charged to readers for the added advertising pages delivered to their homes. Readers in 1980 were not getting the paper for less than cost; they were paying for the advertising.

These calculations understate the payments readers make for ads, which cost as much as three times more to process than news. If the reader lost, the publishers gained. An added recent advantage for publishers is a sharp drop in production costs because of automation and computerization. Large increases in the price of newsprint were more than offset by using thinner paper and shrinking the page size. By 1980 newspapers were getting more revenues per ton of paper than before the sharp newsprint price increases of the 1970s. None of these savings is reflected in prices charged readers.

There is a further understatement of how much readers pay for the advertising in their newspapers. The increase in number of pages from 1940 to 1980, from thirty-one to sixty-six, represents mostly ad pages. But even the increase in nonadvertising pages from eighteen and a half to twenty-three pages is overstated. Most of the added editorial pages were not "news" but were in a gray area between real news and ads, an area called "fluff" in the trade. Most fluff is wanted by advertisers to create a buying mood. The "hard news"—contemporary events and commentary—in 1940 was four pages of the thirty-one-page paper (13 percent). In 1980 there were five pages of hard news of a sixty-six-page paper (7.5 percent). The reader paid more for a rapidly shrinking share of the whole paper.

A prominent editor, Carl E. Lindstrom of the *Hartford Times,* twenty years ago warned that newspapers would eventually sink under the weight of what he called "Revenue Related Reading Matter." Heavy sections of newspapers—like fashions, food, and real estate—were created as advertising bait. Sometimes the material in the special sections is genuinely useful and is produced by professional journalists. More often it is a mixture of light syndicated features and corporate press releases. In recent years some major papers have removed any pretense that their special sections are journalism and have turned over those sections to the newspaper's advertising department to fill with whatever will enhance their selling of ads.

When faced with periodic shortages of newsprint, publishers must decide whether to cut ads or news; they usually decide to cut the news. In 1973, for example, a survey by the Associated Press Managing Editors of 470 daily papers showed that the reaction to shortages of newsprint was 7 to 1 to cut news rather than advertising. Seventeen percent of those who cut the news said they would not restore it when newsprint became more plentiful.

Fluff continues to spread. A study of 1,375 daily papers by the Newspaper Advertising Bureau in 1979 showed that in

1977 and 1978, 23 percent of the country's papers had added "special lifestyle sections" and 24 percent "increased ratio of features to hard news" but only 11 percent "increased ratio of hard news to features."

Between 1971 and 1977, nonadvertising content of daily papers changed in the following ways:

Reduced: news of local and state government, of the national government, of education, about labor and national wage rates, and about minorities.

Increased: puzzles and horoscopes, comics, nonlocal human interest and lifestyle articles, business and finance, and crime.

Changes in newspapers are not made in response to what readers want. Every serious survey, including those by the newspaper industry itself, makes clear that readers want more hard news. In one study a majority of readers, 57 percent, found advertising only "somewhat interesting." But a monopoly can ignore consumer priorities for a long time (although not forever, as a later chapter will show). In the security of their domination of the market, newspaper publishers have been converting newspapers into agencies for merchants. In the words of Harold Evans, former editor of the *London Sunday Times,* the challenge of American newspapers "is not to stay in business—it is to stay in journalism."

The domination of content by commercial advertising took different forms in magazines and broadcasting.

Magazines had existed half a century before the entry of mass advertising. When mass production of merchandise flooded retail stores with surplus goods in the late nineteenth century, magazines attracted attention as the only national medium, and one with higher-quality printing than newspapers. Ads in early magazines were segregated in the back pages since editors assumed they were an intrusion on the reader. But in the 1890s when advertising revenue became important, advertising agencies insisted that ads be moved from the back of magazines to the front. Not long afterward, major advertisers were demanding that their ads appear opposite the opening pages of major articles.

The influence of advertising on magazines reached a point where editors began selecting articles not only on the basis of their expected interest for readers but for their influence on advertisements. Serious articles were not always the best support for ads. An article that put the reader in an analytical frame of mind did not encourage the reader to take seriously an ad that depended on fantasy or promoted a trivial product. An article on genuine social suffering might interrupt the "buying" mood on which most ads for luxuries depend. The next step, seen often in mid-twentieth-century magazines, was commissioning articles solely to attract readers who were good prospects to buy products advertised in the magazine. After that came the magazine phenomenon of the 1970s—creating magazines for an identifiable special audience and selling them to particular advertisers.

Newspapers and magazines have thus entered a stage in which the immediate desires of advertisers have a higher priority than the desires of readers. As Leo Bogart pointed out,

> In its expanding feature content, the daily press increasingly partakes of the character of the magazine—non-threatening and easy to take. Embedded in a tissue of gourmet recipes, instruction on furniture repair, and counsel on premarital sex, the breaking (and unsettling) news is swathed in reassurances.

Broadcasting had the firmest marriage to advertising. When radio became a nationwide medium in the 1920s it was the fastest-growing industry in national history. It was not interested in commercials. The most popular stations were noncommercial, operated by universities, states, municipalities, and school districts. Millions of Americans were tuning in to university lectures, taking correspondence courses by radio, and listening to drama, music, and debates in their communities.

Commercial radio was operated by a private cartel called Radio Corporation of America (RCA) whose chief members were General Electric, Westinghouse, and American Telephone

& Telegraph Company. Under the cartel agreement General Electric and Westinghouse operated radio stations for the purpose of stimulating the sale of home receiving sets that they and AT&T's subsidiary, Western Electric, would manufacture. At this stage the noncommercial stations were considered profitable participants in the plan since their popular programs induced the purchase of radio sets manufactured under the RCA, GE, and Westinghouse labels. AT&T was not to broadcast but was exclusive supplier of all wire connections to studios and transmitters. But in a few years AT&T, using a convoluted interpretation of the cartel arrangement, began operating radio stations (which it called "phone booths of the air"). On August 28, 1922, at 5 P.M., the AT&T station in New York, WEAF, broadcast the first commercial, and broadcasting in America has never been the same.

As the 1920s progressed so did commercials. Soon there were millions of dollars to be made. The educational stations no longer were profitable stimulants to radio sales; rather they were threats because their large audiences reduced the audiences the commercial stations could sell to merchants. Commercial stations and their RCA-related corporations used their influence in government to force educational stations to give up popular frequencies and broadcast times, to shift to lower power, and even to move to other communities. Puzzled listeners to the noncommercial stations would discover that their favorite station was no longer at its regular frequency, which was occupied by a new commercial station. If the listener followed the educational station to its new frequency, he or she might find that it came in faintly because of low power and operated on a strange schedule such as 6 to 7 A.M. or 2:15 to 3 P.M. and shortly afterward was missing even from the new frequency. Corporate owners of commercial stations could challenge educational licenses and they could afford to hire law firms and to send company representatives to attend the hearings of regulatory commissions in Washington while the threatened educational stations, operating on low budgets, could not afford such lobbying efforts. In a dozen years the powerful system of noncommercial broadcasting in the United States had been destroyed, and it has never regained health. By the 1930s, radio made all its money from advertising and created its programs to support advertising.

The broadcast industry had insisted that government regulate radio in order to prevent chaos on the dial (at one time most popular stations operated on the same frequency, jamming each other). Government gave each station a monopoly spot on the dial and made it a crime for anyone else to use that frequency. In return the government asked stations to operate in the public interest. Its standards of "public interest" were vague and, thanks to their influence within government, stations were able to schedule public interest programs at those times of the day when there were no commercials, which meant there were minimal audiences.

Television became a nationwide medium after World War II and evolved as a commercial activity supported almost entirely by advertising (1 or 2 percent of broadcast revenues come from royalty payments for secondary use of broadcast material). In the first years of mass television, whole programs were produced and controlled by single advertisers. These are known in broadcasting history as "the golden age" programs because they were coherent and had unintrusive commercials. Some were popular comedy and variety shows, but the most celebrated programs were original, live dramas. The dramas attracted huge audiences and were important in stimulating sales of television sets. Network stations realized their first large profits from programs like Philco Television Playhouse and Studio One, with plays by authors like Paddy Chayefsky and Gore Vidal.

Then an obscure lipstick company, Hazel Bishop, tried to present a commercial message not attached to sponsorship of a particular show. Hazel Bishop was not a large, established company like the previous sponsors. It had only $50,000 annual sales when it gambled on TV. Within two years Hazel Bishop was grossing $4,500,000 a year. Television was never the same thereafter. Companies, dreaming of similar leaps in sales through the new medium, rushed to buy commercial time. The networks killed the hour-long theater and comedy programs even though their sponsors were willing to pay premium prices. Instead, networks and popular stations instituted the "spot" ad—the ten-second, thirty-second, and sixty-second commercial from different sponsors in one program. Television could make more money each hour from twenty sponsors than from one large sponsor. Networks created a new kind of program that was less emotionally involving than plays by Chayefsky, new programs that created a "buying mood." The thirty-second commercials had advantages for goods whose sales depended largely on creating quick emotional associations rather than on providing product information. Calculated imagery became the main appeal of commercials, which were divided into smaller and smaller periods of time. By selling ever-smaller spots between 1965 and 1975 the industry doubled commercials per hour and in the next decade added another 30 percent.

To growing complaints about proliferation of commercials, television replied that radio and television broadcasting is free, that advertisers give the public something for nothing. The public has never heard the something-for-nothing assumption debated over commercial radio and television or in newspapers and popular magazines. As a result, it has become an article of faith that mass advertising is essential to the preservation of a free press and "free" broadcasting. The parallel argument is that mass advertising saves consumers money in yet another way because it stimulates mass sales, which permit mass production, which reduces the cost of each item.

Unfortunately, the opposite seems to be true. Economists are divided on the issue, as they are on most issues, but a growing body of American and Canadian economists finds that mass advertising often inflates prices rather than reducing them.

Radio and television are not free. Consumers spend much more to receive broadcasts than broadcasters spend to transmit them. The average household with television spends $116 a year in amortized cost of the TV set, antennas, and maintenance.

The "savings" that mass advertising delivers to consumers are similarly dubious. An increasing number of economists find that mass advertising is a major instrument by which big firms keep prices artificially high. The U.S. Supreme Court has said that mass advertising restrains competition by preventing new products from new companies from reaching the public. Advertising is used by many industries to maintain their power in the economy.

Advertising's function of inhibiting competition was recognized early in the Industrial Revolution. In the decades after the Civil War, capital investment in manufacturing machinery more than tripled, enormously enlarging manufacturers' ability to produce quantities of goods, more than had ever been sold before. From 1880 to 1910 the American population grew from 50 to 92 million, thanks to immigration and public health laws that prevented disease and early death. Mass communications began to tie together the expanding country. Mass advertising, riding on those communications, began to sell the mass-produced products to a mass audience.

A single message spread over the whole continent began to be recognized as a commodity of extraordinary value, economically and politically. Another important discovery was that once a message —a set of memorable words or a striking graphic design—had been launched over the continent and was repeated sufficiently, it began to have a value separate from the product it advertised. The familiar brand name with a life of its own has been proclaimed as a public benefaction by the advertising industry. For superior products that has some truth, for deficient products it has the potential for multiplying tragedy. Whether for superior or inferior products, the familiar brand name has another function not publicly celebrated: It has the power to prevent competition.

J. C. Hoagland was a nineteenth-century druggist in Fort Wayne, Ind., who began selling a mixture of cream of tartar and starch, both common materials available to anyone. In baking it was a convenient substitute for yeast. Royal Baking Powder was only moderately successful until Hoagland took out ads in newspapers and magazines, after which sales rose dramatically. He began spending $500,000 a year advertising the brand name. In 1893 he was offered $13 million just for the name of a compound that anyone could put together. The president of Royal Baking Powder, seeing the $13 million offer for the name, calculated that the bidder, had he wished to start a competitive baking powder, would have had to spend more than Royal, about $15 million a year. Thus, he refused the offer of $13 million for the name.

The bidder for the name "Royal" had discovered an important element in mass advertising. Every advertising dollar spent by Royal Baking Powder did two things: It retained existing customers (whose purchases helped pay for the ads) and it attracted new customers. The same dollar spent by a new competitor did only one thing: It attracted new customers. Thus, not only did the newcomer lack a body of existing customers to help finance an ad campaign but new ads were less efficient than the ads for the established firm. Mass advertising with huge budgets introduced a new factor in selling: It began to prevent competition.

Mass advertising could negate the classical theory of supply and demand, which held that success in the marketplace would automatically attract new sellers who would lower prices and keep established sellers from raising their prices to exploit the rush of business. It was a theory that worked in Adam Smith's village square full of farmers selling the same kinds of products to housewives who could test the product by squeezing, smelling, and tasting and who could haggle among the merchants. It was a theory that began to evaporate when the village square was replaced by large, distant corporations making complex products that could not be judged directly by the average consumer—products like automobiles or medicines, or products with purely emotional differences, like perfume, or categories of products that are the same, like aspirin. It is with these products that mass advertising can produce brand loyalty based not on the collective experience of consumers but on the cleverness and persistence of advertising. If a product fails to meet expectations or is considered overpriced, a large advertising campaign reduces the likelihood that a new competitor will enter the scene. The emotional direction of the advertising can shift consumer attention away from the disliked characteristics of the product, or a campaign can sweep the field before a nonadvertising competitor can win approval.

In the 1950s Studebaker, selling its car in smaller quantities for lack of financing for bid ads, nevertheless had to add $64, the cost of ads, to the price of each car. General Motors and Ford, with much larger ad budgets but also much larger sales, could spread their ad budget further and needed to add only $27 in advertising costs to the price of each car. So even before its car had begun to be tested for superiority by consumers, Studebaker had to charge $37 more for its car than GM or Ford. To remain competitive, it had to cut its profit by $37, reducing further its ability to compete with the giants. An additional burden on the smaller company is the volume discount as high as 7.5 percent, given the largest advertisers. With large budgets for mass advertising those differences alone can be fatal to smaller companies, regardless of the quality of their products or their costs of production. Studebaker went bankrupt.

Traditionalists argue that advertising will not work unless it is promoting a superior product. Unfortunately, the history of consumer goods, past and present, includes spectacular commercial success of goods that were either dangerous or ineffective. This was true before the era of advertising, but goods were sold in small volumes, so bad effects were on a small scale.

The biggest line of ads in early national campaigns was for patent medicines. Their impact on the public is a record of unremitting tragedy and fraud. Slogans and claims of healthy results concealed ingredients that were either harmful, like cocaine and heroin, or ineffective, like alcohol and water. For decades one of the most popular medicines was created by mass advertising. Lydia Pinkham's Vegetable Compound for "female discomfort" said in its ads that Mrs. Pinkham "is able to do more for a woman than any physician in America." Whatever other "vegetable compound" Mrs. Pinkham put in her bottles, she was selling, unknown to her customers, 14 percent alcohol.

Lydia Pinkham continues to have imitators. Jeffrey Schrank has noted that in the 1970s advertising raised mouthwash sales to $300 million a year. The National Academy of Sciences has said, "There is no convincing evidence that any medicated mouthwash, used as part of a daily hygiene regimen, has therapeutic advantage over . . . salt water and even water." But because color is added to the mouthwashes and because of associations of color with emotions (red for masculinity, blue for coolness, yellow for warmth), advertising that amounts to $115 million a year sells mouthwash. The public gets mouthwashes that are from 5 to 25 percent alcohol.

Other ads conceal essential realities. All aspirin is the same, for example, so the $130 million spent on aspirin is a social waste. Four of the top ten advertisers on television are drug manufacturers.

For most heavily advertised goods it is doubtful that advertising reduces prices. There is evidence that the opposite is true. When sales sag, dominant firms use advertising—deductible from their corporate taxes as a business expense—as a substitute for reduced prices. For example, despite the language of ads, all liquid bleach is basically the same—a 5.5 percent sodium hypochlorite solution. Price differentials are almost entirely the result of advertising. The consumer walking down the supermarket aisle tends to reach toward the familiar brand name, often unaware that the source of the familiarity most often is the pleasant associations that have flowed out of the consumer's television set. The more advertising or "marketing" such goods receive, the higher the price for the consumer. In the late 1970s, a recession forced many families to buy cheaper, less advertised goods (often called "generic" because their labels emphasize merely the basic nature of the product rather than a commercial brand name). The leading brand of advertised bleach, Clorox, began to lose sales. According to the Clorox 1979 annual report to stockholders:

> The Company is facing several new marketing challenges. *Clorox* liquid bleach volume has been affected by the introduction of "generic" bleaches. These products are not produced to our quality standards, and are priced well below *Clorox*. Several of our other brands have experienced vol-

> ume declines . . . due, we believe, to some softening in con-
> sumer purchases of grocery store products. The Company
> is responding to these challenges with an increased market-
> ing effort.

Standard theory of supply and demand is that the automatic response to lowered demand is lower prices. Because of
advertising—or "marketing"—and consequent market control,
that is no longer necessarily the case.

The bigger the company the more advertising it can afford
and the greater its discount in the cost of its advertising. This
was not a major factor until advertising programs became very
large and required a major resource of cash or credit if any firm
wished to compete in the national consumer market. Any newcomer wishing to invade the market dominance of Procter &
Gamble in soaps, cake mixes, detergents, toothpaste, mouthwash, shampoo, deodorants, cooking oil, and coffee needs to do
more than manufacture the products and establish a distribution
system. The newcomer has to counter the almost one billion
dollars Procter & Gamble spends every year on advertising. And
unless the newcomer has the money for an ad campaign of that
magnitude, it would pay more for each ad than Procter & Gamble because the larger firm gets a discount from the media.

It is not unusual for an industry to spend 5 percent of its
total budget on advertising. This 5 percent is not necessarily
canceled out by lower prices for mass production. More often
the cost of ads is a net addition, in whole or in part, to the retail
price; it is not a negligible added cost. Media-advertised goods
and their percentage of sales spent on advertising are proprietary
drugs, 19 percent; perfumes and cosmetics, 14 percent; liquor,
11 percent; cereal, 11 percent; cigarettes, 8 percent. These heavy
expenditures for ads can raise the purchase price for the consumers. The ads can also maintain the volume of sales, making
it difficult for newcomers to enter the field. The result often is
domination of the market with controlled prices that exceed even
the addition of advertising costs.

One estimate is that heavily advertised industries create
prices that are 15 percent higher than under truly competitive

free enterprise. The "linkage of ads to oligopoly and excess profits costs society from $10 to $20 billion a year."

It is no coincidence that industries considered to have artificially high prices and high barriers to entry by competitors include those industries that advertise heavily in the mass media—liquor, drugs, soaps, autos, photo supplies, cereals, soft drinks, cigarettes, toilet preparations, tires and tubes, large appliances, chemicals, and petroleum products.

The creation of adless newspapers and popular magazines or a well-financed public broadcasting system with nonpolitical public money has been resisted by most of the major media. The adless publication is painted either as a disservice to the public, or as an economic impossibility. An adless newspaper in pre–World II New York, *PM,* ultimately failed, and it has been used by media operators as conclusive evidence that such newspapers are not viable. The success of E. W. Scripps with adless papers is relegated to brief mention in books of journalism history, and the failure of *PM* is never put in the context of the hundreds of failures since that time of newspapers with ads.

The best estimate is that an adless paper costs the reader 70 percent more than a paper with the current level of ads. Though readers pay for the pages of advertising, the high volume of pages printed in a newspaper plant because of ad pages reduces the production cost per page. It is the enormous increase in ad pages that makes for a net increase in the cost of the whole paper. So eliminating those pages would mean smaller printing runs, which would be cheaper in total cost but higher per page by 70 percent. A paper with 1940-level ads, twelve and a half pages, would cost, at most, 14 cents, instead of the 20 cents for the present level of ads, forty-three pages. Elimination of most of the large ads in a newspaper would reduce the cost of many manufactured goods whose makers now add the cost of ads to the price. Today, advertisers spend $400 a year on each newspaper subscriber and about $300 a year on each television household. Even more could be saved by the reduced prices of consumer goods while giving the readers a less expensive paper that would still have twelve pages of ads.

The same calculation could be made for magazines but

with added complexity; magazines vary so widely in their frequency of publication and the nature of their audiences that it is not easy to allocate the cost of advertising to the average subscriber. Much of the billions spent annually by advertisers in magazines could be saved.

Perhaps the easiest calculation is made for radio and television audiences, who are told that their medium is "free," the contribution of advertisers. The user pays for a large part of the more than $30 billion a year in radio and television advertising that is added to the cost of the products advertised, even ignoring the added cost of products whose prices remain artificially high because of market control exercised through advertising.

Saving a large part of the billions spent on ads in newspapers, magazines, radio, and television could have important social and economic consequences. The audience for radio and television could pay a fee for their regular programming, as they now do for newspaper and magazine content, and for cable and pay television. To offset this, they could save much of the $1,000 per household spent annually for media advertising and added to prices of goods. Those net savings could support a different system of announcing new products, prices, and specifications, under the control of the consumer and at lower cost than present media ads. It is possible that if given a choice most consumers would prefer the present system. But today they have no chance to make a choice.

In the latter half of the twentieth century, discussion of these issues is absent in the major media. The taboo permits perpetuation of euphoria about the automatic blessings of advertising, the magic of the infallible marketplace, and other illusions that produce enduring mischief. The euphoria seems untouched by recurring recessions, periodic depressions, and continuing crises in the social and political structure of the country. The simplistic view of commercialized media continues in only slightly more sophisticated form from its origins early in this century.

By 1910 major universities, among them Harvard, were teaching marketing, business promotion, and advertising as a science, including the mystique of mass advertising as a pro-

ducer of competition, of reduced prices, and of the elevation of
the consumer as sovereign.

By 1928 there were thirty-nine universities teaching marketing, business promotion, and advertising. Advertising had
become a big business of its own, growing from $200 million in
1880 to $3.5 billion just before the stock market crash of 1929.
Advertising agencies once limited to placing ads in newspapers
and magazines began to do "creative" work—inventing slogans,
brand names, and artistic designs and, eventually, conducting
social science and psychological research on how to penetrate
the emotions and subconscious of consumers. Especially with
the emergence of television, with vivid images that came and
went in seconds, appeals to the emotions—with sex, ambition,
fear of rejection, and illness—became crucial. Advertising became a vital gear in the machinery of corporate power. It not
only helped create and preserve dominance of the giants over
consumer industries, it also helped create a picture of a satisfac-
tory world with the corporations as benign stewards.

In 1926 the president of the United States, Calvin Coolidge,
said:

> Mass demand has been created almost entirely through the
> development of advertising ... The most potent influence
> in adopting and changing what we eat, what we wear, and
> the work and play of the whole nation ... Sometimes it
> seems as though our generation fails to give the proper esti-
> mate and importance to the values of life ... Advertising
> ministers to the spiritual side of trade ... It is a great power
> ... part of the greater work of the regeneration and re-
> demption of mankind.

If advertising was part of "the regeneration and redemption
of mankind," then the newspapers, magazines, and broadcasters
that got paid for the ads were its appointed agents on earth.
They began the process of adapting their content to the needs
of advertising and of adopting its ideology as their own. They
also adopted the ingenious practice of their advertising spon-

sors: They charged the readers and viewers for propagandizing themselves but told audiences they were getting something for nothing.

Mass advertising is no longer solely a means of introducing and distributing consumer goods, though it does that. It is a major mechanism in the ability of a relatively small number of giant corporations to hold disproportionate power over the economy. These corporations need newspapers, magazines, and broadcasting not just to sell their goods but to maintain their economic and political influence. The media are no longer neutral agents of the merchants but essential gears in the machinery of corporate giantism. And increasingly they are not only needed but they are owned by the corporate giants.

That is why, perhaps, advertising-supported media have not told the complete story of the "miracle" of advertising. Held before the reading and viewing public is the beatific picture of new and liberating goods made possible by mass advertising, of goods at the lowest possible prices, of the vitality of competition kept alive by advertising, and, of course, of the lessened cost to the consumer of newspapers and magazines and the "free" radio and television.

Paul Miller, when he was chief executive officer of Gannett, told his peers:

> And let us remind readers regularly, in editorials, in our promotional advertising, in speeches to civic groups and others, that advertising helps people live better and saves them money. This fact needs constant selling.

William S. Paley, founder of CBS, has said

> I have a theory that television, in particular, has never been evaluated properly. Television, I would say, isn't an advertising medium, it's a selling medium.

The issues of this book are not the inherent merits of advertising and advertisers. But some related points are important. Media consumers pay artificially high prices for goods advertised through their media. They pay high and hidden prices for the media themselves. And the media are no longer neutral agents selling space and time for merchants to promote their wares but are now vital instruments needed by major corporations to maintain their economic and political power.

This raises questions about the role of the mass media in the American economy and politics. Advertising is not a luxury to large corporations but an activity with profound economic and political consequences. The media are now dependent upon these corporations for most of their revenues and increasingly they are owned by such corporations. The media have become partners in achieving the social and economic goals of their patrons and owners. Yet it is the newspapers, general magazines, and broadcasters who are citizens' primary source of information and analysis of precisely this kind of economic and political issue. This raises the question whether our mass media are free to exercise their traditional role of mediating among the forces of society at a time when they have become an integral part of one of those forces.

9

DR. BRANDRETH
HAS GONE TO HARVARD

*What I'd like to know is how you Americans can success-
fully worship God and Mammon at the same time.*
Sir John Reith, director general of
the British Broadcasting Corporation

JAMES GORDON BENNETT, founder of the *New York
Herald*, is one of American journalism's rambunctious bad boys.
In August of 1835 his Ann Street plant suffered a disastrous
fire, but the *Herald* was back on the street nineteen days later
with the pronouncement:

> We are again in the field . . . more independent than ever.
> The Ann Street conflagration consumed types, presses,
> manuscripts, paper, some bad poetry, subscription books—
> all the outward appearance of the *Herald,* but its soul was
> saved.

The *Herald* was "again in the field" but not "more independent than ever." After the fire Bennett was saved by a large
advertising contract from a "Doctor Brandreth," a quack who
sold phony cure-all pills. After the *Herald* was back in circulation, the Brandreth ads appeared in profusion. But so did a
steady diet of "news" stories, presuming to be straight reporting, "more independent than ever," recounting heroic cures
effected by none other than Dr. Brandreth's pills. While other
pill makers complained that Brandreth was getting front-page

news accounts as well as ads, Bennett replied in his news
columns:

> Send us more advertisements than Dr. Brandreth does—
> give us higher prices—we'll cut Dr. Brandreth dead—or at
> least curtail his space. Business is business—money is
> money—and Dr. Brandreth is no more to us than "Mr.
> Money Broker."

Nine months later, when Brandreth canceled his advertising contract, Bennett, in print, called the good doctor a "most
impudent charlatan" who "deceived and cheated," something
any moderately honest reporter could have written from the
start.

In the new dignity of modern American journalism, this
kind of corruption in the news is a thing of the past, having
occurred only in the bad old days before the turn of the century. Modern media, it is said, are immunized by professional
ethics from letting advertising influence editorial content.

Contemporary news and entertainment are, to use Bennett's phrase, "more independent than ever." Newspapers make
75 percent of their revenues from ads and devote about 65 percent of their daily space to them. Magazines, similarly clothed in
virtue, make roughly half their money from ads, though they
used to make more, and they, too, generally insist that their
advertising departments never shape the articles, stories, and
columns produced by professional editors and writers. Radio
and television, the most pervasive media in American life, have
varied nonadvertising content like game shows, situation come-
dies, cops-and-robbers serials, news, talk shows, documentaries,
and musical recordings. These, broadcasters usually insist, are
independent of the thirty-second and sixty-second commercials
dropped into normal programming. In short, nineteenth-century
money changers of advertising have been chased out of the
twentieth-century temple of editorial purity.

It's a pretty picture. Unfortunately, it isn't true.

Present-day Brandreths have changed their technique. So
have the contemporary Bennetts. The advertiser does not barge

through the front door announcing, "I am Dr. Brandreth. I pay money to this network (newspaper, magazine, radio station) and I am pleased to introduce to you the producer (reporter, editor, writer) who, with all the powers vested by society in independent journalism, will proclaim the wonder of my pills." Except for a few clumsy operators, such a tactic is much too crude for the late twentieth century.

Today Dr. Brandreth makes his proper appearance in his ads. He then leaves politely by the front door, goes to the back of the television station (radio studio, newspaper newsroom, magazine editorial offices), puts on the costume of a professional producer (editor, reporter), and in his new guise declares, "I am an ethical professional producer (reporter, editor, writer) whom you have been told to trust. Through professional research and critical analysis it is my independent judgment that Dr. Brandreth's pills, politics, ideology, and industry are the salvation of our national soul."

Modern corruption is more subtle. At one time or another, advertisers have *successfully* demanded that the following ideas appear in programs around their ads.

All businessmen are good or, if not, are always condemned by other businessmen. All wars are humane. The status quo is wonderful. Also wonderful are all grocery stores, bakeries, drug companies, restaurants, and laundries. Religionists, especially clergy, are perfect. All users of cigarettes are gentle, graceful, healthy, youthful people. In fact, anyone who uses a tobacco product is a hero. People who commit suicide never do it with pills. All financial institutions are always in good shape. The American way of life is beyond criticism.

The above messages, to cite only a few, are not vague inferences. Major advertisers insisted, successfully, that these specific ideas be expressed not in the ads but in the ostensibly "independent" news reporting, editorial content, or entertainment programs of newspapers, magazines, radio, and television. The readers, listeners, and viewers do not know that these messages are planted by advertisers. They are not supposed to know. They are supposed to think that these ideas are the independent work of professional journalists and playwrights detached from anything commercial. If the audiences were told that the ideas represented explicit demands of corporations who advertised, the messages would lose their impact.

This is not saying that all journalists and screenwriters are forced to follow ideological lines. There is considerable latitude for description of events and ideas in the news, in magazine articles, and in broadcast programs. But there is a limit to this latitude, established by conventional wisdom in journalism and broadcasting. The most obvious limit is criticism of the idea of free enterprise or of other basic business systems. Some reporters often criticize specific corporate acts, to the rage of corporate leaders. But the taboo against criticism of the system of contemporary enterprise is, in its unspoken way, almost as complete within mainstream journalism and broadcast programming in the United States as criticism of communism is explicitly forbidden in the Soviet Union.

The entry of pro-corporate ideas into news and entertainment is more specific and discernible than the convention against systemic criticism.

Procter & Gamble is the largest advertiser in television. For years it has been a leader in creating promotions in all media, including commercials inserted in television programs. It has always appreciated the power of advertising. The company was created in 1837 with a soap called, simply, White Soap. But in 1879 Harley Procter, a descendant of the founder, read in the Forty-fifth Psalm, ''All thy garments smell of myrrh and aloes and cassia out of the ivory palaces . . .'' Ivory Soap was born and with it the first of the full-page ads for the product. Within a decade Procter & Gamble was selling thirty million cakes of the soap a day. Since then, the company has been spectacularly successful, combining soap, detergent, Christian religion, patriotism, and profit making. After World War II it projected its ideas to television programs in the form of advertising.

They, like most major advertisers, do not merely buy a certain number of commercials, deliver the tapes to the networks and local stations, and let the commercials fall where they may. Some television and radio ads are bought on that basis but not, usually, those of major advertisers. Big advertisers in particular want to know what time of day their commercials will be shown, since that helps define the makeup and size of the audience they are buying. And they want to know the nature of the program into which their commercial will be inserted.

In the early years of television, advertisers sponsored and produced entire news and entertainment programs. This gave them direct control over the nonadvertising part of the program and they inserted or deleted whatever suited their commercial and ideological purposes. NBC's news program in the early 1950s was called "Camel News Caravan" after its sponsor, Camel cigarettes, which banned all film of news that happened to take place where a No Smoking sign could be seen in the background.

After the 1950s, networks produced their own shows and advertisers bought commercials of varying lengths for insertion during the networks' programming. Advertising was allotted six minutes per hour of prime-time evening hours and longer periods at other times of day. But no network produces a program without considering whether sponsors will like it. Prospective shows usually are discussed with major advertisers, who look at plans or tentative scenes and reject, approve or suggest changes.

Major advertisers like Procter & Gamble do not leave their desires in doubt.

The Federal Communications Commission held hearings in 1965 to determine how much influence advertisers had on noncommercial content of television and radio. Albert N. Halverstadt, general advertising manager of Procter & Gamble, testified that the company established directives for programs in which Procter & Gamble would advertise. These policies were to create standards of "decency and common sense . . . I do not think it constitutes control." He then gave the FCC the formal requirements for television programs, as established by the medium's largest advertiser in their memorandums of instruction to their advertising agency:

> Where it seems fitting, the characters in Procter & Gamble dramas should reflect recognition and acceptance of the

world situation in their thoughts and actions, although in dealing with war, our writers should minimize the "horror" aspects. The writers should be guided by the fact that any scene that contributes negatively to public morale is not acceptable. Men in uniform shall not be cast as heavy villains or portrayed as engaging in any criminal activity.

Procter & Gamble was particularly interested in the image of business and business people on television programs:

> There will be no material on any of our programs which could in any way further the concept of business as cold, ruthless, and lacking all sentiment or spiritual motivation.
>
> If a businessman is cast in the role of villain, it must be made clear that he is not typical but is as much despised by his fellow businessmen as he is by other members of society.
>
> Special attention shall be given to *any* mention, however innocuous, of the grocery and drug business as well as any other group of customers of the company. This includes industrial users of the company's products, such as bakeries, restaurants, and laundries.

The company view of religion and patriotism is built into programs. If, in a drama or documentary, a character attacks what the memo called "some basic conception of the American way of life" then a rejoinder "must be completely and convincingly made someplace in the same broadcast."

The same is true of what Procter & Gamble called "positive social forces": "Ministers, priests and similar representatives of positive social forces shall not be cast as villains or represented as committing a crime or be placed in any unsympathetic antisocial role."

The memo specifies, "If there is any question whatever about such material, it should be deleted."

Halverstadt testified that these policies were applied both to entertainment programs in which Procter & Gamble commercials appeared and to news and public affairs documentaries.

Thus, corporate ideology is built into entertainment and

documentary programming that the audience believes is presented independent of thirty-second and sixty-second commercials that happen to appear in the program. It is sobering that these demands are made of a medium reaching eighty million homes for six and a half hours every day.

But insertion of corporate ideology and commercial themes in the nonadvertising portion of television programming is not limited to Procter & Gamble. An executive of Brown & Williamson Tobacco Corporation placed into evidence before the FCC the company's policy on programs carrying cigarette commercials, directives that prevailed until the end of televised cigarette commercials in 1970:

> Tobacco products should not be used in a derogatory or harmful way. And no reference or gesture of disgust, dissatisfaction or distaste be made in connection with them. Example: cigarettes should not be ground out violently in an ashtray or stamped out underfoot.
>
> Whenever cigarettes are used by antagonists or questionable characters, they should be regular size, plain ends and unidentifiable.
>
> But no cigarette should be used as a prop to depict an undesirable character. Cigarettes used by meritorious characters should be Brown & Williamson brands and they may be identifiable or not.

A vice-president of an advertiser of headache tablets, Whitehall Laboratories, told the FCC that the company demanded of networks that "if a scene depicted somebody committing suicide by taking a bottle of tablets, we would not want this to be on the air."

A vice-president of Prudential Insurance Company, sponsor of public affairs programs, said that a positive image of business and finance was important to sustain on the air. The company rejected the idea for a program on the Bank Holiday during the Depression because "it cast a little doubt on all financial institutions."

All major advertisers, it seems, would concur with a statement made by a Procter & Gamble vice-president for advertising

in 1979: "We're in programming first to assure a good environment for our advertising."

Corporate demands on television programs underlie what
many consider the most grievous weakness of American television—superficiality, materialism, blandness, and escapism. The
television industry invariably responds that the networks are only
giving people what the people demand. But it is not what the
public says it wants: It is what the advertisers demand.

At one time Bell & Howell Company attempted to break
the pattern of escapist, superficial prime-time programs by sponsoring news documentaries. The president of the company told
the FCC that this was tried to help counter the standards applied by most advertisers, which he described, disapprovingly,
as consisting of the following requirements:

> One should not associate with controversy; one should al-
> ways reach for the highest ratings; one should never forget
> that there is safety in numbers; one should always remember
> that comedy, adventure and escapism provide the best at-
> mosphere for selling.

Even if a nonescapist program becomes a commercial success, it is likely to be canceled by the networks or major local
stations. In the early days of television there were outstanding
serious programs, including live, original drama: "Kraft Television Theatre," "Goodyear Playhouse," "Studio One," "Robert
Montgomery Presents," "U.S. Steel Hour," "Revlon Theater,"
"Omnibus," "Motorola TV Hour," "The Elgin Hour," "Matinee
Theater," and "Playhouse 90." It was the era of striking television plays by playwrights such as Paddy Chayefsky, who said
he had discovered "the marvelous world" of drama in the lives
of ordinary people.

Erik Barnouw in his definitive history of American broadcasting writes:

> That this "marvelous world" fascinated millions is abun-
> dantly clear from statistics. These plays—akin to genre
> paintings—held consistently high ratings. But one group
> hated them: the advertising profession . . . Most advertisers

were selling magic. Their commercials posed the same problems that Chayefsky drama dealt with: people who feared
failure in love and in business. But in the commercials there
was always a solution as clear-cut as the snap of a finger:
the problem could be solved by a new pill, deodorant,
toothpaste, shampoo, shaving lotion, hair tonic, car, girdle,
coffee, muffin recipe, or floor wax.

Serious programs remind the audience that complex human
problems are not solved by switching to a new deodorant. Con
trary to the network characterization of audiences, a more sophisticated presentation of human affairs was accepted enthusi-
astically by television audiences during the 1950s, if the work
was done with skill and sensitivity. If, in the midst of this, a
commercial resolved serious human conflicts with a new brand
of coffee, the commercial appeared for what it was—silly. A
skillful documentary on assassinations in American politics is
not an ideal "environment" for a commercial arguing that a new
toothpaste with a secret ingredient will give long life, wealth, and
sexual fulfillment.

Even "serious" commercials, like corporate image advertisements, are carefully placed in the most suitable programming.
The manager of corporate communications for General Electric
has said, "We insist on a program environment that reinforces
our corporate messages."

There is another reason networks and advertising agencies
resist serious or nonescapist programs. Networks make most of
their money between the hours of 8:00 and 11:00 P.M.—prime
time. They wish to keep the audience tuned from one half-hour
segment to the next and they prefer the "buying mood" sustained
as well. A serious half-hour program in that period that has high
ratings may, nevertheless, be questioned because it will interrupt
the evening's flow of lightness and fantasy. In that sense, the
whole evening is a single block of atmosphere—a selling
atmosphere.

A major advertiser, Du Pont, told the FCC that the corporation finds its commercials more effective on "lighter, happier" programs. Television is particularly suited to fantasy, im-

agery, and multidimensional effects. Commercials are brief, measured in split seconds. They disappear quickly, permitting no reflection after one image has been implanted before the next appears. The nonadvertising program is designed to leave undisturbed these emotional associations of commercials.

The printed media have not escaped the pressure, or the desire, to shape their nonadvertising content to support the mood and sometimes the explicit ideas of advertisers. Magazines were the first medium to carry sophisticated, artistic advertisements. Magazines had graphic capabilities superior to newspapers, with better printing and color illustrations (the first successful national magazine, *Godey's Lady Book,* begun in 1830, hired 150 women to tint the magazine's illustrations by hand). Until late in the 1800s ads were a minor part of magazine publishing, but once national merchandising organizations grew, this national medium responded. By 1900 *Harper's,* for example, was carrying more ads in one year than it had in its previous twenty-two years.

Before television emerged in the 1950s, successful magazines were 65 percent ads. By that time, most magazines were fundamentally designed for advertising rather than editorial matter. The philosophy of Condé Nast had triumphed. Nast, who had created *Vogue, Vanity Fair, Glamour, Mademoiselle,* and *House and Garden,* regarded his mission "to bait the editorial pages in such a way to lift out of all the millions of Americans just the hundred thousand cultivated persons who can buy these quality goods."

The role of most magazines, as seen by their owners, was to act as a broker in bringing together the buyers and sellers of goods. There was, and still is, a significant difference among magazines in how far they go to sell their readers to advertisers. But the influence of advertisers on magazine content continues.

A 1940 *Esquire* article declared that the guitar is a better accompaniment to singing than a piano. A few months later the magazine ran an apology, "We lost all our piano ads . . . We can and do beg the pardon of the piano manufacturers." By then the fiery owners of the magazine had already been tamed. Two years earlier they had started *Ken,* a magazine of liberal idealism that seemed to start with great promise. Advertisers disliked the liberal ideas in its articles and not only refused to advertise in the new publication but threatened to pull out their ads from *Esquire* as well. So the owners of *Esquire* killed *Ken,* even though it met its circulation plans.

In 1962 Paul Willis, president of the Grocery Manufacturers Association, warned television operators that they had better run more programs boosting the food industry. He boasted that a similar warning had worked with national magazines.

> We suggested to the publishers that the day was here when their editorial department and business department might better understand their interdependent relationships ... as their operations may affect the advertiser—their bread and butter.

The periodical *Advertising Age* said Willis "pointed with pride" to favorable food articles printed thereafter by "Look, Reader's Digest, American Weekly, This Week, Saturday Evening Post, Good Housekeeping, Ladies' Home Journal, Family Circle, and Woman's Day, among others."

If, like Bennett's *Herald,* this was merely the bad old days, there has been little evidence to give comfort in recent years. Condé Nast could create *Vogue* in 1909 with his philosophy of using his articles to get "the cultivated persons who can buy these quality goods." In 1972, with *Vogue* under a new owner (S. I. Newhouse, the newspaper chain, which bought the Condé Nast magazines in 1959), it seemed to make no difference. Richard Shortway, publisher of *Vogue,* sixty-three years after Nast's candid statement, made his own candid statement: "The cold, hard facts of magazine publishing mean that those who advertise get editorial coverage."

Magazines have been the Achilles' heel of corporations who also own book houses. The New York Times Company is a conglomerate involved in magazines, books, and broadcasting, as well as newspapers. In 1976 the *New York Times* published a series of articles on medical malpractice. The news series angered the medical industry, including pharmaceutical firms. They could not retaliate effectively against the *New York Times,* which does not carry much medical advertising. But medicine-related advertisers were crucial to magazines published by the New York Times Company, including a periodical called *Modern Medicine.* Pharmaceutical firms threatened to withdraw 260 pages of their ads from *Modern Medicine,* a loss of half a million dollars, and the Times Company sold its medical magazines to Harcourt Brace Jovanovich.

The sale by the Times raises two interesting questions. How many papers, rather than sell profitable subsidiaries like the Time's medical magazines, would instead have decided not to print the malpractice series or have told their editors not to report such stories again? And what would happen, after the Times sold the magazines, if an author submitted a book manuscript on medical malpractice to the new owner of the magazines, the book publisher Harcourt Brace Jovanovich? Perhaps the more troublesome question is: Without anyone ever saying anything explicit, what would go through the mind of a decision maker at a book company, knowing what had happened at the New York Times?

Reader's Digest Association owns the magazine *Reader's Digest* and Funk & Wagnalls book publishing. In 1968 Funk & Wagnalls prepared to publish a book, *The Permissible Lie,* which criticized the advertising industry. A month before publication date, Reader's Digest ordered its book subsidiary to cancel the book. Reader's Digest advertising revenues in its magazine, at that date, were $50 million a year and the association presumably felt threatened by loss of advertising from its magazine if its book subsidiary offended the advertising industry.

Newspapers are considered the most scrupulous of all the media subsidized by advertising. It has been a sacred edict in official newspaper ethics that church and state—news and advertising—are separate and that when there is any doubt each is clearly labeled. This is a relatively recent change. Thirty years ago it was common for newspapers to resist news that offended a major advertiser. Department store fires, safety violations in stores, public health actions against restaurants that advertised, and lawsuits against car dealers seldom made their way into print. The average paper printed stories about some advertiser or prospective advertiser that were solely promotional propaganda. A standard fixture in almost every newspaper was the memorandum from the business office—B.O.M., or "business office must," meaning that the news department was ordered to run a story for purposes of pleasing an advertiser.

Over the years on most newspapers—but not all—those blatant corruptions of news have diminished or disappeared. But censoring of information offensive to advertisers continues. News that might damage an advertiser generally must pass a higher threshold of drama and documentation than other kinds of news. More common in contemporary papers is the large quantity of "fluff"—material that is not news in any real sense but is nonadvertising material supporting of advertisers.

A 1978 study by the Housing Research Group of the Center for Responsive Law found that

> most newspaper real estate sections serve the real estate industry far better than they serve consumers and general readers . . . Articles that appear as "news" frequently are promotional pieces for developers, real estate agents, or industry associations.

Examples in the study included the following: the *Birmingham* (Alabama) *News* printed four industry press releases without more than cosmetic rewriting on the front page of its real estate section; one issue of the *Sacramento Union* had more than a dozen articles promoting new subdivisions; press releases were substituted for news articles in the *Baltimore Sun, Birmingham News, Boston Herald American, New York Post, Philadelphia Evening Bulletin,* and *Washington Star.*

Bigger papers, including some of the country's most prestigious, often printed more real estate propaganda than did some smaller papers. The report said:

> We were surprised to discover half a dozen smaller newspapers . . . that had a small but respectable real estate section. Their success in presenting real estate news in an ob-

jective, informative fashion compared quite favorably with some much larger newspapers.

These smaller papers were *Indianapolis Star, New Orleans Times-Picayune, Memphis Commercial Appeal,* and *St. Petersburg* (Fla.) *Times.*

The study seemed to have little impact. A year later a number of newspapers not only kept up the flood of industry promotional material masquerading as news but actually took real estate reporting out of the hands of reporters and gave it directly to the advertising department. These papers include the *Van Nuys* (Calif.) *Valley News, Los Angeles Herald Examiner, Houston Chronicle,* and *Dallas Morning News.*

The bulk of "news" in the newspaper is contained in similar special sections. The fashion section, for example, is almost always either taken from press releases submitted by designers and fashion houses or written by fashion editors who attend the fashion shows with all expenses paid by the fashion houses. The result is an annual flood of gushy promotion of exotic garments, all in a "news" section. The contamination becomes more blatant with time. In 1980 John Brooks, director of communications for the *Toronto Star,* said that when the paper created a new fashion section,

> all market research data was turned over to the editorial department so that planning of editorial content would be consistent with the wants and needs of readers and prospective readers. The Family Editor, under whose jurisdiction Fashion/80 would fall, spent a lot of time with advertising department personnel in meetings with advertisers.

The same is true of travel and usually food sections. A survey in 1977 showed that 94 percent of food editors use food company releases for recipes and 38 percent attend food events at the expense of food companies.

The growing trend among newspapers to turn over sections of the "news" to the advertising department usually produces copy that is not marked "advertising" but is full of promotional material under the guise of news. The advertising department of the *Houston Chronicle,* for example, provides all the "news" for the following sections of the paper: home, townhouse, apartments, travel, technology, livestock, and swimming pools. The vice-president of sales and marketing of the *Chronicle* said: "We do nothing controversial. We're not in the investigative business. Our only concern is giving editorial support to our ad projects."

One of the most compelling needs for readers in the 1980s was reliable information about comparative shopping, yet it is one of the weakest elements in American newspapers. The consumer information most needed by families concerns industries with control over the advertising income of newspapers—food, transportation, and clothing. A feature that has always been extremely popular with readers during its spasmodic and brief appearances is the market basket survey. A reporter periodically buys the items on a typical family shopping list and writes a story about price changes in major supermarkets. It is not a story that grocery store advertisers like, so it has practically disappeared in American papers precisely when it is most needed. Even when the market basket surveys are conducted by university researchers, as at Purdue University, most papers refuse to carry the reports, one admitting it bent to advertisers' pressure.

In 1980 the *Washington Star* announced a five-part series on the pros and cons of shopping coupons that have become common in newspapers, but the series was killed after the first story for fear of discouraging advertisers who bought space in the *Star* for shopping coupons.

When small advertisers hurt big ones, the big ones almost always win. A company called Car/Puter International for $10 provides a consumer with a computer printout giving the list prices and dealers' prices of a car and its options. For another $10 the company will order the car from the manufacturer at $125 above dealers' cost, a large savings over ordinary dealer prices. Car dealers are a major newspaper advertiser. More than forty newspapers and magazines refused to run Car/Puter ads, one publisher admitting that the ad's problem was "its direct competitiveness with automobile dealers."

Given the eagerness with which newspapers protect major

advertisers, it is understandable that by now advertisers expect that when the interests of readers are in competition with the interests of advertisers, the newspapers will protect the advertisers.

A senior vice-president of MGM told newspaper executives in 1981 that he had seen too many negative reviews of movies and warned newspapers that the $500 million worth of movie ads

> cannot be taken for granted and you've got to get this word to your editorial counterparts ... Today the daily newspaper does not always create a climate that is supportive and favorable to the motion picture industry ... gratuitous and hateful reviews threaten to cause the romance between newspapers and the motion picture industry to wither on the vine.

Camel cigarettes presumably was not surprised in 1981 when 300 daily newspapers accepted its astonishing offer to run the large Monday morning sports scores not as independent news but imbedded in an advertising display called "Camel Scoreboard." It was the first time a major category of printed news became the property of an advertiser.

Another ingenious method of controlling news was used by Air Canada. In 1978 it notified newspaper advertising managers that its ads would be canceled as long as any news story of an Air Canada crash or hijacking ran in the paper and if its ads were carried within two pages of a news story of any crash or hijacking on any airline.

Daily journalism in the last twenty years has shown more initiative in probing social forces that affect people's lives, reported in the "hard news" sections of papers. But the influence of advertisers and publishers' fears of offending advertisers have created a no man's land of subject matter that few newspapers, or magazines or broadcasters, will enter. These taboo subjects include some of the most critical developments to American life— abuse of land planning in cities, harmful real estate developments, the auto lobby's crippling of public transportation. But perhaps the most shameful money-induced censorship of American news media, a corruption of news that has contributed to millions of deaths, is the decades-long handling of the link between tobacco and heart-lung diseases.

Tobacco first entered human experience sometime in the sixteenth century, as a cure for numerous ailments, an illusion encouraged and sometimes believed by tobacco growers and merchants. But over the centuries doubt grew about the wondrous claims for the weed.

The scientific method applied to medicine has for a long time used circumstantial evidence to end some of the traditional scourges of humanity. Long before the organism of bubonic plague was isolated, that frightening destroyer of whole societies was tamed by systematic observation: People exposed to fleas from sick rats died of the plague while those not exposed did not die. Before any specific agent was identified, the back of typhoid fever was broken by the conclusion that people exposed to contaminated water and milk more often contracted the disease than those who were not exposed. Throughout modern history, killer diseases have been tamed by an analysis of the common experience of those who got sick compared with those who stayed healthy—methods of the science of epidemiology.

Over time, observers using the same methods associated some diseases with smoking. By the 1920s and 1930s medical research in England pointed clearly to tobacco as a danger to humans. In 1933 a team under Dr. Raymond Pearl at Johns Hopkins University began a three-year study of all deaths of patients thirty-five years and older, listing them in categories as nonsmokers, light smokers, and heavy smokers. The study involved 6,813 cases and the results were clear: Smokers became sick and died much earlier than nonsmokers, and on the average the more people smoked the quicker they got sick and died. The report was carried by a standard science service to newspapers and magazines. But, strangely, newspapers, magazines, and radio, which seized upon less conclusive research on the causes of polio, influenza, and tuberculosis, often with overdramatization of evidence, remained silent on the scientifically indicated causes of heart disease and cancer.

On February 24, 1936, Dr. Pearl delivered a paper to the New York Academy of Medicine. His paper concluded that tobacco shortens the life of all users, a piece of genuinely spectacular news affecting millions of readers and listeners. The session was covered by the press, but they either remained silent about the news or buried it. At the time there were eight daily papers in New York City. Six of them carried nothing of the report. The other two, including the *New York Times,* carried only a few paragraphs buried at the bottom of an inside page.

In 1953, the American Medical Association announced that it would no longer accept tobacco advertising in its journals, including the most authoritative medical publication in the country, the *Journal of the AMA.* In 1954, the American Cancer Society released results of a study of 187,000 men. Cigarette smokers had a death rate from all diseases 75 percent higher than nonsmokers. Their death rate from lung cancer was as high as sixteen times greater than that for nonsmokers. It was the start of overwhelming evidence of an epidemic that took more lives than the diseases that regularly hit front pages of newspapers and double-page spreads of magazines. It was increasingly clear that tobacco-linked disease is the biggest single killer in the United States, accounting for more than 300,000 deaths a year, the cause of one in every seven deaths in the country, killing six times more people annually than automobile accidents. But though the statistics are conclusive to medical authorities, to this day they are treated as controversial or non-existent by the news media.

If there is a date beyond which there is no justification for media silence or burial of the link between tobacco and widespread death, it is 1954. In 1953, the year the AMA banned tobacco ads from its journals, the *New York Times Index,* reflecting probably the best newspaper reporting on the tobacco-cancer link, had 248 entries under "Cancer" and "Smoking" and "Tobacco." Ninety-two percent said nothing about the link; of the 8 percent that did, only 2 percent were articles mainly about the tobacco-disease connection, the other 6 percent mostly denials of this from the tobacco industry. In 1954, the year of the American Cancer Society's study, the *New York Times Index* had 302 entries under the same titles. Of the stories dealing mainly with tobacco's link to disease, 32 percent were about the tobacco industry's denials and only 20 percent dealt with medical evidence.

In 1980, sixteen years later, there were still more stories in the daily press about the causes of influenza, polio, and tuberculosis than about the cause of one of every seven deaths in the United States.

There began to be suspicions of a strictly media disease: a strange paralysis whenever solid news pointed at tobacco as a definitive cause of disease and death. For years up to the present, medical evidence on tobacco and disease has been treated differently from any other information on carriers of disease that do not advertise. The print and broadcast media might make page 1 drama of a junior researcher's paper about a rare disease. But if it involved the 300,000 annual deaths from tobacco-related disease, the media either do not report it or they report it as a controversial item subject to rebuttal by the tobacco industry.

It is a history filled with curious events. In 1963, for example, Hudson Vitamin Products produced Smokurb, a substitute for cigarettes. The company had trouble getting its ads in newspapers and magazines and on the air. Eli Schonberger, president of Hudson's ad agency, said, "We didn't create this campaign to get into a fight with anyone, but some media just stall and put us off in the hope that we'll go away."

This is, of course, strange behavior for media who are anxious for as much advertising as they can get. One major magazine told the company its product was "unacceptable."

The tobacco industry spends $4 a year for every American man, woman, and child for its cigarette advertising. The government's primary agency for educating the public about the dangers of cigarettes, the Department of Health and Human Services, spends one-third of a cent a year for every citizen.

National publications, especially the news magazines, are notorious for publishing dramatic stories about health and disease. *Time* and *Newsweek* have both had cover stories on cancer. *Newsweek,* for example, had a cover story January 26, 1978, entitled "What Causes Cancer?" The article was six pages long.

On the third page it whispered about the leading cause—in a phrase it said that tobacco is the least disputed "carcinogen of all." The article said no more about the statistics or the medical findings of the tobacco-cancer link, except in a table, which listed the ten most suspected carcinogens—alphabetically, putting tobacco in next-to-last place. A week later, *Time,* in a common competitive duplication between the two magazines, ran a two-column article on the causes of cancer. The only reference it made to tobacco was that "smoking and drinking alcohol have been linked to cancer." A few weeks earlier, a *Time* essay urged smokers to organize to defeat antismoking legislation.

When R. C. Smith of *Columbia Journalism Review* studied seven years of magazine content after 1970, when cigarette ads were banned from television, he found:

> In magazines that accept cigarette advertising I was unable to find a single article, in several years of publication, that would have given readers any clear notion of the nature and extent of the medical and social havoc wreaked by the cigarette-smoking habit.

The few magazines that refuse cigarette ads did much better at their reporting, he said. (The most prominent magazines that refuse cigarette ads are *Reader's Digest* and *The New Yorker.*)

The magazines that carried accurate articles on the tobacco-disease link suffered for it. In July 1957 *Reader's Digest* ran a strong article on medical evidence against tobacco. Later that month, the advertising agency the magazine had used for twenty-eight years said it no longer wanted the *Digest* as a client. The agency, Batten, Barton, Durstine and Osborn, had $1.3 million in business a year from the magazine. But another client, the American Tobacco Company, which spent $22 million a year with the agency, had asked the agency to choose between it and the *Reader's Digest.*

In 1980 a liberal-left magazine, *Mother Jones,* ran a series of articles on the link between tobacco and cancer and heart disease, after which tobacco companies canceled their ads with the magazine.

Elizabeth Whelan reported, "I frequently wrote on health

topics for women's magazines, and have been told repeatedly by editors to stay away from the subject of tobacco." Whelan, on a campaign to counter the silence, worked with the American Council on Science and Health to ask the ten leading women's magazines to run articles on the growing incidence of smoking-induced disease among women, as these same magazines had done to promote the Equal Rights Amendment. None of the ten magazines—*Cosmopolitan, Harper's Bazaar, Ladies' Home Journal, Mademoiselle, Ms., McCall's, Redbook, Seventeen, Vogue,* or *Working Woman*—would run such an article.

Television, confronted with FCC moves to make it run anti-smoking commercials to counter what the FCC considered misleading cigarette ads, aired a few documentaries, most of them emphasizing the uncertainty of the tobacco link. The best of them was by CBS, in 1965. But Howard K. Smith, of ABC, speaking on a public-television panel, expressed what many have seen as the media's treatment of tobacco and disease:

> To me that documentary was a casebook example of balance that drained a hot issue of its meaning. On that program there were doctors who had every reason to be objective, who maintained that cigarettes have a causal relation to cancer. On the other side, there were representatives of the tobacco industry, who have no reason to be objective, who stated persuasively the opposite. The public was left with a blurred impression that the truth lay between whereas, as far as I am concerned, we have everything but a signed confession from a cigarette that smoking has a causal relation to cancer.

If magazines and broadcasting have been muffled on the national plague, newspapers have been no better. According to medical and other researchers, as well as the editors who produced it, the only lengthy in-depth special feature on tobacco and disease in a standard American daily newspaper was published by the *Charlotte* (North Carolina) *Observer* on March 25, 1979.

The answer lies in a simple statistic: Tobacco is the most heavily advertised product in America, and for a good reason. As the publishing trade journal *Printer's Ink* reported in 1937,

"The growth of cigarette consumption has . . . been due largely to heavy advertising expenditure . . ." In 1954—the year beyond which any reasonable doubt of the link should have disappeared among the media—the trade journal of newspapers, *Editor & Publisher,* criticizing the American Cancer Society and the Surgeon General's reports as "scare news," complained that it had cost newspapers "much lineage and many dollars to some whose business it is to promote the sale of cigarettes through advertising—newspaper and advertising agencies."

It is not surprising that surveys in 1980 by Gallup, Roper, and Chilton found that 30 percent of the public is unaware of the relationship between smoking and heart disease, 50 percent of women do not know that smoking during pregnancy increases the risk of stillbirth and miscarriage, 40 percent of men and women had no idea that smoking causes 80 percent of the 98,000 lung cancer deaths per year, and 50 percent of teenagers do not know that smoking may be addictive.

If there was ever any question that in the bad old days of James Gordon Bennett or in the media of the 1980s advertising influences news and other information given to the public, tobacco makes it unmistakably clear. The tobacco industry since 1954 has spent more than $9 billion on advertising, most of it in newspapers, magazines, radio, and television. Newspapers, magazines, radio, and television have effectively censored news and entertainment to obscure the link between tobacco and death. During that period more than eight million Americans have died from tobacco-linked disease.

Ten years after the crucial findings of 1954, the *New York Daily News,* then the largest daily paper in the United States, carried a headline that read:

CIGGIES ASSAILED AGAIN—HO HUM

The paper commented:

Sure the *News* takes cigarette advertising and likes it and so what?

Unfortunately, the spirit of Dr. Brandreth is alive, though eight million Americans who died prematurely from tobacco are not.

10
DEMOCRACY AND THE MEDIA

Experience is kaleidoscopic: the experience of every moment is unique and unrepeatable. Until we can group items in it on the basis of their similarity we can set up no expectations, make no predictions: lacking these we can make nothing of the present moment.

James Britton, *Language and Learning*

The bond between communities and their news has been strong from the beginning of the American experience. In the eighteenth century, pioneers pushed inland from coastal cities, followed closely by itinerant printers who assumed that every settlement should have its own newspaper. Early radio stations were not limited to national centers like New York and Washington but broadcast in places like Medford Hillsides, Mass., and Stevensville, Mont. To this day newspapers take the names of their cities, and radio and television stations are required to operate in a specified community, with local studios to produce programs about local issues. It is not a quaint eccentricity. It is central to the special nature of governance in the United States.

Most developed countries set all important public policy in their capital. But not the United States. Voters in communities across the United States regularly elect 500,000 local officials to run 65,000 local governmental boards and committees. Local officials govern schools, courts, zoning, water, fire, police, and other vital functions. Even the national government has a locally based democracy in the House of Representatives, with 435 local districts, some consisting of only a few urban neighborhoods. It is a system appropriate for a country with extraordinary diversities of population, local culture, economy, and geography. But it is a formidable responsibility for voters.

Unlike other developed democracies, the United States does not have a parliamentary political system in which voters cast their ballots for parties. Parties in most countries have distinct commitments to differing national programs, differences easily discerned by voters. Citizens voting in those countries know that when they cast their ballots for a party's candidate they are voting for particular policies. In the United States, voters cast ballots for individual candidates who are not bound to any party program except rhetorically, and not always then. Some Republicans are more liberal than some Democrats, some libertarians are more radical than some socialists, and many local candidates run without any party identification. No American citizen can vote intelligently without knowledge of the ideas, political background, and commitments of each individual candidate.

No national paper or broadcast station can report adequately the issues and candidates in every one of the 65,000 local voting districts. Only locally based journalism can do it, and if it does not, voters become captives of the only alternative information, paid political propaganda, or no information at all.

There was never a precise pattern of each voting district with its own journalistic media. But there was once something like it. In 1900, for example, there were 1,737 urban places and 2,226 daily papers. This came close to an average of a paper for every city; most cities had competing dailies and weeklies. Papers were based in a single city, and most papers pursued the intense interests of their particular readers within that city. It meant greater detail of information and political analysis. Readers had strong loyalties to such papers and they provided a greater proportion of those papers' revenues than readers of the 1980s pay for their more bland dailies. In the past it meant more, smaller papers, and smaller papers meant it cost less to start new dailies. If existing papers ignored the interests of a significant part of the community there was a greater likelihood that an entrepreneur or politically oriented publisher would start a new paper to capitalize on the untouched audience. As a result, turn-of-the-century papers more readily reflected changes in the needs and desires of the body politic.

Pursuit of advertising changed the versatility of American print media. It reduced the media's responsiveness to reader desires. Publishers became more dependent on advertising revenues than on reader payments. Ads swelled the size of the paper each day, requiring larger plants, more paper and ink, and bigger staffs, with the result that it was no longer easy for newcomers to enter the newspaper business. As the country's population grew and new communities arose, the old pattern disappeared. Instead of new papers to meet changing political forces, existing papers pushed beyond their municipal boundaries to the new communities and, increasingly, reached not for all the new citizens but for the more affluent consumers. Soon each metropolitan paper was preempting circulation in thousands of square miles with hundreds of communities and voting districts. The newly captured populations were inundated with ever-larger quantities of regional advertising, but the papers, and later the radio and television stations, could not possibly tell each community what it needed to understand its own problems and needs.

From 1900 to 1950 the American population doubled and the number of urban places almost tripled, to 4,700. But the number of daily newspapers dropped from 2,226 to 1,900. The citizens of the new towns and cities, unlike those of an earlier time, learned almost no systematic information about their own communities, and those of older cities learned less than before as their newspapers and broadcast stations turned their attention outward to wider areas.

The vast territory of each metropolitan newspaper and television station intensified a basic change in the country's urban geography. After World War II, affluence and automobiles led many families to the suburbs. "Urban renewal" programs converted downtowns from coherent residential and local commercial centers to regional corporate headquarters. The change removed a major source of newspaper sales. A new interstate highway system encouraged the sprawl of residences, factories, and offices, further diluting the politics and news audiences of the inner cities. Ironically, the programs that destroyed central cities as living complexes were encouraged by metropolitan newspapers, oriented as they were to the desires of real estate and other developers, but all the changes were destructive to the traditional daily sales of newspapers. Demographic changes also hastened the demise of locally owned retail enterprises in favor of ever-larger national and multinational corporations, which, in turn, pushed newspapers and broadcasting farther beyond their community orientation.

After World War II, mass advertising steadily destroyed competitive dailies; monopoly became the norm. In the new suburbs there were new dailies, but far from the number that had grown in American cities of the past. The new monopoly corporations in the central cities pushed outward to the suburbs, preempting the best advertising that might otherwise have supported a new local daily. Existing papers did not cover the new communities journalistically. In 1920 there were 2,722 urban places and 2,400 daily papers in the country. By 1980 there were 8,765 urban places and only 1,745 dailies. Today more than 7,000 American cities have no daily paper of their own.

The new pattern after World War II had a profound impact on the way news was reported. One change was a new category of "news" that was not really news. It was that gray area "fluff," part entertainment of interest to readers but mostly light material designed to create a buying mood as bait for more advertising. The addition of fluff made newspapers larger and drastically reduced the proportion of each paper devoted traditionally to its heart—the breaking news and commentary. The priorities of newspaper companies were quietly rearranged away from the reporting of important political events toward advertising-centered editorial matter. The new emphasis changed staffs, administrative operations, and leadership.

The new form of papers affected the attitude of readers. In 1900 newspaper subscribers paid twice the percentage of their personal incomes for their daily papers as do subscribers of the

1980s. In 1900 each paper meant more to its readers because the news dealt more closely with the reader's community and because each paper was more likely to meet its readers' political and social interests. The responsiveness of earlier papers to their particular readers represented sensitivity to social evolution; as social forces changed, papers were more likely to change with them. Papers in 1900 were more accountable to their readers because their financial fate rested on reader loyalty. The news, which, among other things, meant intense concern with politics and social change, was a more involving experience for individual citizens.

Responsiveness of each paper to its own social group was not an unmitigated advantage for society. It was easier for different segments of the community to see the world differently. Papers' special orientations often increased divisions within the community. But it is not clear that this was worse than the apathy resulting from a bland news system that avoids partisanship in a society whose political system is designed to be partisan. Nor is it clear whether the homogenized news for large areas serves citizens who are asked to make basic political decisions on a specific, local level.

The growth of monopoly and mass advertising diminished the amount of information about each community contained in newspapers. This changed newspapers long before broadcasting became a major news system, though radio and television soon adopted the same doctrine to meet their even greater dependence on advertising.

Newspapers neutralized information for fear that strong news and views pleasing to one part of the audience might offend another part and thus reduce the circulation on which advertising rates depend. Where once it was profitable to pursue particular issues and ideas of interest to the newspaper's particular group of readers, such pursuit now became a threat to larger profits. Newspapers, and later broadcasters, wanted all potential *affluent* consumers regardless of their personal political interests. Consequently, if a group as a whole were poor, as was true of some minorities, papers wished to avoid news of them and their issues. Problems affecting lower-income communities generally did not become news until they exploded and therefore affected affluent consumers.

Blandness in the basic politics of the media became standard. Socially sensitive material of interest to one segment of the population might offend those with different opinions who, regardless of their differences, might possess the relevant quality of interest to newspapers—money to spend on advertisers' products. News became neutralized both in selection of items and in the nature of writing. American journalism began to strain out ideas and ideology from public affairs, except for the safest and most stereotyped assumptions about patriotism and business enterprise. It adopted what two generations of newspeople have incorrectly called "objectivity."

The standard version of "objectivity" holds that it was created to end nineteenth-century sensationalism. To a large extent it did, and that alone made it appealing to serious journalists. "Objectivity" demanded more discipline of reporters and editors because it expected every item to be attributed to some authority. No traffic accident could be reported without quoting a police sergeant. No wartime incident was recounted without confirmation from government officials. "Objectivity" increased the quantity of literal facts in the news, and it did much to strengthen the growing sense of discipline and ethics in journalism.

But the new doctrine was not truly objective. Different individuals writing about the same scene never produce precisely the same account. And the way "objectivity" was applied exacted a high cost from journalism and from public policy.

With all its technical advantages, "objectivity" contradicted the essentially subjective nature of journalism. Every basic step in the journalistic process involves a value-laden decision: Which of the infinite number of events in the environment will be assigned for coverage and which ignored? Which of the infinite observations confronting the reporter will be noted? Which of the facts noted will be included in the story? Which of the reported events will become the first paragraph? Which story will be prominently displayed on page 1 and which buried inside or discarded? None of these is a truly objective decision. But the disciplinary techniques of "objectivity" have the false aura of a science, and this has given almost a century of American journalism an illusion of unassailable correctness.

"Objectivity" placed overwhelming emphasis on established, official voices and tended to leave unreported large areas of genuine relevance that authorities chose not to talk about. It accentuated social forces as rhetorical contests of personalities, with the reporter powerless to fill obvious gaps in official information or reasoning. It widened the chasm that is a constant threat to democracy—the difference between the realities of private power and the illusions of public imagery.

"Objectivity" tended to keep news superficial because too deep a pursuit of a single subject might bore or offend some of the audience. It strained out interpretation and background despite the desperate need for them in a century wracked by political trauma. Recitations of facts about world wars, genocides, depressions, and nuclear proliferation are useful but inadequate; mere recitations imply that all facts are of equal value.

The safest method of reporting news was to reproduce the words of authority figures, and in the nature of public relations most authority figures issue a high quotient of imprecise and self-serving declarations. Physical crime, natural disasters, and accidents were politically safe, which accounts for the peculiar American news habit of reporting remote accidents regardless of their relevance to the audience. News became more official and establishmentarian.

Perhaps the most powerful influence of the doctrine on working journalists was unconscious: It obscured and therefore made more palatable the unprofessional compromises with managerial imperatives and corporate politics. The subtle workings of the doctrine over the years and its rationalization of avoiding judgments made it easy for serious writers to remain silent about social ideas and political forces and to concentrate on contests of personalities. It produced the circular answer to the perpetual question "What is news?"—"News is news." By mid-twentieth century "objectivity" had achieved the status of a received truth.

The first major crisis that "objectivity" created for journalists in this century centered on Senator Joseph McCarthy, who was created largely by the assumption that journalists are not obligated to write what they can demonstrate as true and significant unless it comes from the mouth of authority.

McCarthy paralyzed much of government and created hysteria throughout the country from 1950 to 1954 with lies and distortions. He made increasingly wild claims about Soviet agents in high places, including in the offices of the president of the United States, among generals of the U.S. Army, and in the Department of State. In the vast political wreckage McCarthy left in his wake, the senator did not disclose a single Soviet agent that had not already been exposed. Many competent journalists had evidence that McCarthy's statements were lies or clever distortions, some of it in the private admissions of the senator himself during his jocular drinking bouts with journalists and editors. But most journalistic organizations held to the doctrine that required use only of "official" statements by the most dramatic authority figure, and McCarthy was a United States senator.

Years of reappraisal within journalism after the debacle of the McCarthy years have not prevented subsequent failures of "objectivity" in an apolitical press. Race relations after World War II underwent powerful ferment, politically and socially, but not until they exploded in massive demonstrations and riots did they become major news, reported afterward mostly as police actions rather than as a profound change in the American scene. The same reluctance to report social forces made the persistence of structural poverty in a rich society an unreportable phenomenon until it became a physical phenomenon.

Emergence of broadcasting in the 1920s did not create an alternative news system that might have broadened the spectrum of coverage and provided genuine competition in generating news and analyzing ideas. Instead, broadcasting, with minor exceptions, simply read the printed news in truncated form. Radio and television newscasts, at their longest, provide less information than half a newspaper page. Some distinguished reporting from Europe immediately before World War II was an exception, although the radio journalism staffs that produced it were quickly dismantled. The vivid immediacy of television added a powerful dimension to news but shrank even the narrow spectrum of print.

Television's chief impact on newspapers was commercial, not journalistic. Its stunning ability to sell goods and its inexpensive transmission over thousands of square miles led to a competition between printed and electronic media to reach ever-wider groups of potential customers, the reaches so broad that it was impossible to report news about the specific communities exposed to the ads.

Television has obvious advantages over newspapers in immediacy, motion, color, and convenience. But it has one enormous disadvantage: Each station can transmit only one message at a time. If that message is too long or too controversial for some viewers, those viewers will turn to another channel or commit that terminal horror that haunts television entrepreneurs —turn off the set. Whenever a viewer turns a television dial, a television station loses a customer. Newspapers do not have that problem. If they choose, they can run a long story that will fascinate a particular set of readers. Other readers can move their eyes to the next column or turn the page, where they may find material more to their liking. Moving the eyes or turning the page does not mean that the newspaper publisher has lost a customer.

Television entrepreneurs found from the beginning that they had to maintain maximum attention among a wide disparity of consumers. Far more than in print, TV presentations—in regular entertainment, public affairs, news, or commercials—could not dwell too long on any one subject, and they could not be socially or politically controversial. Television found the answer early in its history. It was the twin sovereigns of attention-getting in history—sex and violence. Sex had to be used obliquely, given the national public morality, so it permeated television by innuendo, in themes of entertainment, in selection of actresses and actors, in double meanings in commercials, and in sophisticated appeals to the subconscious. Violence was easier to stress, given the prevalence of crime as a standard ingredient in printed news and the place of guns and violence in the mythology of the country. Violence could be politically safe in programs of cops and robbers, in which cops won by violence, or spy dramas, in which selected foreign enemies were defeated by violence.

Nothing in the history of public complaints has lessened the combined incidence of sex and violence. Some social scientists, as well as the Surgeon General of the United States, have measured the high incidence and concrete social consequences of sex and violence on television. If television producers momentarily reduce one in the face of organized criticism, they raise the level of the other.

The social and psychological costs of these television twins are incalculable. The Surgeon General's studies have shown that television violence increases actual violence and acceptance of violence in children. Other studies have shown that children who watch a great deal of television are more cynical than are children who watch less television. The television commercial is the most expensive and highly skilled artifact in American society, using the most polished producers, actors, and technical reproduction and spending more for the creation and transmission of a series of thirty-second commercials than some school districts spend to educate children for a year. The artful construction of commercials has created thirty seconds as a basic attention unit, ideal for selling marginal goods but with negative psychological and intellectual consequences for the average American child, who, the statistics show, watches television for twice as many hours as he or she attends school.

It is not simple moral perversity that keeps sex and violence on the air and serious subjects off. It is television executives' desire to maintain as large an audience as possible for as long as possible for the purpose of selling goods and services.

The same persistence, with more subtlety, has characterized emotional manipulation in television commercials. Commercials, too, have been immune to a variety of serious objections from consumer agencies, social critics, and parents. Cynical manipulation in commercials, like that in television programming generally, comes not from capricious malice but from the power of annual profit statements for both the corporations that advertise and the corporations that own the media.

Advertising occupies a powerful place in the American culture. It has become a worldwide symbol of the country's reputation as the land of milk and honey, of endless material possessions for everybody. As an art form, ads are often clever, entertaining, and arresting in their graphics and sexuality. Some are practical and informative. Most ads create a fantasy experience, permitting the national nose to be pressed against the windows of exclusive shops that will never be entered. In all its permutations—as a symbol of national wealth, as a purposeful entertainment, as a guide to useful products, as a clever technique to engage the emotions—advertising has conditioned generations to accept it as an inescapable part of the landscape, as ubiquitous and normal as houses and trees.

Confronted with criticism of commercials, media owners say the public likes ads. Some people clearly do like some commercials, often more than they like the less carefully produced programs in which the commercials are imbedded. But whether the public approves of what it gets in advertising is questionable. The American Association of Advertising Agencies found in a ten-year study, from 1964 to 1974, a significant decrease in public belief that "advertising results in better products for the public" or that it helps raise the standard of living or lowers prices. And there was an increase in public feeling over the ten years that ads often persuade people to buy things they shouldn't and that most advertising insults people's intelligence.

In 1977 a survey by Louis Harris of public attitudes toward leadership of major American activities found advertising at the bottom of the list. The public seems to be repeating what the March Hare says in *Alice in Wonderland*: "You might just as well say that 'I like what I get' is the same thing as 'I get what I like.'"

To counter public resistance to television and advertising,

the manipulation of emotions has become more sophisticated. Social science and psychological techniques have been added to television's arsenal for conditioning human behavior. One firm advises advertisers on whether their products should appeal to the left (analytical) or the right (emotional) side of the human brain. The consultant staff attaches electrodes to scalps of volunteers to measure stimulation and types of brain waves evoked by certain images in commercials. They tell advertisers that ads for products like perfume and beer should be pitched to the right side of the brain; ads for cars and insurance should be directed to the left side. Most TV ads appeal to the emotions. The manager of public opinion research for General Electric says that "much of response to advertising is right-brain."

Another firm uses infrared eye scans to record rapid eye movement in response to test images in television commercials, advising clients on elements of ads like the most effective juxtaposition of sex objects, for example, a woman in a bikini and the brand name of the advertised product. A Manhattan firm measures involuntary larynx reaction and uses computers to test people's reactions to proposed commercials, often determining that even when people say they dislike an ad, it makes a lasting impression. A Texas firm uses electrodes attached to the fingertips of human subjects to see what symbols in commercials— sex, fire, ocean, forests—create the most arousal in connection with a product.

Chuck Blore, a partner in the advertising firm Chuck Blore & Don Ruchman, Inc., has said, "Advertising is the art of arresting the human intelligence just long enough to get money from it."

If that is true, it arrests a great deal of intelligence. It is estimated that the average American child has seen 350,000 commercials by age seventeen and, in the words of Billie Wahlstrom of the University of Southern California, these commercials are "the propaganda arm of the American culture."

The American Association of Advertising Agencies has estimated that 1,600 advertising messages are aimed at a consumer in an average day. The individual obviously is not struck by most of these and does not even become aware of all of them. The average consumer takes momentary notice of about eighty commercial messages. Only twelve make a conscious impression. But in order to maintain sanity and coherence in the midst of this clever and insistent bombardment, each individual has to erect a sensory screen that instantly, often unconsciously, detects the incoming signal and rejects it. A car driver, for example, catches a glimpse of a distant billboard and decides in a fraction of a second that it is of no interest and thus does not engage his or her mind with the content of the ad. The advertising creators know this, so to penetrate the screen that every human being erects to protect the senses, ad agencies need a constant supply of new symbols, images, and ideas.

The sheep's clothing of sex, beauty, a trusted personality, or a semisacred symbol is needed to encase the wolf of the sales pitch. The human being—often referred to by ad agencies as "the target"—on the alert to screen out unwanted symbols he or she has already seen, does not recognize a new image and, before it is recognized as the same old message in a new guise, the unidentified lying object has penetrated the protective screen and made a hit on the deceived mind.

When parent groups and others complain to broadcasters about the impact of sex and violence on the young, broadcasters traditionally answer that sex and violence on television do not change human behavior. That answer has been contradicted by extensive studies and surveys by the Surgeon General of the United States. But each year broadcasters sell more than $10 billion worth of commercial time whose only purpose is to change human behavior. Presumably, the most sophisticated corporations would not continue spending billions of dollars if they thought they were not altering human behavior in their favor.

Furthermore, it is one thing to show that not everyone exposed to a commercial or to regular programming changes his or her overt, physical behavior. But it is another to suppose that there is no emotional or intellectual change from the experience, any more than it would be to argue that the soldier, at any moment untouched by bullets in the battlefield, is emotionally and intellectually untouched by the experience.

The reclothing of ads in ever-new symbols has contributed to the devastating attrition in the lifespan of symbols in modern culture. Advertising is not the only cause of this attrition. All modern communications has a hand in it. Two hundred years ago the common symbols of society were those of rulers and the church, their flags and icons displayed individually and seen solely by live audiences. Mechanical printing and other mass communications changed that. Contemporary society is filled with images, some in a constant state of change like television, or in continuously altered states, as in radio. Printing reproduces words and illustrations in multiples of billions and can be absorbed by millions. Through electronic devices and modern printing processes, flags, crosses, and other emotionally laden symbols can be mass-produced for huge audiences. But no single force has equaled the merchandising process in its use of all the sacred and semisacred symbols to create a culture of material consumption. Advertising is a source of symbol manipulation unknown to earlier generations. The advertising industry spends $1,000 per household in order to break through the resistance of human senses and sometimes of human intelligence. Selling symbols are in continuous flood for six and a half hours of television a day. Printed images are seen on countless billions of magazine pages every week and the four billion newspaper pages printed every day. As viewers and readers get used to the massively displayed symbols, the symbols change to the latest idea or personality or national emotion until it, too, in days or weeks, becomes meaningless, part of the continuous and deliberate slag heap of mass communications.

Sponsoring corporations will even use symbols they dislike and then trivialize them, in their voracious appetite for new sheep's clothing. In the 1960s the psychedelic style in art and clothing, created by hippies as antiestablishment statements, was adopted almost at once in advertisements and editorial illustration by the establishment media, not out of sympathy but as a way of placing inviting and novel garments on old sales pitches.

Symbols and terms of the intense antiwar movement during the Vietnam War were adopted in ads and programming even by corporations engaged in war contracts.

Perhaps the most easily measured damage of the media battle for consumers is inflicted on the American political system. Mass advertising, without intending to, has become instrumental in degrading the basic unit of American government.

News distribution is no longer designed for individual towns and cities. American politics is organized on the basis of the 20,000 urban and rural places in the country, which is the way citizens vote. But the media have organized on the basis of 210 television "markets," which is the way merchandisers and media corporations sell ads. As a result, the fit between the country's information needs and its information media has become disastrously disjointed.

The average television station sends its signal over more than 10,000 square miles, or about fifty counties. Metropolitan dailies, not by coincidence, cover about the same territory. (The *Atlanta Constitution and Journal,* for example, circulates significantly in fifty-five counties, thirty-nine of which do not have their own daily paper.) The average county has twenty-six local governments, of which twenty-two have taxing powers and five are school districts. This means that the average metropolitan newspaper and television station dominate the news for an area that contains 1,300 public policymaking bodies and elects large portions of state legislatures and the U.S. House of Representatives. If each policymaking body in the area met once a week and each metropolitan news medium reported only on those meetings and on no other events in the communities, a typical half-hour newscast would give five and a half seconds to each body, and a newspaper would give thirty-eight words. But in fact TV stations, radio stations, and metropolitan papers do not cover each of the policymaking bodies in the areas of their circulation or even the general news in each of the communities. Nor could they if they tried, given the vast areas and the numerous local districts. In other countries with centralized national policymaking, local news coverage is a negligible need. In the United States local coverage is crucial.

Though big-city TV, radio, and newspapers do not cover each of the communities they reach, they sell advertising to the major merchandisers for their region and thus remove the economic base for indigenous stations and papers. Many of the communities without daily papers have weekly ones and they often serve important functions; the best ones adequately fill the gap. But most communities either have none or have shopping papers with little or no significant social and political news. In fact, most daily papers issue such newless advertising sheets in the smaller communities around their central city to further increase their revenues. By collecting local advertising in that way, they further preempt the basis for an independent local paper.

There is nothing inevitable in this pattern. In 1851 Horace Greeley, testifying before a committee of the British Parliament, described the pattern in the United States in his time:

> When a town grows to have as many as 15,000 inhabitants, or thereabouts, then it has a daily paper; sometimes that is the case when it has as few as 10,000 . . . 15,000 may be stated as the average at which a daily paper commences; at 20,000 they have two, and so on; in central towns . . . they have from three to five daily journals.

If the same pattern existed today, the country would have 4,600 daily papers instead of 1,700. Today 43 percent of the U.S. population lives in counties with no local daily paper. If radio licenses were granted on the basis of political and social needs, each county could have at least three indigenous stations instead of the present concentration of radio and TV stations in a small number of major metropolitan merchandising markets.

This disparity between citizens' and merchandising needs has made American elected office the prize of rich men and women or candidates backed by rich men and women. Traditional elective politics demanded that the candidates appear in person before special groups of voters. This produced a generous diet of rhetorical sound and fury, sophistries, cynicisms, and simplistic proclamations. But because the candidate appeared in person, often before groups who had intense interest and knowledge of issues that affected them, the effectiveness of empty rhetoric was limited. Farmers might accept sophistries about urban factory workers but they would have a high level of critical judgment about agricultural economics, and they would not hesitate to press the candidate for details. The same would be true for auto workers, corporate executives, railroad operators, or labor union chiefs. Each would want to pursue in depth the subjects that most concerned them. The mosaic of these interests put together by a candidate would decide success or failure at the polls.

But if a candidate could avoid firm positions, it increased the possibility of giving the appearance of being all things to all voters. For this, television seemed a perfect medium. It is an established American habit. Favorite programs are watched by a large, predictable audience. The insertion of emotional commercials into programs had become an accepted practice for a variety of products—perfume, laxatives, toilet paper, automobiles, underarm deodorants, adhesives for dentures, hemorrhoidal ointments. A commercial for a political candidate could fall easily into the accepted brief interval in regular programs. A carefully taped, meticulously edited political presentation with all the immediacy and simulated sincerity of a commercial, but without serious content, could be projected into homes where viewers would be most vulnerable.

Television stations reach more people than a candidate, other than a presidential candidate, wants to reach. But the candidate has no choice but to "buy" voters not needed for election, and at enormous cost. (The fact that most of the candidate's message is irrelevant to most of the audience means that a portion of the audience might switch channels, which in turn means that television stations resist political commercials if they can.) A candidate for the U.S. House of Representatives from a district in metropolitan Chicago would find the economics of TV advertising impossible without heavy financial backing. The typical House district has 150,000 households. A Chicago-based television station that reaches a typical district also reaches three million households in thirty-five counties in four states. The candidate either pays for the 2,850,000 unwanted households or loses the television access to his or her district that a richer candidate can buy. (A prime-time, thirty-second commercial for a major sponsor can cost more than $250,000 to produce. Few political commercials cost as much, but the cost even for less elaborate political ads on television is so high that it has created an ominous barrier to entry into American politics.) Thirty-second commercials must be repeated to be effective. The thirty-second political ad on a Chicago station, repeated ten times, would cost more than $50,000 just for air time. The ad would then be broadcast over a station that reaches so large an audience that 95 percent do not vote in the candidate's district.

Few candidates can afford to buy a fifteen-minute or thirty-minute block of television time, a period so long in commercial television for a nonentertainment program that most stations would refuse such a sale for fear of losing most of their audience. Even if a candidate wanted to buy this time, there are disadvantages: The longer the time, the harder it is to avoid serious issues. (In Ronald Reagan's 1980 campaign for the presidency, the most expensive in history, 70 percent of his network time was for thirty-second commercials, 25 percent for five-second commercials, and only 5 percent for thirty-minute talks.) So, inevitably, television electioneering, which, combined with direct mail, is now the major mechanism of American campaigns, deals mostly with imagery and emotional manipulation engendered by the five-second and thirty-second commercial. It has displaced the phenomenon of the live candidate before live audiences and almost eliminated coherent debate. A whole generation of voters has not heard serious content in election campaigns; that this generation of voters increasingly does not bother to vote may not be unrelated.

If a Chicago candidate for the U.S. House decided to turn to a Chicago newspaper to reach his or her 150,000 households, he or she would not find a substantial difference in cost or effectiveness. A major Chicago newspaper is distributed in thirty-seven counties with a population of seven million. To buy a half-page ad repeated ten times could cost $100,000.

Running successfully for public office is highly expensive, and the biggest spenders have been winning the campaigns at a rate of 4 to 1. Abraham Lincoln won by spending $100,000; McKinley in 1900 spent less than $4 million; Roosevelt in 1932, less than $3 million; Kennedy in 1960, $10 million; Nixon in 1968, $25 million; Reagan in 1980, $152 million. Between 1976 and 1980 the total cost of campaigns for all public office in the country doubled, to $900 million.

In California, where some of the best records are kept, the cost of a campaign for the U.S. House of Representatives rose 45 percent between the election of 1976 and that of 1978; the cost of a U.S. Senate race in those two elections rose 72 percent. Today it can cost a quarter of a billion dollars to get elected president and multiples of millions to become a senator or a representative in Congress. Not surprisingly, the role of wealthy, special-interest groups in campaigns has risen dramatically.

The inappropriate fit between the country's major media and the country's political system has starved voters of relevant information, leaving them at the mercy of paid political propaganda that is close to meaningless and often worse. It has eroded the central requirement of a democracy that those who are governed give not only their consent but their informed consent.

Part III

MASS MEDIA
WITHOUT MASSES

11
MASS MEDIA
WITHOUT MASSES

By 1990, publishers of mass circulation daily newspapers will finally stop kidding themselves that they are in the newspaper business and admit that they are primarily in the business of carrying advertising messages.

A. Roy Megary, publisher,
Toronto Globe and Mail

WILL IRWIN, an American journalist, writing seventy years ago, said:

> It was an axiom of old-time journalism that the newspaper must at least assume to stand for popular causes . . . The newspapers . . . pretend to speak for the people; and the public which reads the newspapers expects this service.

Irwin, fearful of the detachment of most newspapers from the average citizen before World War I, would feel the fruition of his fears in the 1980s: There is a steady decay in public loyalty to the media. There is hostility or indifference toward modern newspapers, and the same fate is hovering over television.

Newspapers have been making record profits for decades, but they have been profiting at the cost of a hemorrhage in their most valuable commodity, the loyalty of their readers.

The best quantitative measure of the newspaper's standing in society is how many papers are sold daily per one hundred households. It has not been a heartening index:

1930 132
1940 118

195

1950	....	124
1960	....	111
1965	....	105
1970	....	90
1980	....	79
1986	....	72

A drastic drop in household sales of newspapers during a period of record newspaper profits seems paradoxical, but it is a paradox with a number of causes. Disappearance of competitive papers always causes loss of sales. When dailies merge, the surviving paper never keeps all the readers from both papers; some readers are interested only in the paper that has disappeared and other readers who used to buy two or more papers a day when they were available can buy only one when there is a monopoly.

In the years after World War II the decay of both central cities and mass transit meant that metropolitan papers no longer had customers pouring out of downtown offices and factories looking for a newspaper to read on the bus or train ride home. New suburbs without their own papers and workers' commuting by car have diminished the newspaper-reading habit of millions of families.

If metropolitan dailies try to transport their afternoon edition to suburbia before the workers reach home, they encounter an ironic barrier. On the clogged highways at rush hour, newspaper delivery truck and commuting reader block each other in a race for the suburban doorstep.

There are purely logistic discouragements to newspaper reading, barriers erected largely by policies of newspapers themselves. In the new primary mission of newspapers to serve advertisers rather than readers, newspapers have become greatly enlarged. In 1980 the average paper had two and a half times more pages than in 1946. This requires longer and more complicated press runs. To accommodate the longer press runs, deadlines for news have been pushed earlier: By the 1980s many afternoon papers had to go to press by 8:00 A.M. or earlier for suburban editions. Those papers would not be read by most subscribers until 5:00 P.M. or later. The afternoon paper has no news of that day, or at least none significantly more recent than the reader may have seen in the morning paper. (Morning papers printed for the suburbs might go to press at 11:00 P.M. but between that time and the reading of the paper at 7:00 A.M. not much news would have transpired.) So afternoon newspapers have little real news to offer. Most afternoon papers consist of "soft" non-news or fluff, and the result has been drastic declines of circulation among metropolitan afternoon newspapers (which is a convincing plebiscite of public attitude toward newspapers that emphasize something other than news).

The massive modern American newspaper is staggering to deliver and to read. The *Los Angeles Times* averages 123 pages daily and 512 pages on Sunday. The boys and girls who used to deliver such papers have been replaced by adults in vehicles. The reader must plow through masses of pages of no interest and, in all probability, find no news of his or her own community and then pay, or have the tax-supported municipality pay, to haul away the daily remains.

These factors contribute to reduced public buying of newspapers, but the most obvious cause is the growth of broadcasting.

Radio began the change in the national pattern of delivering news. From 1920 to 1930 it grew from an exotic technical device to a household appliance in 40 percent of American homes; by 1940 it was in 80 percent of homes.

Radio killed the "Extra," the unscheduled edition of newspapers once printed when dramatic local or national news occurred between regular press runs. Radio became a dramatic presence when families in their living rooms could hear the live words of American newsmakers like Franklin Roosevelt and Father Coughlin and foreign leaders like Hitler, Mussolini, King George, and Winston Churchill.

Between 1930 and 1940 there was a substantial drop in newspaper buying, but the impact of radio is obscured by the concurrent impact of the Great Depression of 1929–1942 in which millions of families had to question all purchases that were not life-sustaining. After the Depression, losses in newspaper readers were not great. By 1950 radio was in 93 percent of homes (television in 9 percent) but between 1940 and 1950 newspaper sales per household dropped only 6 percent. By 1960 radio was almost universal and television was in 87 percent of homes. Even with those twin alternative sources of news, newspaper sales dropped only 11 percent. By 1965 there was at least one television set in 93 percent of American homes; a figure close to that had been true for almost a decade. Family television watching had been a habit for years, with the average set in use five and a half hours a day and with network evening news established as a national ritual. Yet there were still 105 newspapers sold each day per 100 households.

Curiously, the greatest loss in newspaper reading did not come until years after radio and television had made their inroads into family time and the pattern of news delivery. From 1965 to 1980 newspapers sold per 100 households dropped from 105 to 79. In the thirty-five years in which broadcasting became entrenched, from 1930 to 1965, newspaper sales dropped 21 percent. But in the fifteen years from 1965 to 1980 sales dropped 25 percent.

The loss came in the face of some developments that should have helped newspapers. Before World War II, half the adult population barely finished junior high school, but by 1980 half the adult population had some college. The number of people who could read significantly and who constituted potential newspaper customers increased from 19 to 92 million. People who learn to read fluently also undergo other changes like employment in higher-level jobs, achievement of stable families and residence, and greater involvement in the political process, all characteristics of high newspaper readership.

Another positive change in the population in favor of newspaper reading was a large increase in disposable personal income. In the 1945–1980 period, this income multiplied fourteen times, far more than inflation. Yet it was during this period that newspapers suffered their worst loss of readers.

If there were obvious factors that would diminish newspaper reading, most of these factors had peaked before 1965. Both radio and television had already established their place in society by then. The suburban flight had leveled off. Local newspaper competition had already disappeared in 97 percent of American newspaper cities by 1960.

It was in the 1965–1980 period that American mass media, especially newspapers, came under maximum control of national and multinational corporations. The ownership of a local paper by a distant corporation is not in itself a deterrent to newspaper reading. If papers remained truly unchanged under absentee ownership, changed titles of incorporation would be irrelevant to most readers. But corporate ownership changed the form and content, the strategies of operation, and the economics of newspapers.

Newspapers and other media bought by large corporations as investments come under new pressures for maximizing profits. The parent firm competing in world markets must attract shareholders with high dividends and gross revenues, and distant owners remain insulated from local objections to changes made in order to extract maximum profits.

In addition, the new corporate ownership hastened the conversion of newspapers to primarily carriers of advertising. Advertisers want affluent readers between the ages of eighteen and forty-nine. Magazines and broadcasting want the same audience. Magazines control their readership by sending subscription solicitations only to mailing lists that include affluent eighteen-to-forty-nine-year-old men and women (and sometimes not sending renewal notices to those in postal zones with too low a median income). Broadcasters cannot keep the nonaffluent and elderly from watching or listening to their programs, but they design the content to attract younger, affluent viewers. Newspapers control the readership by not reporting significantly on neighborhoods of low-income and elderly populations and by promoting their circulation in affluent neighborhoods with the desired characteristics.

The "unwanted American population" that is systematically discouraged by advertising-supported media is not small. In 1984, families with less than median combined income, an undesirable income level for major media, constituted 50 percent of all American families. Seventy percent of black families and 64 percent of Hispanic families are below the median income level. Even this understates the exclusion of blacks and Hispanics from media audiences, because many families with incomes higher than the median are forced by housing patterns to remain in neighborhoods shunned by the media. Standard American newspapers and broadcasters would deny that they are racist. But their policies on reporting the news are indistinguishable from policies that would deliberately exclude minorities from news of their own society and normal news of minorities from the rest of the population.

Like the nonaffluent, those who do not meet the age criterion cannot always be prevented from buying a newspaper or magazine or watching a television program, but the content of news and its distribution does its best to exclude them. Yet the unwanted population of the "wrong ages"—younger than eighteen and older than forty-nine—constitutes 54 percent of Americans; those older than forty-nine make up 26 percent of the population. In the perpetual surveys and promotions to counter loss of readers, the newspaper industry has never addressed itself to its deliberate exclusion of a third to a half of the American population.

The industry has also indulged in periodic attempts to make newspapers more interesting by altering the styles of newspaper writing. In the 1950s, experts said the ideal copy consisted of words of minimum syllables and of sentences with few words. The results were largely incomprehensible. Later, "precision journalism" was the fashion, applying statistics and survey techniques to make stories more scientific, a reasonable technique for some stories and nonsense for others. More recently, "writing coaches" have been in vogue, reviewing articles as though formulas of word use can lead to engaging writing. But none of the institutional therapies against reader boredom has addressed itself to the enormous increase in material of superficial content and of minimal interest to readers but of maximum interest to advertisers.

At first glance the modern American newspaper appears to

be the product of irrational publishers. Faced with a major competitor, television, they have stressed "fluff" or light entertainment content, which television can produce more vividly and effectively than any printed medium. And publishers have de-emphasized local and detailed news, which is what readers want and which is television's weakest offering. Furthermore, publishers' emphasis on fluff flies in the face of a history that has shown long-term stable profits for papers that establish themselves as carriers of serious news while industry cemeteries are full of papers that tried to lure readers with games, fluff, and brief news items. Local news has shrunk in metropolitan papers even though papers that have gained the most circulation since World War II are those in which local news is a large element.

If long-term profits and stability come from local news and larger portions of detailed and analytical news, why have newspaper publishers gone in the opposite direction? The reason is not irrational if short-term profits are the goal.

Unfortunately, short-term profits are now imperative in the major media almost without regard for the future of media institutions. Newspapers no longer depend solely on their readers. They must satisfy advertisers, Wall Street investors, and parent corporations. The reader may have a primary civic stake in long-range stability of the local paper but for all the others that newspapers must satisfy, long-range stability is, at best, a secondary consideration. Wall Street investors look for dividends and rising stock prices every day or every three months and are not moved to behave today by considerations of the more remote future. Advertisers demand immediate sales based on the appearance of their ads, and parent corporations, needing high stock prices and cash flow for their operations, can always sell or liquidate media subsidiaries that don't serve short-term demands.

In the race for short-term profits, the American newspaper is no different from other large American corporations in the last half of the twentieth century. But the newspapers represent an institution which, unlike steel mills and automobile companies, affects the roots of the democracy.

Magazines similarly have adopted a strategy that enhances

immediate high profits at the expense of long-term stability. When the Magazine Publishers Association advertises, as it does, that magazines are for the "77,136,000 . . . movers and shakers" and not for "window-shoppers" who do not buy luxury products, the publishers desire only 35 percent of the population. And even the content designed for that 35 percent of the population gives little reason for the "movers and shakers" to be deeply loyal to their magazines.

Television is the quintessential short-term medium. Like jugglers, television lives for the split second. Its relationship to viewers is measured in tiny fractions. Solemn hierarchies of men and women react to overnight program ratings with something approaching nervous breakdowns because one percentage point in ratings can mean a difference of $30 million profit a year. The result of this manic concern is to design programming that will serve the split second of attention-getting rather than humanistic substance that will stay with the viewer; the ratings race serves the advertiser's needs, not the audience's.

The presumed hold of television on its audience is becoming doubtful as the public is offered an alternative. The vision of an American population as a nation of addicts, grateful for the lowest common denominator in entertainment and news, began to erode in the 1980s, even as sales of newspapers previously eroded for the same reason. There had appeared a choice. In 1982 a study commission by the National Association of Broadcasters showed that Americans who had a choice had already reduced their television viewing by as much as 29 percent. The alternative was cable and pay television which gave viewers the ability to select programs or an offering of higher-quality programming without advertising. The television stations that lost the smallest number of viewers were public television, which has the most serious programming of all and no commercials.

Another set of statistics points to the deadening effect of printed and televised news as produced by American standard media. The data apply to newspapers, but they may have meaning for all social and political information. American publishers sell fewer papers per capita than publishers in most other developed countries.

According to the 1982 edition of the *World Press Encyclopedia*, the ranking of countries in daily newspapers sold per 1,000 population was the following:

Sweden	572
Japan	526
East Germany	472
Luxembourg	447
Iceland	431
Finland	425
Norway	412
Switzerland	402
Soviet Union	397
Israel	394
Australia	394
Great Britain	388
New Zealand	376
Hong Kong	349
Denmark	341
Austria	320
Netherlands	315
West Germany	312
Czechoslovakia	300
United States	287

Greater reading of newspapers in foreign countries may have several causes. Cultural differences in family and work patterns could affect newspaper reading. No country exceeds the United States in the amount of time television preempts, of all other family activities, including reading. In some ways, American monopoly papers serve the combined functions of specialized foreign daily papers in politics, finance, sports, and gossip.

But the magnitude of newspaper reading in other developed countries seems to transcend individual cultural differences. Japan, like the United States, has high average television viewing and high use of newspapers. East Germany subsidizes papers used for government purposes, but West Germany does not and still has a higher reading rate than the United States. Sweden has high personal income that could enhance newspaper buying, but Czechoslovakia, which has very low personal income, still has more newspaper buying than the United States.

The main difference, I believe, is a greater sense of involvement in the meaning of the news among foreign audiences. In the other countries news is not presented as a series of isolated facts and public events but rather in a context of political and social meaning. The style of news and the environment of explicit social forces permit the facts of the news to be seen as an explanation of life around the individual or the family. Even when the political content is suspect or worse, as must be true for many readers in authoritarian states, the political setting of the news is significant if only because it makes plain the intent and strategy of the ruling forces.

Political and social ideas are standard ingredients in the news of other societies, including democratic ones; they are minimized in American news.

A commentator in the book *Reporting U.S.-European Relations* notes of news in the United States:

> The world of fact—that is, of observed events, demonstrable trends, quoted statements, and the other classic ingredients of what goes by the name of "objective" reporting—is the province of the *"news"* columns. Anything that moves beyond such description to a judgment of merits, a recommendation for action, or even a speculative interpretation is somehow set apart and labeled . . . such as "News Analysis" . . . By contrast, Continental newspapers expect their reporters to pass judgment on what they see, hear, and write about . . . A correspondent who holds back from suggesting to the reader how to understand the merits of a public issue or an official action falls short of doing his or her whole job.

Even this statement exaggerates the social context permitted standard American journalism. Articles labeled "news analysis" or run as opinion are generally devoid of genuine political analysis and identification of social forces. Typically, they simply exercise greater freedom in describing the personalities and tactics involved in mechanical changes in events.

Besides producing greater emphasis on soft content detached from serious news, the concentrated corporate control of newspapers and other news media also strained out extreme political writing that in the past, ironically, was overwhelmingly sympathetic to corporate values. Until the 1960s newspapers typically carried at least one syndicated or local political column and these were, with rare exceptions, narrowly right wing. No standard paper carried a columnist on the left who was the counterpart of the prevailing columnists on the right. As monopoly developed and as the pressure for increased advertising revenue was applied with corporate ownership, expression of explicit politics, even sympathetic corporate politics, was moderated to prevent alienation of a new generation of affluent readers. Newspapers began carrying a variety of political columns, but none, right or left, strayed very far from centrist positions and none was permitted to stress anticorporate ideas. It was a clear demonstration of neutralizing the news to make papers more efficient carriers of advertising. But it produced social sterility and silence on fundamental forces behind major news events.

The consequences for American politics have been serious. One assumption of the "objectivity" doctrine of reporting is that every side of a dispute has an equal and opposite side. No "extreme" views are considered legitimate, though the characterization "extreme" is often applied to politics considered normal in other democracies. Anything beyond the status quo is in danger of being seen as either communist on the left or fascist on the right. Most of the significant ideas in Western democracies and in developed authoritarian states as well are neither communist, fascist, nor limited to the corporate ethic of American politics. As a result, some of the most significant social forces of the 1980s remain nameless in social and political reporting and, consequently, they remain beyond public discourse and cannot be dealt with intelligently in society.

This is more than a problem in semantics. If all kinds of apples were required to be called simply "apples" and not Gravenstein, Delicious, Macintosh, or Pippin, then it would be impossible to have an intelligent discussion about the most appropriate apple for each purpose. If the daily news, in print and broadcasting, is perpetually cast in terms of largely physical events related to personalities and devoid of political and social meaning, the public is without a way of identifying, analyzing, and assessing the value of alternative social forces. The social and political sterility of American reporting leaves most citizens without a coherent view of politics. In an inevitable circle of indifference, this leaves most citizens without a sense of involvement in the news. Political news becomes personal melodrama carefully strained of explicit political and social significance.

Broadcast news is widely watched because it is attached to family evening entertainment, and has thus evolved to meet entertainment standards. Newspapers, which for fifteen years have accelerated their entry into the entertainment field, have, to a lesser but still significant degree, adopted the same entertainment ethic in all their news.

The news media—diluted of real meaning by apolitical and sterile context, homogenized with the growth of monopoly, overwhelmingly more of a service to merchants than to the audience, and filled with frivolous material—are a threat to their own future but also to the body politic.

When sterility of news writing fails to relate political and social events to real forces in society, it produces something worse than "nothingness." By removing significant context from events, it leaves the average citizen looking at what James Britton has called a "kaleidoscope." If it is left as isolated fragments, Britton says, "We can make nothing of the present moment." And if people can make nothing of the present moment they tend to remain static and bewildered, left at the mercy of whoever acts with power. That, almost inevitably, means perpetuation of power without accountability. By following these policies of news, American media corporations benefit from the political sterility of the media. A population unable to select alternative patterns of power sustains the status quo.

Media executives have always insisted that they merely give people what people want. They say that they are governed solely by the public interest. David Sarnoff, ex-NBC head, defined "public interest" as whatever the public chooses to watch on television. Former CBS chairman Frank Stanton said, "A program in which a large part of the audience is interested is by that very fact . . . in the public interest."

The Sarnoff and Stanton assertions are sometimes true and sometimes not. But they are fallacious as operating principles. A passerby may watch a street gunfight in horror, but it is not necessarily in his or her best interest. Children would probably watch public torture if it occurred on their way home from school, but that fact does not make public torture in the public interest. Soviet plebiscites show that voters give remarkable acquiescence to what is offered them, far higher even than American network television ratings. But this is not necessarily what people want. It is what they get.

The product of the news media, the content of which is not designed primarily to serve the purchaser—the reader— but to please a third party—the advertiser—has begun to lose its vigor as an institution. When the news is designed to exclude a third or a half of the population, it has sacrificed much of its standing as a democratic mechanism. And if it delivers accounts of events without relating them to the real world it has begun to fade as an important force in any society.

12

THE GROWING GAP

It appears to have five outpouchings. . . . A container of some sort?

Oliver Sacks
The Man Who Mistook His Wife for a Hat

IN 1986 WHEN General Electric, through its acquisition of RCA, became the owner of NBC, it raised familiar questions about new ownership patterns in the American media.

General Electric activities periodically become subjects in the news. The country's tenth largest corporation and a major defense contractor, it is the biggest producer of electric lamps, a major manufacturer of power plants, nuclear reactors, jet engines, nuclear missiles, locomotives, and of almost every link in the production and distribution of electricity. Through its board of directors it interlocks with still other industries also sensitive to their treatment in the news.

To promote its business, General Electric, like most large corporations, expends formidable energies to shape its public image in positive, even heroic terms. Like other corporations, it uses whatever influence it can to sell its commercial products and win government contracts. An important part of the promotion is intensive work by public relations staffs and, on occasion, top executives, to influence the news in its favor. Now, if it desires favorable treatment it no longer has to plead with at least one major American news organization. It owns one.

Only time will tell how this will affect NBC. But the power

208

and politics of General Electric are not very different from those of other large corporations that in the last twenty-five years have acquired control of the country's major media.

General Electric's record illustrates the problem. Throughout its history it has had public embarrassments. Each time, uncontrolled news reports damaged its advertised image as a benevolent force selling helpful household appliances. Some news stories have periodically weakened its image as a conscientious government contractor.

In 1932, for example, one of its engineers testified that the company cut the life of light bulbs a third in order to increase sales during the Great Depression. In 1941 it was convicted of an illegal agreement with Germany's Krupp company, particularly embarrassing because World War II had started and Krupp was a major supplier for the Nazi war machine. In 1942 General Electric was convicted of fraud in supplying cable for U.S. Navy warships. In 1948 it and Westinghouse were convicted of a conspiracy to fix bids on street lighting for American cities. In 1961 it was the largest of a group of companies found guilty of having conspired for years to rig bids on electrical generating equipment; three GE executives were sentenced to jail terms.

In 1982 news stories disclosed that though GE had 1981 pretax earnings of $2.66 billion, it had paid no income tax and actually received a $90 million rebate from the Internal Revenue Service, legal under a new law but still embarrassing. In 1985, the year before its acquisition of NBC News became final, it pleaded guilty to forging 100,000 employee time cards in order to shift expenses from one of its private contracts to a Department of Defense project for intercontinental nuclear missiles.

Over the years it has taken special pains to promote its preferred politics. In the 1950s, for example, it launched Ronald Reagan as a national political spokesman by paying him to make nationwide public speeches against communism, labor unions, social security, public housing, the income tax, and to augment the corporation's support of right-wing political movements.

It is still interested in politics. Shortly after General Electric bought control of NBC, the GE executive who was appointed the new president of the National Broadcasting Company, announced

that NBC should start a political action committee and contribute
money to strengthen the company's influence in Washington. The
new network president made it clear that failure to cooperate would
raise questions about the employee's "dedication to the company." The president of NBC News had to announce that news
employees would be exempted.

Question: If General Electric had owned NBC during its
earlier episodes of criminal convictions and other public embarrassments, would NBC News have reported them?

Fifty years ago the answer would have been an almost certain
no. Newspapers and broadcasters did not publicize bad news about
their owner.

The answer in 1986, however, would probably be yes.

If General Electric in 1987 experienced a major criminal
conviction, NBC News would probably report it in a straightforward way.

Another question: If NBC did report the news item of the
conviction, would NBC also proceed to produce a documentary
on criminality and carelessness in defense contracts, with General
Electric as an obvious recent example? If it were disclosed that
the company paid no income taxes during three years of multi-
billion profits, and General Electric owned NBC at the time, would
the network produce a documentary on inequities in the national
tax system?

One has to speculate, but the answer is probably no. It is
unlikely that any corporate-owned medium would do so, but General Electric, recently embarrassed, might be less likely to.

These differing answers symbolize the paradoxes and problems of concentrated corporate control of the major media. The
new corporate ownership has not canceled an outstanding strength
of American news reporting—accurate reporting of facts—but it
has increased some of the most troublesome weaknesses in the
integrity and usefulness of American news.

*   *   *

It has been two generations since American media suffered
sweeping corporate suppression of the media. The investigative
and political reformist magazines of 1900–1912 included some of

the most prestigious in the country—*Harper's, Scribners, Century*—and a dozen others. The "muckraker" magazines' exposure of systematic bribery of government by banks and industry, and abuses by monopolies and trusts, were an important force in the political movements that elected mayors, governors, and, finally, a reformist president, Theodore Roosevelt. That was too much, and in a series of abrupt acts J. P. Morgan and the Rockefeller interests simply bought controlling interest in the magazines—*Harper's, Scribners, Century*, and a number of others—installed their own managers, and announced that the public was tired of reading exposés of banks and business. It ended an era of American journalism and national politics.

Corporate power to influence public information has not changed, but American journalism and its audience have altered the way it is done. History seldom repeats itself precisely. In the latter half of the twentieth century, the holders of corporate media power are, like their fellow citizens, a different breed in a different time.

Compared to the years before World War II, the quality and seriousness of daily breaking news in the United States has improved significantly, thanks largely to a remarkable alteration in the perceptions and expectations of the American public.

World War II ended any remaining innocence about the horrors possible in the human race, and wiped out illusions that any society can insulate itself from the rest of the world. Nowhere was this change more significant than in the United States, where two underlying beliefs had been the inevitability of human progress and the beauties of isolation from a troublesome outside world.

Ever since, the message has been clear that, like it or not, Americans have a personal stake in unfolding history, and that awareness has created a public demand for more relevant daily news.

Shocks like the Vietnam War, the gasoline shortage of the 1970s, and hijackings of the 1980s have removed any remaining doubt that the lives of individuals are profoundly altered by remote forces. In domestic life, society changes with ever greater speed. Whole industries are born while others die, occupations alter almost overnight, sons and daughters no longer assume they will do the same work or live in the same place as their parents. Radical technologies that prolong individual life can also terminate all human life.

The demand for better public information during World War II was furthered by an almost revolutionary move in its aftermath. After World War II, the G.I. Bill promised free higher education to the 14 million men and women who had been in the armed services. That ended the perception of university education as an elite privilege, and began an alteration of the intellectual, occupational, and cultural character of the American population. Today a majority of adult Americans have had some college education and that figure is rising. With widespread travel and international communication, cosmopolitan tastes and values are growing. The American public developed wider sources of information, in textbooks, lectures, and experience with new cultures.

Journalists have been part of that transformation. Today, journalists are not only better educated, but they are more concerned with individual professional ethics than would have seemed possible fifty years ago. The conventions against lying, fictionalizing, and factual inaccuracy are strong and widespread. Collection of accurate facts is a high priority in American reporting.

The devotion to accurate facts and the rarity of suppression of dramatic public events are strengths of American reporting.

Unfortunately, that admirable professional standard in American news does not extend to other crucial kinds of news treatment.

*　　　*　　　*

Despite raised standards in journalism, American mainstream news is still heavily weighted in favor of corporate values, sometimes blatantly, but more often subtly in routine conventions widely accepted as ''objective.'' One is overdependence on official sources of news. Another is a peculiar lack of social context for facts in the news, which removes much of the meaning. Third is a pattern of selective pursuit that results in some subjects regularly developed in depth and others of equal or greater importance systematically avoided.

Just Credentialed Facts

Facts supported by important figures form the bulk of contemporary news. Someone in authority makes a statement, a law is enacted, the government or a corporation releases data, an accident occurs, a natural phenomenon is reliably observed—all can be cited and proved as objective entities.

There are sound reasons for it all. Facts supported by named authorities are crucial social artifacts, whether it is a secretary of defense reporting on performance of a new weapons system or a local police chief on the subject of a crime. Citing responsible sources has reduced the worst curses in worldwide reporting—the propagation of baseless rumor, lying or lazy reporters, anonymous falsehoods planted for cynical purposes. Unless there is a body of unambiguous fact, there is no basis for reality in public discourse. And those who wield social power deserve special attention. They have a major impact on public affairs and what they say in public is part of their public accountability.

The highly credentialed fact is also commercially and professionally convenient. If a fact comes from a named source with an impressive title, it is less easy to accuse the reporter, editor, or news organization of introducing personal judgments or bias.

But overemphasis on news from titled sources of power has occurred at the expense of reporting "unofficial" facts and circumstances. In a dynamic and changing society, the voices of authority are seldom the first to acknowledge or even to know of new and disturbing developments. Officials can be wrong.

Overreliance on the official view of the world can contribute to social turbulence. Unable to attract serious media attention by conventional methods, unestablished groups have had to adopt melodramatic demonstrations that meet the other media standards of acceptable news—visible drama, conflict, and novelty. If they are sufficiently graphic, the news will report protests, demonstrations, marches, boycotts, and self-starvation in public places (though not always their underlying causes). But in the end, even that fails. Repeated melodrama ceases to be novel and goes unreported. Social malaise or injustice often are not known, or can be ignored, by officialdom. Unreported or unpursued, these realities have periodically led to turbulent surprises—such as the social explosions that came after years of officially unacknowledged structural poverty, continuation of racial oppression, or damage from failed foreign policies.

Over the years, the exaggerated demand for official credentials in the news has given the main body of American news a strong conservative cast. This is not peculiar to the United States, though many other democracies avoid it. Where there are not genuinely diverse voices in the media the result inevitably is an overemphasis on a picture of the world as seen by the authorities, or as the authorities wish it to be.

Fear of Context

Accurate facts are indispensable, but by themselves they can be misleading; a single dramatic event may be unrepresentative of the whole, or even contrary to the nature of the whole. Simple recitations of data seldom lead to public comprehension. Most naked facts are comparatively meaningless. Context is crucial.

There are good reasons to exercise care in providing context. Incompetent or propagandistic context can distort rather than clarify meaning. Simple personal opinion of the reporter should not be mistaken for informed context. Furthermore, in a news system characterized by local monopolies, there is an obligation to be attentive to the border between clarifying context and politicizing news.

But there is a difference between partisanship and placing facts in a reasonably informed context of history and social circumstance. American journalism has not made a workable distinction between them. Too often the social significance of American news is avoided for the wrong reasons.

There are powerful commercial pressures to remove social significance from standard American news. Informed social-economic context has unavoidable political implications which may disturb some in the audience whose world view differs. Those readers and viewers might grudgingly accept the briefly announced, indisputable fact but not the display of its similarly indisputable implications. In the late 1980s, for example, failures of local banks were routinely reported, but seldom the ominous growth in annual bank failures and what this could mean for the national economy. Both advertiser and owner want the audience to remain in an accepting attitude toward both the news and the advertising. The result is unnecessarily bland and unintegrated information, which too often leaves the public without a true understanding of the facts in the news.

Most serious editors agree that some interpretation is periodically needed. But the doctrine of just-the-facts is so strong that with rare exceptions the interpretations are done with self-canceling circumlocutions in order to remove any impression that political and economic judgments are being made.

The overemphasis on austere factuality makes much American news insufficiently descriptive. In the drive for rigid neutrality, American reporting style has become the journalism of nouns, at the expense of verbs of action and adjectives of states of being.

While not all journalists have the background knowledge, analytical skills, or personal insights to provide a valid context for the news, there is a large reservoir of journalists who have those qualities in their own fields.

Too often the experienced journalist is forced to imitate the patient described by Oliver Sacks (*The Man Who Mistook His Wife for a Hat*). The patient, an educated and cultivated man, suffered from a neurological disorder that kept him from perceiving the function of common objects. Shown an ordinary glove, the patient stared at it and said, ''A continuous surface, infolded on itself. It appears to have five outpouchings. . . . A container of some sort?'' The patient's perceptual system did not permit him to recognize its function and name the word *glove*. With too much vital news, American journalism is forbidden to call a glove a glove.

Exaggerated dependence on facts that carry the imprimatur of the authorities, combined with limitations on giving the context for facts, has left American journalism relatively defenseless when authorities lie or evade relevant facts. A generation ago, Senator Joseph McCarthy created years of chaos by lying or misusing facts.

This was known by reporters covering him, but the constraints of journalism permitted the lies and distortions to prevail for years before they became plain to the public.

It is a highly cultivated art form in contemporary life for leaders to pretend to address cogent issues while evading them; almost always there are knowledgeable journalists who recognize the emptiness, but who must solemnly report the words accurately without the context that places the spoken ''facts'' in their real meaning, or lack of it. The limitation has contributed to the debasement of public discourse. Public and private leaders who lie with enough charm or evade compelling questions with sufficient artfulness, can usually rely on the conventions of news to tolerate it. The system penalizes truth and rewards its avoidance.

Dig Here, Not There

There is no journalistic convention for dealing with the ''butcher's thumb'' of owner prejudice in deciding which news events will be pursued, which will be repeated with emphasis.

The pattern is clear in American journalism: in general, items are more likely to be pursued in depth if they portray flaws in the public, tax-supported sector of American life, and less likely to be pursued if they portray flaws in the private corporate sector. Items about high costs or flaws in welfare and labor unions are likely to be emphasized and repeated. Items such as General Electric's conviction for cheating on its defense contract in 1985 are not as likely to be pursued by a series of articles in depth on flaws in defense contracting. Over long periods of time, this results in the public impression that public-sector activities are essentially flawed and should be limited while private enterprises are essentially sound and have no need for change.

The dilemma is vexing. Deciding which news to pursue in depth and which to drop quickly is legitimate, normal, and necessary. It is the most important single step in journalism. Yet, current professional standards give journalists little or no power to question systematic failures to pursue some important subjects and overemphasis on other subjects. Reporters take for granted that they have the right to resist an order to write a falsehood. There is no comparable convention for resisting the avoidance of important issues or the pursuit of self-serving ones.

When an editor makes a news decision based on corporate orders, or knowledge of ownership wishes, the editor seldom states the real reason. Thanks to raised journalistic standards, it is too embarrassing before professional subordinates. It violates the prevailing dogma of American journalism that serious news is the result of whatever is true and significant, let the chips fall where they may. It is a religious value in journalism, and like most religious values it is subject to official interpretation.

For example, it is normal and necessary for every editor to make decisions based on a variety of concerns—the inherent importance of the subject, its possible special meaning in a particular community, the strength of evidence to support a story, existence of special problems such as bad taste, unfair defamation of individuals, or whether the special interests of the owning corporation will be harmed. If the real "special problem" is the owners' private interests, the editor seldom announces the real reason. The item is dismissed for another, professionally acceptable reason, such as being insufficiently documented, or of no interest to the public.

As cited earlier in this book, 33 percent of American newspaper editors said they would not feel free to print an item damaging to their parent firm. They were not asked whether, if they decided against printing such items, they would announce the true reason to their staffs.

Overt punishment for embarrassing owners has lasting effects. In almost every news organization there has been, at some time, an editor who permitted publication of a legitimate story that unexpectedly brought retribution from the owner. A reporter or editor is fired, demoted, or otherwise reprimanded. That lesson is observed by everyone in the news organization. Future items of that nature are not aired or published. For years, no one has to speak to the editor or the news staff to know that the organization does not consider that subject "news." Eventually, the prohibition is no longer a conscious one. After a passage of time, long after the punished malefactors have disappeared, the professional staff may say, with sincerity, that owners exercise no influence on the news because they have never been told or seen a memorandum stating the prohibition. Journalists quickly learn that whatever is regularly printed in their newspaper or broadcast over their station is the definition of what is "news."

This internalized bias has special meaning in an era of ownership by a few large corporations, all with similar political and economic goals. Eighty years ago the Morgan and Rockefeller interests did not hesitate to buy politically toublesome magazines and set them in a different direction. Today, corporations whose contemporary goals are not that different from the Morgan and Rockefeller goals eighty years ago already own the most important media.

There are laudable exceptions to the prevailing pattern of news organizations avoiding pursuit of subjects that could hurt the financial interests of their owners. As cited earlier, the *Charlotte Observer* did this with tobacco. CBS in its 1971 documentary "The Selling of the Pentagon" showed waste and impropriety in the Pentagon at a time when CBS was a significant defense contractor. In 1978 CBS produced a documentary on growing concentration of ownership in newspapers (though CBS owned no newspapers it is not usual for one medium to stress problems of ownership in another). But these are rare. They are becoming more so.

The butcher's thumb that quietly tilts news in favor of corporate values has survived the rise in journalistic standards. The tilt has been so quietly and steadily integrated into the normal process of weighing news that the angle of the needle is now seen as "zero."

*　　*　　*

There is another paradox in American journalism, a seeming contradiction between heightened standards of news and a worsening deficiency. The country's newspapers and broadcast stations are rapidly, if unwittingly, abandoning a vital need of their audience. They are literally redrawing the map of American news.

The average voter in the United States is probably better equipped to consider public policy problems than the average citizen in any other major country. (The American public is too often unfairly compared with the elite of foreign countries, and it is forgotten how often those elites have blundered.) But Americans are required to know more.

Other democratic countries deal with serious issues only in national voting; practically all their primary government functions are controlled at the national level. Furthermore, most have a parliamentary system in which voters select not hundreds of individual candidates but, in effect, one of several parties, each with a distinct set of programs and policies. Consequently, the voter in other democracies makes clear choices from a relatively small number of alternatives. These choices are dealt with in the several competing national papers available to all.

Unlike voters elsewhere, Americans must know local candidates and issues as well. Each community makes its own decisions on education, land use, police, property taxes, and much else.

Presented on election day with an array of local, state, and national decisions, this is complex enough. But the task is made infinitely more complicated because political candidates in the United States, though they may run with a party label, are not committed to a party platform. For both local and national offices, the voter is supposed to know about each individual candidate. Consequently, United States citizens face a formidable task in trying to vote intelligently. They need to be informed routinely about their local schools, highways, and zoning and property taxes, something no national news medium can provide. And since every office, local and national, will be filled by a winner who is not bound by party discipline, the voter, theoretically, should know about each candidate's personal public history, including voting record, position papers, and other specific information that would permit matching the voter's wishes with each candidate.

There are strengths and weaknesses in both the parliamentary and the American system. But to be effective, the American system must be served by appropriate news about its civic governments: the map of the political system and the map of news reporting ought to have basic similarities. But the two maps are becoming more dissimilar with each passing year, a difference accelerated by the new corporate ownership.

Two gaps are widening. The first is the media's decreasing interest in news aimed at those who are not affluent or who are fifty years old or older. The second is the decreasing fit between the geographic boundaries the news media have established as their fields of operation, and the political boundaries by which people vote.

A century ago almost every city and town had its own daily paper, with systematic information about civic bodies and other politics affecting that particular community (see chapter 10). This has changed radically. The number of daily newspapers has diminished, from 2,000 in 1900 to 1,676 today. During the same period, the number of urban places increased from 1,737 to 8,765 today. Cities and towns without a paper are now the majority.

A new philosophy of American news distribution coverage has made the disparity even worse. It is a swift reversal of past patterns when newspapers, and broadcast stations, concentrated on particular municipalities. The names of American newspapers have always included colorful references to local place names— the *Oil City* (Pennsylvania) *Derrick,* or the *Bad Axe* (Michigan) *Tribune*—but colorful or not, the name of a city was an integral part of the newspaper title and the station identification.

But newspapers are rapidly eliminating their place names. For example, in California, which has more daily papers than any other state, two-thirds of all the daily papers have no city name showing on page one of their title.

The rapid disappearance of home cities in newspaper titles and in most broadcast station identifications is not an accident.

Most newspapers and broadcast stations no longer direct themselves to a particular municipality. They design themselves— and their content—to reach a particular retail market. The focus of circulation is no longer City Hall but the shopping mall.

There are 19,000 municipalities in the United States but only 210 markets. A market covers dozens and sometimes hundreds of municipalities, counties, school districts, and state and federal legislative districts. Newspapers and broadcast stations aimed at markets cannot and will not cover those hundreds of districts in any systematic way.

Candidates do not run from markets. They do not represent shopping malls. Political districts and public agencies whose actions directly affect the public do not draw their lines according to the 210 retail markets but according to the 19,000 municipal boundaries. Yet the American newspaper and local broadcast industries are in the process of a revolutionary rearrangement of their circulation and content strategies to service the market areas and to move away from focusing their primary efforts on municipalities. As a result, the country suffers from a growing gap between what the average voter in a particular city needs to know and the pattern of content and coverage by the news media.

The new corporate owners of the media did not cause the gap, but they have rapidly widened it. They have done this not out of a desire to debilitate intelligent voting, but because of the greater pressure on large corporations to maximize quick profits of their news subsidiaries. The most direct way of doing this is to rearrange their circulation to appeal to large regional advertisers, and to compete with television stations whose broad geographic reach has defined the 210 markets.

Similarly, new corporate owners of newspapers and broadcast stations have more swiftly altered their content to deal with affluent consumers instead of the whole adult population. It is an ingredient of the ''better resources'' and ''higher managerial skills'' often offered to the public as an advantage of corporate ownership.

The widening gap is the result of commercial decisions, not journalistic ones, about what each community needs to know. It is undoubtedly a contributor to the steady decline in the percentage of eligible citizens who actually vote.

Professional journalists, including their top editors, are largely powerless in determining the areas of strategic news coverage. That task has been taken over by market analysts and business consultants. The focus of journalistic effort has shifted from what the community needs to what the advertiser wants.

The average American voter is getting steadily less information about civic institutions and candidates from standard news.

But neither the voter nor the professional journalist has the power to regain the lost coverage.

*　　　*　　　*

Defenders of the narrowing control of the media point, accurately enough, to the large numbers of media outlets available to the population: almost 1,700 daily papers, more than 8,000 weeklies, 10,000 radio and television stations, 11,000 magazines, 2,500 book publishers, more than a dozen movie studios, plus cable systems, home videotapes, and more—the usual number quoted for individual outlets is 35,000.

Unfortunately, the large numbers deepen the problem of excessively concentrated control. If the number of outlets is growing and the number of owners declining, then each owner controls ever more formidable communications power.

Furthermore, the growing numbers, ironically, accompany a growing uniformity of content. In the last generation all newspapers have become more similar in content and approach. Most magazines have become specialized in content but major magazines that deal with political, social, and economic information are increasingly similar in political and economic orientation. There is such imitativeness in radio and television that it is almost arbitrary which station is heard. Major books and movies retain more variations, though mass advertising and distribution techniques tend to favor imitative books. Cable and videotapes are almost entirely duplications of the already uniform content of commercial television.

As the country approaches the end of this century, the major media are extremely profitable and closely organized in a few powerful corporations. But underneath the spectacular annual profits and corporate self-satisfaction, there is a disturbing separation of most major media from the true nature of their country's population, a separation that threatens not only the future usefulness of the media, but the vitality of the American political process.

13

TO UNDO EXCESS

So distribution should undo excess,
And each man have enough.

King Lear, 4.2

TO GIVE CITIZENS a choice in ideas and information is to give them a choice in politics: if a nation has narrowly controlled information, it will soon have narrowly controlled politics.

This book has described a threat to that need for broad choices: the alarming concentration in the control of information during the last half of the twentieth century. Today the integrity of news and other public ideas depends on corporate self-control, on the hope that the large corporations that now control most of the media will never use that power as an instrument to shape society to their liking.

The history of those who hold great power inhibited solely by self-control is not reassuring. It was the morbid record of absolute power left to its own devices that led to the formation of democracies in general and the United States in particular.

The threat does not lie in the commercial operation of the mass media. It is the best method there is and, with all its faults, it is not inherently bad. But *narrow* control, whether by government or corporations, *is* inherently bad. In the end, no small group, certainly no group with as much uniformity of outlook and as concentrated in power as the current media corporations, can be sufficiently open and flexible to reflect the full richness and variety of society's values and needs.

223

The answer is not elimination of private enterprise in the media, but the opposite. It is the restoration of genuine competition and diversity.

Consolidated control over the mass media has congealed at a tenuous time in national history. Democracy's strength is its ability to adapt nonviolently to changing needs, and in the last quarter of a century the United States has developed a special need for openness to new ideas and diversity of information. It must deal with the threat of nuclear annihilation, with growing global tensions between rich nations and poor ones, while within its own borders there is a parallel polarization between haves and have-nots, whites and nonwhites, old and young.

In periods of prolonged and basic change, societies that survive with any coherence need a social glue that holds them together. Today there is a weakening of national patterns that once constituted an automatic glue. In times past, within small communities, people of different classes may not have approved of each other but at least were forced to recognize each other. In public schools the children of the poor and the children of the rich came to know each other before the social status of their parents pulled them apart.

But in the last quarter of the twentieth century, Americans no longer know each other as they once did. In large cities the inhabitants have become strangers. They no longer attend the same schools or ride the same public transportation. The automobile has become a social as well as a mechanical isolation chamber in which the rich and poor pass each other in unseeing insulation.

In this new urbanized world, the glue of personal contact is weakened and something else is needed to maintain common bonds and mutual understanding. The "something else" should include publicly supported institutions, like schools, libraries, community centers, and some private institutions like the mass media. But public institutions are being starved when they are most needed, at the behest, largely, of corporate political values that dominate contemporary politics and promote private-sector affluence and public-sector poverty. The parent firms of most of the major media are part of the corporate political power that has pressed for inadequate tax support of public institutions.

The media themselves are rapidly evolving into a service for the material ambitions of eighteen-to-forty-nine-year-old affluent citizens. That is not the kind of glue that helps hold together a democratic nation.

* * *

In an earlier edition of this book I avoided suggesting remedies that seemed politically impossible. In that edition, I argued as I do in this one, that the media power of a handful of industrial giants is dangerously excessive as an element in American democracy. So there is a certain logic to the proposition that if the concentration is too great it ought to be diluted; it would seem to be common sense that if one corporation has too many outlets for the country's economic and social health, the corporation ought to divest itself of the excess. I believe that it is logical and makes common sense.

But for logic and common sense to emerge from the democratic process, the public requires adequate information. Other themes of this book suggest that when it comes to the issue of the media's corporate power, the media have never permitted news and commentary to make their corporate power a subject of common knowledge, let alone of public debate.

Political leaders take their cues of public interest from what is emphasized in the mass media. Politicians do not often take issue with a corporation that controls their public image. It is unlikely that any administration in the foreseeable future will use antitrust law to reduce holdings of dominant media corporations. A bill merely to study the degree of concentration in important industries, including the media, was introduced in 1977 by Representative Morris Udall; it died in committee without a whisper.

Because it is politically unrealistic to expect divestiture by the giants, in an earlier edition of this book I did not suggest it as a remedy. In retrospect I think that was wrong. The political realities are unchanged. But what is logical and good ought to be expressed even if it appears unachievable at the moment.

In the gravitational field of Washington, the idea of rigorous divestment by monopolistic corporations has no present weight. Yet the acceleration of control has been so unrestrained that at some point the reality of czarlike media control may break through even media indifference to the issue.

Antitrust laws are generally applied to corporations whose market power tends to limit competition and restrain healthy trade. But there has been a basic error in applying this law to daily newspapers and broadcast stations. Traditionally, the law has been applied to control of the national market. But the American newspaper and broadcast-station market is not national, it is local. Today, for example, no newspaper chain has more than 10 percent of the national market but most of the individual newspapers they own have from 80 to 100 percent of their local markets. In antitrust law, 10 percent of a market is meaningless. But 80 or 100 percent control normally would arouse even the most somnolent administration.

In broadcasting, with only a few exceptions, each station has a local, not a national market. In each local market the profits are regularly divided among the three network affiliated stations. Their market share (profits), despite near hysteria over shifting rankings between one and three, seldom vary more than 15 percent from first to third. It is usual for the three together to control from 80 to 90 percent of their markets. It is a classical oligopoly but it happens to be local. Recognition is long overdue that the market boundaries of newspapers and broadcast stations, with only a few exceptions, are not national.

The ideal ownership pattern for newspapers is one for each owner. That is how the best American dailies developed, and they did so for obvious reasons. A single owner concentrates energies, skills, and managerial and journalistic resources on one newspaper and has the power (and often the economic motivation) to reinvest surplus profits in the long-term strength of that paper and its relationship to that one community. A chain owner does the opposite. With rare exceptions, reinvestment into the long-term health of individual daily papers is a low priority compared to the inexorable demand of its parent firm for maximum profits, often for expansion elsewhere.

If there were one daily paper per owner, something else of importance would be gained. As long as most newspaper revenues come from advertising, there would still be local monopoly. But one thousand or more separate local owners would increase the chance for a wider spread of political and economic values than the chiefs of a dozen national and multinational corporations.

There is no good social or economic reason for a single corporation to control more than one local monopoly. Individual daily newspapers are economically viable. Yet two corporations own more than ninety local papers, all but a few monopolies. Other chains own dozens of monopolies. Consequently, it is generous, and more politically feasible, to suggest that no newspaper company should have a controlling interest in more than thirty local monopoly daily newspapers. Nor should any firm control monopoly papers that constitute more than 3 percent of national daily circulation. (In the 1980s, 3 percent would be about 1,800,000 papers sold daily.) Papers operating with direct competition would not come under the limitations.

If such a law were passed, the sudden sale of hundreds of newspapers would depress their market values. Even though most owners have already earned back their purchase prices many times over, a solicitous regard for owners' habits of generous profit-making might give corporations fifteen years to divest themselves of their surplus newspapers or circulation.

No corporation already at the new legal limit could buy another monopoly paper without selling one in order to keep within the legal limit.

Forbidding anyone, including a corporation, to publish a newspaper raises a constitutional question. The First Amendment prohibits governmental interference in freedom of the press, which has been interpreted to mean that anyone can print anything without prior restraint. A law forbidding a corporation to publish more than a fixed number of newspapers could be interpreted as a violation of the First Amendment freedom to publish anything anywhere. Consequently, a divestment law restricting the newspaper ownership of corporations should be limited to corporate acquisition of existing monopolies. Any corporation, regardless of its ownership of other daily papers, would always be permitted to create a new newspaper. Such a policy might also help put excess profits into creation of new enterprises rather than merely collecting existing ones.

Magazines would require a more complex formula, given their variety of specialties and frequency of publication. But there, too, a limit on degree of market share, measured against revenues for the entire magazine industry, and for the specialties of subject matter of magazines, would be applied only to acquisitions of existing magazines, and not limit creation of new ones.

Broadcasting presents no constitutional problem to governmental regulation of ownership. It is a regulated industry because of limited channels and at its own insistence that government protect assigned frequencies from competitors.

The same argument for one newspaper per owner is even stronger for broadcast stations. The potential number of newspapers is unlimited, since paper and presses are for sale to all. But there is a limit to the number of available broadcast channels. Ownership should be limited to one AM, one FM, *or* one television station per owner, not one of each.

Book publishers, like magazine owners, should be limited in the share of market they can attain by acquiring existing properties, but not be limited by expansion of their own companies.

Movie studios should be more restricted than they are now to ownership of movie theaters that give them guaranteed bookings.

There should be severe limits on cross-ownership of the media. When confronted with the accusation that they have monopolies and near-monopolies, most owners insist that they face competition from other media, newspapers from radio and television, magazines from newspapers, books from movies, and so forth. While this is generally exaggerated, if taken at face value, they should not be permitted to buy their competitors. But there are better reasons to forbid cross-ownership than forcing the media to take the consequences of their exaggerated claims of competition. Media that truly compete with each other produce more variety and innovation and they monitor their competitors' business practices more closely.

The deadening effect of cross-media ownership is clear in

the sad loss of the original dream of cable. The great promise of cable—one that started to be realized twenty years ago—was copious channels for each city, organized as a public utility. A block of channels carried standard commercial programs from existing television stations, others provided a variety of specialized national and local subject matter for small clusters of listeners, and still other channels were devoted to noncommercial and educational uses. In return for the exclusive franchise given by a municipality, the cable operator would provide some channels free of charge for civic uses.

Cable would become a common carrier, like the electric and phone company, guaranteed a reasonable profit in return for an agreed-upon level of public service. The cable operator would be in the business of renting cable time with an almost unlimited supply of channels available. Like the electric and phone companies, the more customers for channel time, the higher the profit. Just as the electric and phone companies do not control how its customers use the service, the cable operator would not control what buyers of channel time did on their programs.

Under these conditions, there would be the possibility of "narrowcasting," devoting numerous low-cost channels to smaller audiences, each of which had a deep interest in a special subject—school board meetings, home repair, local sports, hometown debates on local issues, local lectures, amateur dramatics and music, and other activities that once took place in town halls and school auditoriums when communities were small. It would not be necessary to attract a maximum, generalized audience, profitable for mass advertising, which is the dynamic that now produces the bland and imitative programming of through-the-air broadcasting. This new direction was the promise of modern cable, thanks to the technology that made possible systems of eighty or more channels.

The original dream for cable is all but lost. There are enlightened exceptions, but for most communities the original idea has been reversed, thanks to lobbying that produced changes in congressional law and policies of the Federal Communications Commission. When these changes were being considered, most newspaper and broadcast news was silent on the profound consequences of the changes. It is not coincidental that most cable systems are owned by companies who already are owners of other media—newspapers, radio, television, and magazines.

* * *

Mass advertising is the engine that drives much of the media into giantism, toward monopoly, toward socially insignificant editorial content, and raises barriers to new media entrepreneurs. A progressive tax on advertising would reverse or slow the present self-feeding process.

Mass advertising has shifted consumer power in the economics of newspapers, broadcasting, and magazines. For example, in the past, the readers of newspapers were sovereign: they were the majority support for each paper and if the paper did not satisfy the high priorities in readers' interests, the paper lost its major economic revenue. Either the paper changed or new papers filled the gap. The result was not only competition, but a diverse presentation of information that more accurately reflected the varieties of group interests in the community. It was the era that Horace Greeley spoke of when every community of 15,000 people had competing daily papers.

Today the advertiser is sovereign in newspapers, broadcasting, and magazines. It is not sovereign in the sense that the advertiser necessarily dictates the nonadvertising content explicitly, though that may be a significant practical effect. The advertiser is sovereign by the simple businesslike decision to place its ads in the newspaper, broadcast station, or magazine that reaches the most affluent consumers in the most precisely targeted way and with content that most maximizes the selling power of the ads. The form and content of contemporary American newspapers, magazines, and broadcasting are, of course, a combination of what the advertiser and what the audience wants. But with each passing year, newspapers and broadcasting have put more weight on what makes for effective advertising than on inherent community interest and need.

Increasingly, the nonadvertising content in American newspapers, magazines, radio, and television is what in television is called "LOP," the Least Objectionable Programming. It does not meet the greatest needs and interests of the audience but it is mildly interesting to many. It is good for advertising. It is not an adequate method of deciding what the public needs for self-government and cultural variety.

A progressive tax on advertising would reduce its volume and elevate the public's needs in the media's selection of non-advertising content. Reduced advertising would not eliminate its socially useful functions—announcing new goods, providing specifications and prices, and permitting consumers to make comparisons. But beyond a certain level of a company's total budget, advertising spending would be subject to a tax that increases with the excess over the limit.

* * *

Lowered postal rates for publications with little or no advertising have been a part of postal philosophy in the past. Historically this was crucial in stimulating new newspapers and magazines and permitting the wide distribution of all printed matter. Printing is now less expensive than in the past, thanks to modern technology. But the most formidable barrier to new printed media is the crushing cost of distribution. Postal regulations that acknowledge the educational as well as the profit-making function of mail service would greatly increase the availability of new and different noncommercial voices. But that requires alteration of the philosophy that attempts to evaluate all governmental functions on the ability to make a profit (except, of course, in defense contracting).

* * *

A sacred principle in journalism has been the wall of separation between "church and state," that the reporting, writing, and selection of news shall never be influenced by the business side of the news organization. It is considered unethical for any money interest to influence the selection of news. The only legitimate criterion for news is what the journalist perceives to be true and significant in the life of the nation and community, and what may be humanly interesting. It has always been a somewhat porous wall, but it is the one principle almost every journalist would agree is central to uncorrupted news.

Among contemporary working journalists in the United States, respect for "the wall" in their personal finances is higher than ever. When some journalists violate the rule, they are held in contempt by their peers. Most of the companies that journalists work for stress the same principle; the individual reporter found altering news to fit a personal financial interest is usually fired or otherwise penalized. Many news organizations spell out the prohibition for the individual journalist in forceful terms.

But the wall of separation between American news and the business interests of the companies who control the news is being systematically dismantled at institutional levels of journalism. The problem is no longer the reporter or editor who accepts money or favors to insert or delete a piece of news. It is more widespread and insidious. Executive editors throughout the country are being trained not to select news of interest to their community as a whole, but only for those people who live in selected neighborhoods that have certain characteristics wanted by major advertisers. The news thus becomes profoundly altered for financial reasons unconnected to the principle of never permitting business advantage to influence the news.

What is properly forbidden the individual reporter is increasingly demanded of the reporters' professional superiors. The practice of selecting news in order to make advertising more effective is becoming so common that it has achieved the status of scientific precision and publishing wisdom. Corporate headquarters send out experts to train editors in its fine points. Editors are supplied with the location of postal zones of most interest to major advertisers, are shown the census data about the characteristics of residents of those postal zones, and are instructed to select national news and cover local news with those zones and those characteristics in mind. The result is the rapidly growing exclusion in standard American newspapers and broadcast operations of the activities and interests of the less affluent and the older people who live in the circulation area of the standard media.

Excluding coverage and news of interest to the nonaffluent and elderly is growing more rapidly because new corporate owners are under more pressure than independent ones to show ever higher profits in order to maintain their competitiveness in the stock market. They use their news subsidiaries to subsidize their corporate acquisitions elsewhere. It is becoming more deeply imbedded into journalistic decision-making by giving bonuses to top editors based on their paper's annual profits, with implied and sometimes explicit threats of demotion or undesirable transfer if their paper, regardless of the reason, fails to achieve its annual assigned profit margin.

Because the country's top editors are being integrated into the managerial imperatives of the corporation, journalists, through their editor, become less responsible for the integrity of the news and more for the profitability of the whole enterprise. That is not journalism. It is advertising and marketing. Combining journalism with advertising and marketing ultimately will destroy the integrity of the news.

Newspapers are not alone in the practice. It is true as well in commercial broadcasting—and increasingly in noncommercial broadcasting that is now dependent on corporate support—and with magazines. But destruction of the "wall" in newspapers is particularly alarming. Newspapers are the central news gatherers in the United States. In general, local broadcast news is primarily concerned with physical drama and entertaining items; it depends on printed sources for serious subjects. Magazines are not basic originators of news. When the interests of the residents of the "wrong" postal zones are ignored, when the optional news that will not attract advertisers is excluded, there is no daily alternative in broadcasting or magazines.

A change in the governance of professional journalists in the American news media would slow the destruction of the supposedly sacred wall of separation. Newspaper professional staffs should elect their own top editor, as is the case in distinguished daily papers in Europe. This would alleviate the growing pressure to alter news to fit merchandising.

American journalists confronted with the idea of electing editors sometimes respond that it would create office politics. It would. But office politics concerned with elevation to editorial power already exists, but with decisions deeply influenced by factors irrelevant to journalistic leadership. Judgment of peers would lessen managerial pressures on an editor to conform to corporate wishes in the news.

The election of editors sometimes raises the issue of staffs voting for the most easy-going or charming peer. The desire among newspaper staffs for low standards and lackadaisical work is close to nonexistent. One does not have to entertain illusions of professional perfection. But it is not an illusion that this generation of American journalists is moved—as are other kinds of workers, such as doctors, chemists, physicists, and professors of English— by the desire for the respect of their peers. Like academics in the best universities, they should have control of their professional work.

Few collective votes of a reporting staff would be directed at an editor who was known to be incompetent, a bad administrator, or had displayed disrespect for journalistic standards. Contemporary newspaper journalists almost universally condemn sloppy reporting, blatant personal bias, lazy collection of information, and clumsy writing. They are as interested in their incomes as any other worker, professional or not. But when it comes to the opportunity to perform at the highest possible levels of competence and responsibility, American journalists, almost universally, try to work for newspapers, networks, and broadcast news operations known to have high standards.

The basic barrier to election of editors is the removal of an owner's traditional property right to manage his own possession, including the selection of serious news. Election of top editors could not occur unless owners suspended that proprietary right. At least a third of chain editors have said they would not feel free to publish news harmful to the interests of their parent firm. Owners will be reluctant to relinquish that feeling in their editors. That is the reason they *should* relinquish it.

The growth of monopoly and of unprecedented control by a few giant corporations will, sooner or later, raise the issue of undemocratic control of public information. Inserting one institutional barrier to corporate abuse could diminish not only the real abuses, but the public's fear of abuse. Permitting professional staff members to elect their editors for fixed terms would be a way not only of moving toward greater professional integrity in the news, but would relieve owners of some of the public concern with excessively concentrated control of the media, especially in newspapers, almost all of which are monopolies.

*   *   *

The 1988 presidential elections revealed how sterile the national political dialogue has become. A major cause is the mass media's treatment of politics, specifically the failure of their reporting to reflect the full range of ideas and programs that exist in American thinking and expertise. It is not surprising that, in each election since 1960, when television became the main vehicle of campaigning, a smaller percentage of those eligible bother to vote.

The paucity of ideas and alternatives in national politics reflects the dominant role commercial television has come to play in campaigns and issues. Television is the main medium of national and regional electioneering, mostly ten-second to thirty-second campaign commercials that are devoid of content. It is the chief reason the cost of running for office has become prohibitive for all except the rich and those supported by the rich.

The Federal Communications Commission has the power to assist electoral democracy. It should do what some other democracies do: forbid paid political campaign commercials, and mandate substantial free prime-time for representatives of all parties that have polled 5 percent or more in the previous election. The time should be in multiples of fifteen minutes, not chopped up in seconds.

In politics and where socially important information is at stake, the public should become more aware of the lively alternative press that exists regionally and locally, and support those publications that speak to their needs. The alternative papers often pursue subjects and air opinions squeezed out of the mainstream local press. Some of their investigative reporting regularly stimulates the first public awareness of flaws in the institutions the mainstream media tend to protect, such as utility companies, banks, and major advertisers.

At issue is an extraordinary national resource whose diversity is vital to the maintenance of true democracy. There are tens of thousands of individual outlets of news, commentary, entertainment, ideas, and popular culture. They are potentially capable of a broad spectrum of ideas and perceptions. Yet the manic rush of media giants toward market dominance has made the thousands of outlets increasingly imitative and narrow, a sameness that flows from huge bureaucracies with identical goals and strategies.

Embedded in this resource are the 100,000 trained professionals in news and public affairs. They have rising standards of ethics and competence. They are free of government censorship. Their numbers and skills are potentially capable of richness and self-correction. But the emphasis and direction of their work is channeled by superiors more concerned with fast profits, market share, and corporate expansion than with reflections of the real world beyond the balance sheets.

Unless the trend is reversed, a few giant corporations will control the major media for years to come. Monopoly and near monopoly will not change. Irresponsibly excessive profits will continue to weaken the vitality of a crucial institution. Glib financial manipulators will repeat more pious speeches even as their media treat the public mind with contempt. Honest operators, repulsed by their greedy brethren, will continue to remain silent; in the cathedral of corporate life it is a sacrilege to cry out during the sacrament of the quarterly earning.

There is a chance to reverse the tide. It lies in public awareness of the danger. But because the media are not going to make an issue of their own power, the initiative must come from others. A serious, sophisticated public commission, supported by foundations or other private money, could produce a comprehensive picture of the extent to which diversity and accountability of the marketplace has been lost, and of the financial excesses that threaten the long-term strength of the mass media. But the study cannot be dominated by those who are the problem.

If it dared risk the hostility of the media, Congress could conduct such a study. In the past, it has produced scholarly-like basic studies. When done well, some, such as studies of banking by the late Representative Wright Patman, were serious attempts to save the private sector from its own excesses. But the Congress would have to resist its own temptations to use the media and, as with any other study, avoid capture by the forces it would study.

Concentrated control of the media is not the most urgent danger facing society. It pales before more compelling threats— imminence of economic disorder, deterioration of the planetary environment, growing violence between the world's rich and the poor, and the possibility of nuclear annihilation.

But the ability to cope with larger problems is related to the peculiar industries we call the media, to their ownership and the nature of their operation. They create the popular base of information and political values out of which all critical public policy is made. In a world of multiple problems, where diversity of ideas is essential for decent solutions, controlled information inhibited by uniform self-interest is the first and fatal enemy.

The "enemy" is not wicked individuals who operate the dominant media. The enemy is avarice married to arrogance. It is the insidious power that comes with unchallenged dominance over the information of others. The object of reform is not to silence voices but to multiply them, not to foreclose ideas but to awaken them. For it is in diversity and openness that the genius of the United States can flower.

AFTERWORD

AS THE WORLD PREPARES to deal with the twenty-first century, United States society as a whole and the country's mass media find themselves in the same conflict—between what is good for business and what is good for the quality of life in society.

A robust economy and social equity have always been intertwined, and government played an intricate role in the relationship. But in the United States during the decades leading to the millennium, both national politics and most of the country's commercial media have created the notion that social and economic well-being are in a state of conflict.

America's major media are crucial parties to the creation of this artificial conflict. The media do not speak in total unison. Some occasionally present arguments and proposals for a more balanced view. But all are wedded to the ultimate need to satisfy the major source of their income, corporate advertising.

Consequently, corporate decision making is the most powerful single force in socializing and politicizing the American public. Leading corporations own the leading news media and their advertisers subsidize most of the rest. They decide what news and entertainment will be made available to the country; they have direct influence on the country's laws by making the majority of the massive campaign contributions that go to favored politicians; their lobbyists are permanent fixtures in legislatures.

This inevitably raises suspicions of overt conspiracy. But there is none. Instead, there is something more insidious: a system of shared values within contemporary American corporate culture and corporations' power to extend that culture to the American people, inappropriate as it may be.

239

It is no exaggeration to call the artificial conflict between the need for social equity and a healthy economy, on the one hand, and the corporate world's consistent attack on taxes, on the other, a crisis in American democracy. Taxes are indispensable to support the public institutions that are crucial to social equity, and the corporate world's powerful opposition to such taxes lies at the center of this crisis.

On the national social scene, for example, there is an urgent need for increased funding for public education, including libraries and all the supportive activities on which real education depends. Schools need limits to class size, proper teaching of the arts, and adequate pay for teachers. For a rich country that has the lowest taxes among the industrialized nations but is forever telling its youth that education is the key to success, that is both hypocrisy and a self-imposed crisis.

There is a desperate need for universal decent housing and neighborhoods. Inhabitants of deprived areas suffer high unemployment, and wretched neglect of the governmental services that are required even more than in affluent neighborhoods. Too many of the residents are devastated by drugs and crime. The central solutions to these problems are clear: good education, meaningful employment, and proper housing. But those demonstrated remedies are sidetracked by a national program to build more prisons. That is a crisis.

There is a similarly urgent need for universal health care. The United States is the only developed country in the world without it. A high proportion of the population has no regular access to doctors or clinics. The result is an enormous number of unhealthy citizens, near-epidemic illnesses and malnourishment in the country's poorest regions, and higher costs when some turn in desperation to overburdened emergency rooms. That is a crisis.

Cities are smothering in air pollution, traffic jams, lavish use of fuel resources and a measurable loss of both work and home time because the auto and highway lobbies have successfully defeated support for adequate urban mass transit. Among affluent urban nations the United States is close to the bottom in readily available mass transit. That is a crisis.

Congress once passed a law guaranteeing full employment, but never did much about it. The human, social, and economic damage caused by high levels of unemployment and jobs at poverty-level wages is not a mystery. It is preventable. Yet the country still tolerates shameful rates of unemployment during long periods, and endemic underemployment most of the time. At the same time, the compensation of America's top corporate executives is the highest in the world, and the income gap between executives and their employees is the widest in the world. The corporate sector speaks constantly about the need for U.S. workers to increase productivity, but most citizens are not aware that American workers are already the most productive among industrial countries. Unlike their workers, the high compensation of executives has been proven to have no relationship to the executives' productivity for their corporations, as measured by the standard criteria of business itself. That is a crisis.

Politicians speak constantly of the importance of parents and family in raising each generation of young Americans—and they are correct. But the same politicians refuse to guarantee a living wage for every worker. When both parents need to work outside the home but have no access to affordable, reliable day care, that is a crisis.

Because commercial television is such a powerful socializing force in the country, it is sometimes a more potent influence than parents, schools, and religions. It "educates" each new generation of Americans. Stripped of its public relations pretensions and constant trumpeting of a few benign programs, television remains a national school for crime and aggression. Day and night it demonstrates to children and adults how to kill and maim other human beings, creates an image of a world of ever-present evil and danger, and glorifies violence as the conflict resolution of choice. Alongside this televised curriculum is the teaching of commercials and testimonials that without the correct soft drink, athletic shoes, and clothing, an American child is not socially acceptable. That is a crisis.

Perhaps most dangerous of all are rising levels of cynicism about our own democracy. Citizens are justified in their growing assumption that individual voting means less and less, and that corporate money in politicians' pockets counts more. Buying votes in the Congress and state legislatures is open and lavish. Most voters are disgusted. An appalling number don't bother to vote. That is a crisis.

These are not the issues considered compelling news in the commercial media.

There is no need for our media to become a funereal chorus of impending doom. A better organizing principle was symbolized by the social essayist Life Jensen, in a cartoon of a robed and bearded city prophet carrying a placard reading: "The world is not coming to an end. We will have to learn to cope."

The propagation of unsupported ideas and the avoidance of central issues are characteristic of many media. Some of the illusions they foster also have historical roots. But the chief contemporary culprit is the one most of the American population depends upon for news and a sense of priorities in public life—commercial television.

Resistance to genuine reform in commercial television is rooted in an item of sanctity in corporate life—the seemingly holy creed of a born-again, uninhibited free-market ideology that emerged triumphant in the 1980s and 1990s. It claims that the profit motive producing results every three months should be applied to as much of society as possible. It preaches that the quest for profit should never be restrained by government. The constant iteration that the federal government has few legitimate roles beyond defense has energized efforts to cut tax support for basic social institutions like public schools, libraries, municipal and other governmental services, like retraining the unemployed, and assisting the poor and the elderly.

Sooner or later, the citizens of the country will have to face the crises and make decisions. Unfortunately, based on past performance they can expect little help from their most common source of news and public affairs discussions, commercial television. Instead, the industry continues to create its artificial world designed by the advertising of large corporations.

Deeply involved in its pursuit of maximum profit making without social obligation, commercial broadcasting has worked behind the scenes with its corporate allies to keep noncommercial television at a minimum, or to kill it completely.

There are democratic countries that have demonstrated that business health and social justice need not be at war with each other and that a healthy tax-supported noncommercial broadcasting system can operate side by side with a healthy commercial one. Britain and Germany are examples. But Congress regularly condemns the idea as "socialism" and a heresy against some sacred American business theology.

The desire for reform is not limited to a cultural elite. There is a growing gap between what a majority of citizens have said they want and what television gives them.

Media industry executives insist that their high profits prove that they have met their obligation to the public. Commercial television operators, for example, argue that if American audiences didn't like what they saw, they could simply shut off their sets. The majority of the public does not shut off its sets and the industry continues to make high profits. Therefore, the argument goes, no matter what surveys of public opinion may show, the public is voting with their off-on switches.

It is not an argument that can be dismissed out of hand. The data on audience habits do show massive continued listening and watching. The majority of the audience continues to have television sets in operation about seven hours a day. The difference between what people say they want and what most actually do has the appearance of a paradox. But it is not.

The level of violence on commercial television, for example, remains invulnerable to change, yet the data show that nonviolent programs have 33 percent more viewers than violent ones. A Times Mirror poll in 1993 showed that 53 percent of Americans want less violence and 80 percent agreed that TV violence is harmful to society. Even the majority of local station managers have said there is excessive violence in the programs networks and syndicators send them—but the same managers make profits by passing on to their local viewers the programs that they and their audience say they do not prefer.

Why the broadcast industry behaves that way is not hard to explain. The necessity of filling as many as fifty channels with eighteen to twenty-four hours a day of programming favors easily duplicated formulas. Though all operators provide the same general content, imitative programming pays. An increase of one percent in the number of households watching nationwide can give a program's network more than $50 million in added profit a year. Total advertising revenues remain so huge that even losers in the ratings race make handsome profits.

But that does not explain why the audience at home does not turn off their sets in higher numbers.

The basic answer to the seeming paradox lies in the history of television's original impact on society. When, by the mid-1950s, television sets had become a near-universal appliance in the country's living rooms, they changed more than national entertainment. Television produced a radical transformation in the way American families arranged their lives.

Before television, families typically used after-dinner time to read newspapers, magazines and books, play games, do homework, listen to the radio, gather around the piano to sing songs, or socialize with their friends and neighbors. When they could, parents took the family downtown to a restaurant and a movie.

Compared to the older pattern, mass television was stunningly fascinating, convenient, and inexpensive. Social and after-dinner habits changed rapidly. The downtowns of most cities became wastelands after dark as movie houses and restaurants closed. Their former customers were able to watch movies and live programs on their own small screen in the living room without dressing up, leaving the house, eating dinner in a downtown restaurant, or paying admission to a theater.

It is worth noting, however, that in those formative years that produced such a profound alteration of national habits, mass television was essentially nonviolent. It carried far more pleasant, unaggressive children's programs; it lacked today's endless staccato of commercials, and it was almost entirely family oriented.

With that content, the electronic box became a permanent fixture in the living room and the pattern was established of "free" home entertainment. It is "free," that is, if one does not count the cost of commercials, which is added to the price of products people buy (1997, almost $20,000 a year per capita disposable income). It is free if one disregards the amount of money spent on the goods television advertises most successfully—non-essential, marginal goods promoted through short, emotionally-laden messages. It is free if one ignores the loss of this national spending for central social needs like education and health care.

Once the national habit of staying home to watch free news and entertainment was established, a profound national social pattern was set. But there was an ironic aftermath. As detailed earlier, television emerged as the most powerful merchandizing tool in human experience. Progressively, more channels have been added, and with each addition the competition for viewer attention has increased proportionately.

The frantic competition was compounded by what seemed to be an innocent, convenient and simple invention. The hand-held, portable remote-control switch permitted viewers to remain comfortably seated while changing channels. It increased the pressure on broadcasters to fix the viewer's immediate attention by physical melodrama and fast-moving actions. There are golden industry rewards when viewers stop "to see what happens next."

Growing billions in advertising revenues were at stake in keeping the audience transfixed by some compelling action. Imminent murder, flaming car crashes, blazing gunfights, and sexual couplings became money in the bank, or, more likely, in the quarterly earnings on which Wall Street determines the success of broadcasters and their programs.

Government regulation of commercial broadcasting has become an important part of the national debate on the role of government in all of society. Most of the public gets most of its news from commercial television; it is the most common form of entertainment for children and adults. The country would benefit from national news and discussions about the best way to use the airwaves, since the public owns them.

But the record so far shows that the public cannot trust the commercial media to raise the issue, let alone tell them the truth, the whole truth, and nothing but the truth.

In recent years, the protests of parents and educators have grown louder, asking for change in antisocial programming and other inappropriate material for children. But they are faced with new obstacles.

There has been increasing insistence by the corporate world that the free market dogma must prevail with no governmental interference. And the broadcast industry has taken to proclaiming its "First Amendment rights."

The historic, legal, and pragmatic truth is different.

In private, few in the corporate world want total fulfillment of their public demand to "get the government out of the way of business." And broadcasting, despite its constant claim, does not have literal First Amendment rights.

Although the simple idea that business practices should be left solely up to business firms is a commonly held one, "public choice in a free market" is not in fact the undiluted goal of all commerce. Few corporate leaders want to fly in an airplane that has not been tested and approved by the government. They do not want their families eating food unprotected from contamination by toxic chemicals. They don't want their seriously ill children taking powerful prescription medicines produced under the free market mantra of "let the buyer beware." Nor would their corporations accept checks drawn on banks that had never been subjected to a government audit.

It is beyond argument that the First Amendment in the Bill of Rights of the U.S. Constitution forbids government from abridgment of freedom of the press and of expression. And it is beyond argument that this freedom is crucially important in American democracy. Under the First Amendment, it is unconstitutional for government to require anyone to have a license in order to print or write anything.

When it comes to broadcasting, however, neither law nor history is so simple.

The First Amendment applied to print and speech is close to absolute on grounds that speaking and writing are open to anyone. Anyone can publish criticisms of government and the established press; people and groups (and authors of books like this one) do so constantly. Owning a press is a big advantage, but with all its modern complications in both theory and practice, the First Amendment gives Americans more freedom to speak and publish than do laws and practice in any other major democracy.

But broadcasters do not have the "First Amendment rights" that forbid government regulation of writing and printing. In their private and more honest moments, broadcasters know this; it is the commercial broadcasters themselves who insist on government regulation—and with good reason.

As described in Chapter 8, in early, unregulated radio after World War I, commercial and amateur operators sent out signals on any frequency they wished. Some poached on the frequency of popular broadcasters, or sent out such powerful signals that they interfered with distant transmitters. The result was a chaos of jamming and static that threatened the entire enterprise and satisfied no one.

It was the broadcasters themselves who demanded that government regulate the industry by granting each operator a monopoly on a particular frequency, and who insisted that government punish anyone who intruded into their channel monopoly. As previously cited, the government has in fact imprisoned and fined citizens who have broadcast without a government license.

In return for this monopoly protection of their frequencies, the Congress insisted that the licensed stations must operate "in the public interest." The government wisely did not define "public interest," but said that during the license period a broadcaster should provide ample news and educational programming, and access to religious and other civic groups. When time came to renew the station's license, the overall record of that broadcaster could be reviewed in a process open to public comment. While public participation in license renewals exists more on paper than in actual practice, it is there for citizens who want to pay the costs of exerting their right.

Even the new Telecommunications Act of 1996, which granted the telecommunications industry most of what it desired, requires operation "in the public interest," but broadcasters have successfully narrowed the meaning of that phrase almost to the point of disappearance. The Fairness Doctrine once required broadcasters to devote a reasonable time to discussion of controversial public issues, and to permit reasonable opportunities for opposing views to be heard if an adversarial position was presented. Broadcasters pushed for repeal of these provisions and, with their special power within government, they won.

Since the 1980s, the federal government has largely ignored the legal "public interest" requirement and has increasingly adopted for broadcasting the dogma of the free market, endorsing whatever pays the most profit.

As mentioned above, the refusal of the major media properly to address central public concerns has created a crisis in democracy. A public inadequately informed about the substance of the arguments that affect its most important social policies has lost the substance of citizenship rights. If voters do not have easy access to central facts and ideas concerning public issues, voting becomes meaningless. Increasing numbers of voters understand this and are becoming cynical. Cynicism poisons free societies.

That is why when citizens are inundated with frivolous or minuscule fragments of public debate, there are social consequences that go beyond "merely business" or "what pays the quickest cash profit." The most common broadcast news today is either a litany of crime or happy talk about private lives of "personalities," in which the media decide how a "person" becomes a "personality." Or "discussions" of public issues become insult-slinging contests by paid gladiators of the air.

One side effect of this vulgarization of national discourse has been an artificial limitation of choice in the discussion of what roles broadcasting should have in American society. The false limitation can be characterized as The Fallacy of the Two-Model Choice.

One model of broadcasting is presented as undiluted government propaganda if any tax support is involved. In the rhetoric of commercial broadcasters and their supporters in politics, using taxes to help finance noncommercial broadcasting is equated with dictatorial "government propaganda" and "socialism." The rhetoric offers the examples of broadcasting under Hitler and Stalin.

The alternative model, in the "two-model fallacy," is presented as the only one acceptable for the United States. In this model, broadcasting is totally commercial and therefore automatically "free and democratic"; there is a minimal place, or no place at all, for noncommercial broadcasting—which leaves the field open solely to corporate control.

The reality, of course, is that there are many other free and democratic models of broadcasting in the world. These exist in minimal degree even in the United States, and they flourish in vigorous fashion elsewhere today. In many democracies, tax-supported broadcasting is not authoritarian, and usually there is a strong parallel commercial system. There are such systems all over the world, many of which provide creative, open access to a wide range of citizens and citizen groups.

In United States congressional and media discussions of how best to use the new and powerful methods of mass communication, however, there is almost total silence about existing alternative systems and continued propagation of the false image of "the two-model choice."

Forgotten except to historians of the media, and sometimes even by some of them, is the irony that in the 1920s, during the early years of widespread broadcasting in the United States, the most common and popular stations were noncommercial ones operated by municipalities, universities, and state public agencies.

Today, the closest the United States has come to a departure from the two-model image is the public broadcasting network and other nonprofit stations. But they live on the knife-edge of unstable political appropriations and conservative attacks. Most stay alive by endless efforts to raise their own money from subscribers, and are forced to run commercials that duplicate those on the commercial stations. As a result, a real spectrum of noncommercial radio and television in the United States has remained skeletal.

Noncommercial broadcast operations in this country consist mostly of National Public Radio, television's Corporation for Public Broadcasting, the Pacifica radio stations (a small set of Alternative radio stations), and a variety of stations operating at low power on tiny budgets, usually by a school or other educational institution.

The objection of conservatives to public broadcasting is ideological. There is no practical impact on tax rates or the federal budget. The Corporation for Public Broadcasting obtains less than 14 percent of its money from the federal government, a negligible tiny fraction of one percent of the federal budget. The rest of its funds comes from states, municipalities, commercial support, and voluntary contributions.

When the conservative Congress of 1994 proposed to kill public broadcasting by law, politicians were surprised by a poll commissioned by the Public Broadcasting Service, which found that of those surveyed—Republicans, Democrats, and Independents—84 percent wanted Congress to increase funding for public television or maintain it at current levels. The response was not limited to people with high levels of education or "high culture" tastes. The congressional budget-cutters discovered that the children's television program "Sesame Street," for example, is such a beloved American household presence that parents of every political coloration rose up in angry protest at the thought of its loss. Other public programs and documentaries had similar strong support at many levels of society.

In Britain, when Prime Minister Margaret Thatcher, pressing the conservative ideological drive for maximum privatization, made a similar suggestion for the BBC, there, too, public protest prevented a total turnover to private operators. (Without use of BBC programs, American television would be even more deficient in serious drama than it is today.)

The general public in the United States has received little information either from political debates over broadcasting or from their major media about differing broadcast models in Canada, Britain, the Scandinavian countries, Belgium, Netherlands, Germany, Japan, and other developed democracies. None of these foreign systems is exactly the same, but they all have stable, copious financing through a variety of plans that provide public access to civic groups with large memberships, and they are usually operated by quasi-trusteeships, supported by financing from fixed taxes.

In Belgium and the Netherlands, for example, civic and other organizations, including "listener associations," have guaranteed access to broadcast time based on the size of their memberships.

Within the United States, major foundations, consumer advocates like Ralph Nader, and others have suggested alternatives to the two-model illusion of choice. They have demonstrated, often with carefully evolved plans, that there are tax-supported alternatives appropriate to the United States.

The struggling alternative stations (and the illegal pirate ones) remain lonely voices against the national silence on the many ways broadcasting could develop if we do not have to limit ourselves to choosing between broadcasting that is governmental propaganda and broadcasting as a product designed for maximized corporate profit making.

In the 1995 and 1996 congressional debates and in most major media reporting on the future of American telecommunications, mention of any successful, established, foreign democratic systems was notably absent. Yet ironically, Japan's Nippon Hoso Kyokai (NHK), which is one of the world's largest noncommercial broadcasting systems, is a United States creation.

Today NHK is a leader in broadcast technology (it was the first to develop high-definition television and direct broadcasting from satellite), and, with the BBC, it is one of two remaining public systems financed by license fees charged like taxes to the public. NHK has multiple channels, with more than 6,000 television stations (some of neighborhood range); 3,000 of these stations are general in content and 3,000 are devoted to education. It operates alongside commercial networks and stations.

NHK was born with a resounding declaration by the American government on the need for noncommercial broadcasting with tax support. After the United States defeated imperial Japan in World War II and reconstituted a new, democratic political system, U.S. authorities insisted that no modern democracy should be without a well-financed, nonpolitical and noncommercial public broadcasting system. But ever since, similar suggestions for the United States itself have been met with hostility in Congress, in commercial broadcasting, and in most mainstream American news.

One result is that American commercial television, which started as inexpensive, nonviolent home entertainment, has become focused almost entirely on merchandising and on catching viewer attention with antisocial violence and indiscriminate, gratuitous sex.

This afterword began by citing a series of crises facing many of the country's basic institutions. American commercial broadcasting is intimately involved. Television, in particular, has profound obligations. It mostly fails them.

As the communications medium the public most depends on, television has become the nation's baby-sitter, chief news source, and ever-present entertainer. When broadcasters and their corporate sponsors fail to deal seriously, fairly, and regularly with the country's urgent issues, in a very real way they are using the nation's own property to rob its citizens of the knowledge necessary to cope with their most urgent needs and challenges.

The public needs a constant reminder:

The airwaves do not belong to the broadcasters. They do not belong to the advertisers. The owners, by law, are the people of the United States.

NOTES

Introduction (pages lii-lvii)

lii   "The dream of every leader." Colin Blakemore, *Mechanics of the Mind* (Cambridge: Cambridge University Press, 1977), 170.

liv   There are 1,700. Bureau of the Census, *Statistical Abstract of the United States, 1981* (Washington, D.C., 1981), 564, 568, and Benjamin M. Compaine, ed., *Who Owns the Media?* (White Plains, N.Y.: Knowledge Industry Publications, 1979), 223.

lv   "You really have to." George Morris, quoted by John Perham in "The Embattled Corporate Secretaries," *Dun's Review*, July 1971, 38.

lv   When Fred Friendly resigned. David Halberstam, *The Powers That Be* (New York: Knopf, 1979), 419.

lv   "Wall Street didn't." Allen Neuharth, quoted in the *Los Angeles Times*, 7 September 1978, 30.

lvi   "I made the first talk." John Knight, *Editor & Publisher*, 27 June 1981, 37.

1. The Endless Chain (pages 3-26)

4   Predictions of massive. John C. Busterna, "Trends in Ownership of Daily Newspapers," 1920-1986, *Journalism Quarterly* (Winter 1988), 833, plus updating for later mergers and acquisitions; *Forbes*, 5 November 1986, 111; *Washington Post*, 27 November 1988, 1ff. See also *The Media Monopoly*, 2d edition (Boston: Beacon Press, 1987).

4   The same dominant. *New York Times*, 23 January 1989, C-9; and *Los Angeles Times*, 4 January 1989, C-1.

5   Money: Market dominant. *Financial Times*, 12 January 1989, 24.

5   Few investors believe. *presstime*, November 1986.

6   A few newspapers. *Chicago Tribune*, 1 August 89, 1-E; and *Business Week*, 8 May 1989, 119.

7   When a corporation. *presstime*, November 1986.

7   When a large corporation. William B. Blankenburg, "A Newspaper Chain's Pricing Behavior," *Journalism Quarterly* (Winter 1986), 275ff.

7   When the same corporations. *Advertising Age*, 9 November 1988, 10.

8   The claim that. See Mark Hertsgaard, *On Bended Knee* (New York: Farrar, Straus & Giroux, 1988).

9   Even the most. From CBS-TV documentary, "The Business of Newspapers," producer, Irina Posner, July 1978.

11   Media lobbyists. Sheila Kaplan, "The Powers That Be," the *Washington Monthly* (December 1988), 36ff.

11   In 1986. *Executive Enterprise Briefing Book*, 20–21 October 1986, New York City.

12   Most of the country's. Frank Luther Mott, *American Journalism*, 3d ed. (New York: Macmillan, 1962), 550.

13   Concentrated ownership. Erik Barnouw, *A Tower of Babel*, vol. 1 (New York: Oxford University Press, 1966), 57ff.

15   But there are. Deborah Lipstadt, *Beyond Belief* (New York: The Free Press, 1986).

18   There are fourteen. *John Morton Newsletter*, 10 March 1988, 5, with updating for later mergers and acquisitions. Magazine data from *Advertising Age*, 26 December 1988, with updating. Radio and television from *Advertising Age*, ibid. Book data from *BP Report*, 3 November 1986, with updating. Motion picture studio dominance data from A. D. Murphy data in *Variety*, 10 January 1989.

19   If one considers. *Advertising Age*, 26 December 1988, 11.

19   It is claimed. *Books in Print* (R. R. Bowker, 1988–89).

20   In recent years. *Wall Street Journal*, 14 April 1988, 34.

22   Newspapers. *'89 Facts About Newspapers* (Washington, D.C.: Newspaper Publishers Association, April 1989).

25   A 1979 study by Peter Dreier. "Interlocking Directorates," *Columbia Journalism Review* (November/December 1979), 51–68.

25   Louis Brandeis. Louis Brandeis, "The Endless Chain," *Harper's Weekly*, 6 December 1913, 13.

2. Public Information as Industrial By-Product (pages 27–45)

27 One day in 1979. Conference between authors and Nan Talese is based on interviews with Mark Dowie, Geoffrey Cowan (proposed co-author), and Nan Talese. Rejection of book proposal by Richard Snyder, president of Simon & Schuster, based on interviews with Mark Dowie and Geoffrey Cowan, notes from Geoffrey Cowan, interview with Nan Talese, and letter dated 16 October 1979 from Talese to Cowan describing result and tenor of lunch meeting with Snyder. Before this book was first published, Simon & Schuster threatened legal action in order to review the manuscript on grounds that it considered the account defamatory. This extraordinary censorship demand was denied. The original Simon & Schuster incident appears in this and earlier editions as originally written. See also *Publishers Weekly*, April 22, 1983, p. 19.

28 Gulf + Western was a leading producer. Annual editions of *Moody's Industrial Manual;* Gulf + Western's 10-K report; and Milton Moskowitz, Michael Katz, and Robert Levering, eds., *Everybody's Business Almanac* (New York: Harper & Row, 1980).

30 But a survey. *Special Report: News and Editorial Independence. A Survey of Group and Independent Editors*. Ethics Committee, American Society of Newspaper Editors, April 1980, Easton, Pa.

31 "It is incredible." *New York Times*, 28 May 1978, 16.

33 On Monday, August 27, 1973. Memorandum from Claude McCaleb to Noam Chomsky and Edward Herman, undated.

36 Walter Cronkite and Ed Asner. *San Francisco Chronicle*, 19 August 1982; *New York Times*, 18 May 1982, respectively.

37 In August 1982. *Wall Street Journal*, 16 August 1982, 17.

38 The reviews were good. *New York Times Book Review*, 15 December 1974, 5; *Publishers Weekly*, 7 October 1974, 14.

38 William Daly. *Gerard Colby Zilg* vs. *Prentice-Hall, Inc. and E. I. Du Pont de Nemours & Company*, 78 (CIV). 130 (CLB). U.S. District Court, Southern District Court of New York.

39 The quick empathy. *Wall Street Journal*, 6 November 1979, 1.

39 The *Los Angeles Times* is owned. KABC-TV, "The Life and Times of Citizen Chandler," 18–29 October 1979.

40 Most of which. Nadine Joseph, "Water, Water Everywhere," *Columbia Journalism Review*, January/February 1981, 8–9.

40 In 1978 the Samuel Horvitz Trust. *Editor & Publisher*, 8 March 1980, 10.

40 In Atlanta. *Columbia Journalism Review*, September/October 1979, 27.

41 Media companies, large and small. *Washington Post*, 13 May 1980, A7.

41   Bruce Ware Roche. University of Southern Illinois, Carbondale, 1975.

41   Walter Annenberg. *Fortune*, June 1970: 130; and John Cooney, *The Annenbergs* (New York: Simon & Schuster, 1982), 292–295.

41   When the Du Ponts. Ben H. Bagdikian, "Case History: Wilmington's 'Independent' Newspapers," *Columbia Journalism Review*, Summer 1964, 13–17.

42   *Houston Chronicle*. Ben H. Bagdikian, "Houston's Shackled Press," *Atlantic Monthly*, August 1966, 88.

42   When General Electric. *Grassroots Editor*, March/April 1969, 9.

42   When the Amalgamated. *Columbia Journalism Review*, Winter 1979–1980, 5.

42   In the years after. George Seldes, *Never Tire of Protesting* (New York: Lyle Stuart, 1968), 26.

42   Television KPIX. *Grassroots Editor*, July/August, 1971, 6–10.

42   In 1949, for example. *Texas Monthly*, March 1978, 99–100; W. A. Swanberg, *Luce and His Empire* (New York: Dell, 1972), 408, 597; Marshall Frady, *Billy Graham* (Boston: Little, Brown, 1979), 199–202.

43   "Joe gave me a call." Lindsay Chaney and Michael Cieply, *The Hearsts, Family and Empire—The Later Years* (New York: Simon & Schuster, 1981), 128.

44   The general public. *New York Times*, 9 December 1984.

45   The myth of union wages. *Forbes*, 13 August 1984.

3. "Won't They Ever Learn?" (pages 46–66)

46   "There are still." Kenneth A. Randall, president of the Conference Board, quoted in the *Los Angeles Times*, 3 December 1980, 1. The Conference Board, a policy study group, is supported by major industries.

46   He was impressed. Don Carlos Seitz, *Joseph Pulitzer* (New York: Simon & Schuster, 1924), 35. Pulitzer's trustee device did not save the *New York World*. The paper continued to enjoy prestige and influence because of its writers, among them Walter Lippmann, Heywood Broun, Alexander Woollcott, Frank Cobb, Herbert Bayard Swope, and Franklin P. Adams. But Pulitzer's will of 1904 and codicil permitted relatives to succeed original trustees, and family heirs had different ideas for the paper. After years of high profits, and a few years of reduced ones, the heirs killed the most famous paper, the morning *World*, then they killed the *Sunday World* and sold the evening *World* to its New York competitor, the Scripps-Howard *Telegram*, where it became the *World-Telegram*.

48   Since the start of the Industrial Revolution. From Oliver S. Owen, *Natural Resource Conservation*, 2nd ed. (New York: Macmillan, 1975); hazardous waste data from *Time*, 22 September 1980, 58.

49 Later that same year. Grant McConnell, *Private Power and American Democracy* (New York: Knopf, 1966).

49 Its survey of industrial leaders. *Harvard Business Review,* January/February 1977, 57.

49 Two separate 1976 surveys. *Business Week,* 31 January 1977, 107.

50 Nevertheless, nothing in government. *San Francisco Chronicle,* 17 July 1979, 40.

50 Or lessened corporate crime. Department of Justice, Law Enforcement Assistance Administration, *Illegal Corporate Behavior,* October 1979.

50 Conservative foundations give judges. Gregory C. Staple, "Free-Market Cram Course for Judges," *The Nation,* 26 January 1980, 78–81.

50 In the 1961 conviction. Ovid Demaris, *Dirty Business* (New York: Harper's Magazine Press, 1974), 10.

50 When the Aluminum Company of America. *New York Times,* 15 July 1979, 1.

50 Through the Internal Revenue Service. Data provided author by IRS.

50 When the Firestone Tire. *The Nation,* 11–18 August 1979, 101.

51 In 1974, for example. G. William Domhoff, *The Powers That Be* (New York: Random House, 1978), 44.

51 Defense industry executives. Senate Committee on Government Operations, *Advisory Committees,* 1970.

51 The most powerful business lobby. Mark Green and Andrew Buchsbaum, *The Corporate Lobbies* (Washington, D.C.: The Public Citizen, February 1980).

51 In the public schools. Sheila Harty, *Hucksters in the Classroom* (Washington, D.C.: Center for the Study of Responsive Law, 1979).

53 Among the most commonly suppressed. Each year a national panel is asked to select the most important developments untouched or de-emphasized by the major media. The panel is directed by the Department of Sociology, Sonoma State University, California.

53 In their Political Action Committees. James North, "The Effect: The Growth of the Special Interests," *Washington Monthly,* October 1978.

54 "People in business." *Wall Street Journal,* 27 July 1977, 1.

54 "There is a basic bias." *Dun's Review,* May 1977, 76.

54 "All too frequently." *Broadcasting,* 27 April 1981, 76.

55 "I have brought." Senate Subcommittee on Administrative Practices and Procedures, *Sourcebook on Corporate Image and Corporate Advocacy Advertising,* 1978, 882.

55 Lawrence K. Fouraker. *Editor & Publisher,* 8 December 1979, 10.

55   A. Kent MacDougall. Series in *Los Angeles Times* beginning 3 December 1980, 1.

55   Leonard Matthews. *Editor & Publisher*, 24 November 1979, 15.

56   But of 1,110 members. *Editor & Publisher*, 19 May 1981, 116.

56   An authoritative study. Stephen Hess, *The Washington Reporters* (Washington, D.C.: The Brookings Institution, 1981).

56   "Only 8%." *Wall Street Journal*, 4 August 1976, 32.

56   "The media." John Brooks, "Profile," *The New Yorker*, 5 January 1981, 41.

56   The year Wriston. Bureau of the Census, *Statistical Abstract of the United States, 1980* (Washington, D.C., 1981), 487, 481.

57   David Finn. David Finn, *The Business-Media Relationship* (New York: American Management Association, 1981), 50.

57   "Because business has countenanced." "There is a tendency." *Dun's Review*, May 1977, 81.

57   "Businessmen are always." Quoted in *Mother Jones*, February/March 1980, 32.

58   "It presents the corporation." Senate Subcommittee on Administrative Practices and Procedures, *Sourcebook on Corporate Image and Corporate Advocacy Advertising*, 1978, 78.

58   The publication *Media Decisions*. Senate Committee on the Judiciary, *Sourcebook*, 581.

59   Mobil Oil is the second largest. Michael Gerrard, "This Man Was Made Possible by a Grant from Mobil Oil," *Esquire*, January 1979, 62.

59   In 1980 the company agreed. *Broadcasting*, 29 September 1980, 46.

60   "Any restraint on free discussion." *The Nation*, 24 May 1980, 609.

60   But shortly afterward. *Broadcasting*, 12 May 1980, 30.

60   The ad exploited. *Columbia Journalism Review*, September/October 1981, 26. The Mobil ad described an energy-saving project of the Benedictine Sisters in Erie, Pa. Mobil had asked the sisters to grant it permission to use them and their project in its ads. The Benedictine Sisters refused. Mobil nevertheless did use the sisters and their project in the Mobil ad that ran in ten major newspapers. When the prioress wrote to each paper disassociating the sisters from the ad, only the *Los Angeles Times* printed her letter. The papers that refused were the *Wall Street Journal*, the *Denver Post*, the *Chicago Tribune*, the *Washington Post*, the *New York Times*, the *Boston Globe*, the *Dallas Times Herald*, the *Houston Post*, and the *Christian Science Monitor*.

60   Other Mobil editorial ads. Gerrard, "This Man Was Made Possible."

60   The cynicism of ads. *New West*, 16 July 1979, 24.

61 The top twenty oil companies. "The Big Oil Shuffle," *New West*, 16 July 1979, 24.

61 Mobil itself was investing. Gerrard, "This Man Was Made Possible"; Milton Moskowitz, Michael Katz, and Robert Levering, eds., *Everybody's Business Almanac* (New York: Harper & Row, 1980), 513–17.

62 It was a study of oil company revenues. Department of Energy, Financial Reporting System, *Performance Profiles of Major Energy Producers, 1979*, June 1981.

62 Shortly after Roby's story. Edward F. Roby, UPI Story A262, 5 June 1981.

62 A Mobil ad appeared. The ad ran in eleven major newspapers, including the *New York Times*, on June 18, 1981.

63 In 1977 Representative Benjamin Rosenthal. House Committee on Ways and Means, *Recommendations of the Task Force on Foreign Source Income*, 8 March 1977; House Committee on Government Operations, *Foreign Tax Credits Claimed by U.S. Petroleum Companies*, 24th report, 1978; *The Foreign Tax Credit and U.S. Energy Policy: Report to the United States Congress by the Comptroller General* (Washington, D.C.: 10 September 1980), particularly i and ii.

64 (Recently officials in China.) Testimony of Jack A. Blum, Counsel, Independent Gasoline Marketers Council, before the House Committee on Government Operations, 13 March 1979. Also Hobart Rowen, "Chinese Shuffle Trade Policy to Accommodate U.S.," *Washington Post*, 24 December 1978.

64 Roby had reported what was. Edward F. Roby, UPI Story A221, 6 July 1981; UPI Story A271, transmitted 7 July 1981 for use 11 July 1981. The story that some major oil companies had written Secretary Watt to request reduction in acreage open for bids also appeared in major newspapers in stories written by other reporters: Andy Pasztor, "Offshore Energy Leasing Plans Trimmed as Interior's Watt Retreats Amid Criticism," *Wall Street Journal*, 6 July 1981; Charles R. Babcock, "Watt Defies Critics of Oil Plan for Oil Leases," *Washington Post*, 7 July 1981. Similar stories also appeared in trade papers, including *Oil Daily*, 9 June 1981. But only Roby and UPI were mentioned in the counterattack by Exxon and petroleum public relations agencies.

64 Exxon in teletypes. Teletype on Exxon's national public relations wire: "To Business Desks, PRW3/Press Relations Wire Wash 347-5155. For Immediate Release 07/10/81. EXXON USA SUPPORTS CHANGES IN OFFSHORE LEASING PROGRAM. Several news reports recently have misrepresented Exxon's position on the Department of Interior's proposed changes in the offshore leasing program . . . FYI, UPI moved a story 8 July 81 for weekend use . . . by Edward Roby . . ." The same message was sent by printed press release to editors around the country: "NEWS, Exxon Company, U.S.A. . . . July 10, 1981. EXXON USA SUPPORTS CHANGES IN OFFSHORE LEASING PROGRAM. Houston—Several news reports . . ." Roby was similarly named.

65 "I know of no company," Press release of American Petroleum Institute, Washington, D.C., 28 July 1981: "NOTE TO EDITORS: The attached statement by Charles J. DiBona, president of the American Petroleum Institute, is provided in response to inquiries from the news media about offshore leasing proposals of Interior Secretary James G. Watt . . ."

65 "We hope this ad." Quoted in *Editor & Publisher*, 4 July 1981.

4. From Mythology to Theology (pages 67–89)

67 "No Gannett newspaper." From Neuharth, "Newspapers: Dominating Their Markets; Gannett: Never a Down Quarter," address to the New York Society of Security Analysts, 11 March 1976.

67 Homer was Europe's. *Encyclopaedia of the Social Sciences* (New York: Macmillan, 1930), s.v. "folklore," 228, and "myth," 180.

68 In the beginning. From Frank Luther Mott, *American Journalism: A History, 1690–1960* (New York: Macmillan, 1972), 649; and Carl Lindstrom, *The Fading American Newspaper* (New York: Doubleday, 1960).

69 "Nobody must ever." Lindstrom, *The Fading American Newspaper*, 90.

69 "Not newspapers for profit." Alfred McClung Lee, *The Daily Newspaper in America* (New York: Macmillan, 1937), 196.

69 One year later. Bryce W. Rucker, *The First Freedom* (Carbondale: Southern Illinois University Press, 1968), 21–22.

70 A. R. Graustein. Senator George W. Norris. Lee, *Daily Newspaper in America*, 112.

71 "Would William Allen White." *Editor & Publisher*, 16 February 1963.

71 "As the newspapers' interest." White quoted in George Seldes, *Lords of the Press* (New York: Julian Messner, 1938), 274.

72 "Frank Munsey." William Allen White, *The Autobiography of William Allen White* (New York: Macmillan, 1964), 629.

72 Allen Harold Neuharth arrived. Personal observations and the *Los Angeles Times*, 7 September 1978, 1.

73 In 1967, Gannett had 28 newspapers. *Broadcasting*, 25 May 1981, 65; *Editor & Publisher*, 8 August 1981, 10, and 19 September 1981, 27.

73 The failure rate. "Reports of an Exaggerated Death," monograph by the author, 1976.

74 While all manufacturing return. "Notice of Special Meeting and Joint Proxy Statement," Gannett Co., Inc., Rochester, N.Y., 25 January 1979.

74 30 to 50 percent a year. From memorandums to Gannett local publishers made available to the author.

74 But in one respect. Lee, *Daily Newspaper in America;* Federal Trade Commission, Bureau of Competition, *Proceedings of the Symposium on Media Concentration*, vol. 1, 14–15 December 1978; *Editor & Publisher Yearbooks; Yale Law Journal*, vol. 74 (1965), 1339.

74 "If a newspaper is noncompetitive." Otis Chandler, quoted in *Business Week*, 21 February 1977, 59.

75 In 1979. *Editor & Publisher*, 10 March 1979, 16.

75 Not surprisingly. *Circulation 80/81*, 19th ed. (Malibu, Calif.: American Newspaper Markets, 1980).

75 "Gannett prints." *Value Line Investment Advisory Service*, 22 September 1979.

75 "Gannett believes." From *Washington Journalism Review*, October 1980.

76 A black media group. National Black Media Coalition, "Gannett-Combined Communications Merger: Background and Policy Implications" (Washington, D.C., 7 June 1978).

76 Gannett resorted. *John Morton Newspaper Research Letter*, 30 June 1979, 2.

77 "In Pumpkin Center." From Neuharth, speech to 93rd Annual Convention of American Newspaper Publishers Association, 23 April 1979, reported in *Editor & Publisher*, 18 October 1980, 16.

78 The local team is given. From Gannett memorandums made available to the author.

79 Former discounts. Cassandra Tate, *Columbia Journalism Review*, July/August 1981, 51–56.

80 She cited. Tate, *Columbia Journalism Review*.

80 In 1974 Gannett supervisors. *Rochester Patriot*, 23 October–5 November 1974, 1.

80 The new owner sued Gannett. Jon O. Newman, U.S. District Circuit Judge, "Memorandum of Decision," *Gannett Co. Inv. v. The Register Publishing Co.*, Civil No. B-74-123, 10 April 1980.

80 "Diversity of news." *Editor & Publisher*, 23 June 1979, 14.

80 A large ad. *New York Times*, 6 March 1979.

81 How can one know. *Los Angeles Times*, 7 September 1978, 1.

81 From 1973 to 1978. *John Morton Newspaper Research Letter*, 31 January 1979, 8.

81 While Gannett was losing circulation. *Editor & Publisher Yearbook*, 1974 and 1978, citing circulation data for previous years from Audit Bureau of Circulation.

81 "A total of 74." Neuharth, address to American Society of Newspaper Editors, 2 May 1977, published by Gannett Company.

81 (The *New York Times* won eight.) Calculations by the author.

82 "Coffeyville, Kansas." *Emporia Gazette*, 2 October 1979, 4.

82 "It was my first meeting." *Emporia Gazette*, 30 September 1979, 4.

82 The *Coffeyville Journal*, it turned out. *Publishers Auxiliary*, 5 November 1979, 1, 3.

82 "Its neighbors." *Parsons Sun*, 1 October 1979, 6.

83 "One of the state's best editors." *Emporia Gazette*, 30 September 1979, 4.

83 "Higher prices and lower quality." Pam Eversole, "Consolidation of Newspapers: What Happens to the Consumer?" *Journalism Quarterly*, Summer 1971, 245.

83 Another study at Brookings Institution. *Straus Editor's Report*, 13 December 1969, 1.

83 A 1978 study at George Washington University. *Help: The Useful Almanac, 1978–1979*, Washington, D.C., 398.

83 A separate study by Kristine Keller. "Quantity of News in Group-Owned and Independent Papers: Independent Papers Have More," master's thesis, Graduate School of Journalism, University of California, Berkeley, 15 June 1978.

84 In 1966, before Gannett began. Annual summaries of *Editor & Publisher* and *John Morton Newspaper Research Letter*. Employment figures for Gannett newspaper employees from John C. Quinn, senior vice-president for news for Gannett Company. In 1966 Gannett had 6,500 employees of all kinds in its newspapers. In 1980 it had 15,755, of whom 4,122 were engaged in news operations (as opposed to production, sales, and the like). Quinn stated that the company had no record of 1966 figures for newsroom employees but did have such records for 1974. I applied the 1974 percentage of newsroom employees, as given by the company, to the 1966 figure for all newspaper workers in the chain and obtained the estimate of 1,430 newsroom workers in 1966. This is probably slightly in error, though not substantially, because the 1966 total had not yet been reduced by automation in nonnews functions, as the total of workers was by 1974. My calculation is that the 1966 estimate could vary by as much as 57 newsroom workers for the entire chain, a maximum variation that would not affect the basic conclusion. Despite the addition of many papers and new editions, the average size of Gannett papers remained remarkably close from 1966 to 1980. In 1966 the average Gannett daily paper had a circulation of 44,539; in 1980 circulation was 43,988.

84 The Cox chain. Scripps-Howard. Daniel B. Wackman, Donald M. Gillmor, Cecile Gaziano, and Everett E. Dennis, "Chain Newspaper Autonomy as Reflected in Presidential Campaign Endorsements," *Journalism Quarterly*, Autumn 1975, 411–20; *Editor & Publisher*, 4 November 1972, 9–11; *New York Times*, 29 October 1972, 21; *Wall Street Journal*, 26 September 1980, 1.

84 Panax has fired. From CBS-TV, "The Business of Newspapers," 14 July 1978.

84 Copley Newspapers. *Editor & Publisher*, 20 April 1968.

85 Freedom Newspapers. Lloyd Gray, "From 'Moderately Liberal' to 'Doctrinaire Libertarian,' " *Bulletin of the American Society of Newspaper Editors*, February 1981.

85 "Is not helpful." Ralph R. Thrift, Jr., "How Chain Ownership Affects Editorial Vigor of Newspapers," *Journalism Quarterly*, Summer 1967, 329.

85 Chains tend to hire. Stephen Hess, *The Washington Reporters* (Washington, D.C.: Brookings Institution, 1981), 136–66.

85 Gannett has another way. "New Cash System Gives Gannett Extra Funds," *Editor & Publisher*, 1 December 1979, 13.

86 "To tighten the golden handcuffs." *Editor & Publisher*, 10 January 1981, 55.

86 "From long association." *Editor & Publisher*, 4 December 1976, 10.

86 Both companies." *Editor & Publisher*, 25 December, 1976, 8.

86 "In keeping with Gannett's policy." *Editor & Publisher*, 14 July 1979, 9.

87 "We believe completely." *Los Angeles Times*, 7 September 1978, 1.

87 "The *New Mexican*." "Mr. McKinney has developed." *Santa Fe New Mexican*, 27 February 1976, 1.

87 Watkins was given. Peter Katel, "When the Takeover Doesn't Take," *Bulletin of the American Society of Newspaper Editors*, February 1981, 23.

88 "It could be printed." Katel, "When the Takeover Doesn't Take."

88 "Look, this is the way." Judge Santiago E. Campos, "Memorandum Opinion," *Robert M. McKinney v. Gannett Co., Inc., and* The New Mexican, Civil No. 78-630 C, 17 March 1981, 19–20.

88 "This worried Watkins." Campos, "Memorandum Opinion."

89 They depicted. Supplied to author by Gannett Company.

5. "Dear Mr. President . . ." (pages 90–101)

90 "More people are bribed." Jonathan Daniels, "An Editor's Diagnosis," *Saturday Review of Literature*, 30 April 1955, 11.

90 Berlin was asking. Berlin correspondence obtained by the author through Freedom of Information Act.

90 The Hearst Corporation owned. From annual editions of *Editor & Publisher Yearbook;* Christopher H. Sterling and Timothy R. Haight, *The Mass Media:*

Aspen Institute Guide to Industry Trends (New York: Praeger, 1978); Federal Trade Commission, *Proceedings of the Symposium on Media Control,* vols. 1 and 2, 1978.

91 Lionel Van Deerlin. *Progressive,* July 1979, 39.

91–92 Frank Leeming. Katharine Graham. Joseph Costello. The National Association of Broadcasters. *Congressional Quarterly,* 2 August 1980, 2179.

93 That night no television network. Nick Kotz, *Progressive,* July 1979, 40.

93 "When word of this." Senate Subcommittee on Antitrust and Monopoly, *Hearings,* pt. 6, in consideration of Newspaper Preservation Act.

94 In 1981 two editors. *Editor & Publisher,* 18 April 1981, 222.

95 Berlin wanted President Nixon's. Senate Subcommittee on Antitrust and Monopoly, *Hearings,* 1967–69.

97 In June, before the Berlin letters. Christopher Lydon, "Aide Says Nixon Opposes Easing of Trust Laws for Weak Papers," *New York Times,* 21 June 1969, 30. Weeks later, the Department of Commerce, taking a position on the Newspaper Preservation Act for the first time in the three-year history of the proposal, issued a statement for the Nixon administration in favor of the bill. Eileen Shanahan, "Nixon Supports Newspaper Bill," *New York Times,* 26 September 1969, 94.

99 But in early October. Dirks Brothers *Newspaper Newsletter,* 31 October 1972, 1.

99 A study of major papers. Ben H. Bagdikian, "The Fruits of Agnewism," *Columbia Journalism Review,* January/February 1973.

99–
100 In 1972, after passage. Paul Delaney, "Cox Tells Papers to Endorse Nixon," *New York Times,* 23 October 1972.

6. Only the Affluent Need Apply (pages 105–17)

105 "We make no effort." Nizen, quoted in *Editor & Publisher,* 3 January 1981, 15.

106 Most people in the industry. Number of ad pages, revenues, and dividends from annual reports of F-R Corporation.

107 The onset. Origins of the Schell article, its consequences, and statements of William Shawn from personal interview with Shawn, editor of *The New Yorker,* 14 May 1981.

109 After 1966, *The New Yorker* audience. From periodic readership studies by *The New Yorker* and from Simmons Surveys.

110 "We had to deliver." *Wall Street Journal,* 4 June 1981, 14.

113 By the 1980s. *FOLIO: 400*, September 1981, 32.

113 "Kids and dummies." Paul Klein, quoted in *Broadcasting*, 9 January 1978, 32.

114 When word of this title, *Broadcasting*, 9 January 1978, 32.

114 WOMEN 18–49. *Broadcasting*, 10 November 1980.

114 WANTED. *Public Relations Journal*, November 1978.

115 At the time advertisers spent. From Bureau of the Census, *Historical Statistics of the United States* (Washington, D.C., 1975); Bureau of the Census, *Statistical Abstract of the United States, 1981* (Washington, D.C., 1981).

116 "The traditional view." John C. Ginn, speech before Newspaper Forum, reported in *John Morton Newspaper Research Letter*, 9 April 1980.

116 "The lost subscribers." Monograph by William B. Blankenburg, "Newspaper Ownership and Circulation Behavior," University of Wisconsin, Madison, 3 August 1981.

116 "The target audience." Transcript of interview with Chandler by KABC-TV, Los Angeles, 18–29 October 1979.

116 "We arbitrarily cut back." *Washington Post*, 24 July 1977.

117 Years after the near-fatal disease. *Profiles of The New Yorker Subscribers and Their Households* (New York: *The New Yorker*, n.d.). Though undated, the book reports a 1980 survey.

117 A MAGAZINE DOESN'T. *The New Yorker*, 5 October 1981.

7. Monopoly (pages 118–33)

Descriptions in this chapter of Washington, D.C., as a one-newspaper city refer to the period after the failure of the *Washington Star*. In 1982 a new daily was started that was subsidized by organizations connected with the Reverend Sun Myung Moon. Because it is subsidized, it conceivably could survive despite the monopoly-producing impact of advertising.

118 London has eleven dailies. *Editor & Publisher Yearbook, 1982*.

119 The American newspaper industry is fabulously profitable. Profits of the newspaper industry are not uniformly published since papers that are not publicly traded are not required to declare their profit figures and seldom do. However, publicly traded companies account for most of the national circulation. These data plus private studies of large samples such as members of the Inland Daily Press Association give generally accurate estimates of the level of profit for papers as a whole. In 1980, for example, publicly traded newspaper companies had 17.1 percent return on stockholders' equity. The only industrial groups with a higher percentage were petroleum, mining and oil, broadcasting, tobacco, and pharmaceuticals. Bureau of the Census, *Statistical Abstract of*

the United States, 1981 (Washington, D.C., 1981). According to the *John Morton Newspaper Research Letter* of April 15, 1982, the publicly traded newspaper companies had 1980 stockholders' equity return of 17.1 percent and had five-year averages of 18.5 percent. Pretax profit margin in 1981 was 17.3 percent with a five-year average of 18.3 percent and a ten-year average of 17.4 percent. Return on sales for newspapers generally ranges from 15 to 28 percent.

120   At times they complain. Cassandra Tate, *Columbia Journalism Review*, July/ August 1981, 51–56.

120   In the last two generations. Bureau of the Census, *Historical Statistics of the United States*, vol. 1 (Washington, D.C., 1975), 846–49.

121   Newspapers, magazines, and broadcasters in 1981. Bureau of the Census, *Statistical Abstract, 1981*, 572.

121   Four of the fifty largest. *Advertising Age*, 10 September 1981, 1. The four media companies among the fifty largest advertisers are Gulf + Western, RCA, Time, Inc., and CBS.

122   By 1970 attrition. *Editor & Publisher Yearbook, 1971*.

123   In 1970 the same large ad. Open line rates, *Editor & Publisher Yearbook, 1970*. The open line rate is the fundamental unit accepted in the trade for calculating ads in newspapers; it represents one fourteenth of a column inch. There are many variations of this rate when discounts are applied to large ads or a series of ads by the same advertisers or for different types of ads.

124   Exceptions to monopoly newspaper cities. New York City, alone among American cities, has three dailies—the *New York Times*, the *New York Daily News*, and the *New York Post*. In seeming contradiction to the concept that the leading paper triumphs over all, the *Times*, with 1982 circulation of 887,000, was the only paper of the three making a profit, while the *Daily News* with 1,483,000 was not and the *Post* with 663,000 was losing millions of dollars. This is unique among American newspaper cities, largely because the *New York Times* is an elite paper with half its circulation outside metropolitan New York. It is favored for advertising, despite its smaller circulation compared to the *News*, because the *News* and the *Post* are seen as having low-income readers while the *Times*, reaching a stratified upper-income audience, is more profitable for the high-priced stores whose ads dominate its pages. This segmentation of the audience by class has happened in New York because of New York's large population and partly because of the momentum of history. The *News* as recently as 1975 was highly profitable. In past decades it, like newspapers of the period, made most of its money from subscribers. Beginning in the 1960s New York became an extreme example of a demographic trend in all large cities, a polarization between the rich, who lived in expensive apartments and townhouses, and the poor, who lived in ghettos, while the middle class moved to the suburbs. The affluent, as the prime advertising audience, traditionally buy the *Times*, and the *Times* consequently gets the profitable ads. The poor in New York buy the *News*, but the *News*, having shifted to an advertising

base for its profits, is not perceived by large advertisers as an appropriate carrier for promotion of largely luxury items, so the *News* began losing money. The *News's* attempt to become a middle-class paper with more serious news coverage has been only partially successful. The *Post* showed a profit under a former ownership that ran serious commentary and some serious news. Under the ownership of Rupert Murdoch it has lost large amounts of money despite increases in circulation. Murdoch, obviously misunderstanding American newspaper economics, turned the *Post* into a sex-and-sensation paper like some of his profitable Australian and English tabloids, and to his surprise it is losing money.

124 (In 1982, for example.) *Editor & Publisher Yearbook, 1982.*

126 "A newspaper . . . must at all times." Negley D. Cochran, *E. W. Scripps* (New York: Harcourt, Brace, 1933), 235.

127 "Tax luxuries." W. A. Swanberg, *Pulitzer* (New York: Scribner's, 1967), 75–76.

127 "Which would be better." "This newspaper hopes." "Shall organized capital." Arthur Brisbane, *Editorials of the Hearst Newspapers* (New York: Albertson Publishing Company, 1906), 152.

128 The *Times* decided. Personal interview, 1962, with Orvil Dryfoos, publisher of the *New York Times*.

128 The publisher of the *Miami Herald*. Personal interview with Lee Hills, former editorial chairman of Knight-Ridder newspapers, publishers of the *Miami Herald*.

129 "With the best of intentions." Leo Bogart, *Press and Public* (Hillsdale, N.J.: Lawrence Erlbaum Associates, 1981).

8. The High Cost of Free Lunches (pages 134–51)

134 "With no ads." *Nation's Business,* October 1979, 88–89.

135 In 1940 daily newspapers. Calculations are made on the basis of standard data, on newspaper size and percentage of advertising, listed in Bureau of the Census, *Historical Statistics of the United States,* vols. 1 and 2 (Washington, D.C., 1975) and annual volumes, Bureau of the Census, *Statistical Abstract of the United States* (Washington, D.C.). Various cost indices are from *Historical Statistics* and the *Statistical Abstract*. Using either the consumer price index or the producers price index did not result in significant differences in this calculation. Changes in production costs for the period 1940 to 1980 was 185 percent, or 1980 costs almost triple 1940 costs. Average cost of daily papers in the United States for 1940 and 1980 is from American Newspaper Publishers Association.

135 By 1980 newspapers were getting. Newsprint Information Committee.

136 Most of the added editorial pages. Ben H. Bagdikian, "Fat Newspapers and Slim Coverage," *Columbia Journalism Review*, September/October 1973, 15. Statistics were updated for this book.

136 "Revenue Related Reading Matter." Carl Lindstrom, *The Fading American Newspaper* (Magnolia, Mass.: Peter Smith Publishers, 1960).

136 A survey by the Associated Press Managing Editors. "APME Poll Indicates Cut in the Newshole," *Editor & Publisher*, 13 October 1973, 66; Leo Bogart, *Press and Public* (Hillsdale, N.J.: Lawrence Erlbaum Associates, 1981), 34.

136 A study of 1,375 daily papers. *Editor & Publisher*, 5 April 1980, 36.

137 In one study a majority of readers. Bogart, *Press and Public*, 212; *Broadcasting*, 24 March 1975, 29.

137 Newspaper publishers have been converting. An added move of newspaper publishers in the direction of primary service to advertising is the printing and distribution of "shoppers," free papers devoted entirely to advertising, now produced in conjunction with their newspaper operations by a majority of American publishers (Bogart, *Press and Public*).

137 "Is not to stay in business." Bill Ostendorf, "A British Perspective," *Byline*, Winter 1980, 27.

137 Ads in early magazines. Theodore Peterson, *Magazines in the Twentieth Century* (Champaign: University of Illinois Press, 1975), 21.

138 "In its expanding feature content." Bogart, *Press and Public*, 173.

138 When radio became. Erik Barnouw, *A Tower of Babel* (New York: Oxford University Press, 1966).

140 In the first years of mass television. Erik Barnouw, *The Image Empire* (New York: Oxford University Press, 1970).

141 By selling ever-smaller spots. *Broadcasting*, 31 January 1977, 28; *Los Angeles Times*, 26 November 1981, 1.

142 The U.S. Supreme Court. *FTC v. Procter and Gamble Co.*, 386 U.S. (1967).

142 J. C. Hoagland. Frank Presbery, *The History and Development of Advertising* (New York: Doubleday, Doran, 1929), 392.

144 In the 1950s Studebaker. Harvey J. Goldsmid, H. Michael Mann, and J. Fred Watson, eds., *Industrial Concentration* (Boston: Little, Brown, 1974); William S. Comanor and Thomas A. Wilson, *Advertising and Market Power* (Cambridge, Mass.: Harvard University Press, 1974), 31.

144 Lydia Pinkham's Vegetable Compound. Presbery, *History and Development of Advertising*, 44.

144 Jeffrey Schrank has noted. Schrank, *Snap, Crackle and Popular Taste* (New York: Delacorte, 1977).

145 Other ads conceal. Schrank, *Snap, Crackle*.

145   "The Company is facing." Clorox Company Annual Report for the year ended June 30, 1979, 2–3.

146   Media-advertised goods. Federal Trade Commission, Bureau of Economics, *Statistical Report: Annual Line of Business Report, 1976* (Washington, D.C., 1982), 11.

147   "Linkage of ads." William S. Comanor and Thomas A. Wilson, "The Effect of Advertising on Competition," *Journal of Economic Literature*, June 1979.

147   It is no coincidence. William G. Shepherd, *The Economics of Industrial Organizations* (Englewood Cliffs, N.J.: Prentice-Hall, 1979), 373.

147   The best estimate. Ben H. Bagdikian, *The Information Machines* (New York: Harper & Row, 1970), 217.

148   Saving a large part. 1980 figure from Bureau of the Census, *Statistical Abstract, 1981*, 572.

148   By 1910 major universities. Presbery, *History and Development of Advertising*.

150   Advertising had become a big business. Bureau of the Census, *Historical Statistics*, vol. 2 , 855.

150   "Mass demand has been created." Presbery, *History and Development of Advertising*, 619.

150   "And let us remind readers." Miller, quoted in *Editor & Publisher*, 16 September 1961, 16.

150   "I have a theory." Paley, quoted in *Broadcasting*, 31 May 1976, 36.

9. Dr. Brandreth Has Gone to Harvard (pages 152–73)

152   "What I'd like to know." Sir John Reith to a delegation from Columbia Broadcasting System, January 1930, quoted in Erik Barnouw, *A Tower of Babel* (New York: Oxford University Press, 1966), 248.

152   In August of 1835. Frank Luther Mott, *American Journalism* (New York: Macmillan, 1972), 231.

153   "Send us more advertisements." Alfred McClung Lee, *The Daily Newspaper in America* (New York: Macmillan, 1937), 317.

155   This is not saying. For a description of the line between reporting corporate misdeeds and analysis of faults in the system, see Ben H. Bagdikian, "A Case of Split Personality at the *Wall Street Journal*," *Washington Journalism Review*, July/August 1981, 35–39.

155   The company was created. Frank Presbery, *The History and Development of Advertising* (New York: Doubleday, Doran, 1929), 396.

156   NBC's news program. Erik Barnouw, *Tube of Plenty* (New York: Oxford University Press, 1975), 170.

156   The Federal Communications Commission held hearings. Federal Communi-
      cations Commission, *Second Interim Report by the Office of Network Study,
      Television Network Program Procurement* (Washington, D.C., 1965).

156   "Where it seems fitting." Senate Committee on Interstate and Foreign Com-
      merce, *Report* (Washington, D.C., 1963), 446–53.

156   Individual verbatim testimony in FCC hearing is from *New York Times*, 27
      September 1961, 28 September 1961, 29 September 1961, 30 September 1961,
      3 October 1961, 4 October 1961, 5 October 1961, 7 October 1961, 8 Octo-
      ber 1961.

159   "We're in programming." *Fortune*, 31 December 1979, 70.

159   At one time Bell & Howell. *New York Times*, 28 September 1961, 83.

159   "That this 'marvelous world.' " Barnouw, *Tube of Plenty*, 163.

160   "We insist on a program environment." *Broadcasting*, 5 November 1979, 52.

160   "Lighter, happier" programs. *New York Times*, 27 September 1961.

161   Magazines were the first medium. Theodore Peterson, *Magazines in the Twen-
      tieth Century* (Urbana: University of Illinois Press, 1975), 5.

161   "To bait the editorial pages." *Time*, 28 September 1942, 51–52.

161   A 1940 *Esquire* article. Two years earlier. Peterson, *Magazines in the Twentieth
      Century*, 279.

162   "We suggested." "Look, Reader's Digest." *Advertising Age*, 19 November
      1962, 1.

162   "The cold, hard facts." *Advertising Age*, 17 April 1972, 85.

162   In 1976 the *New York Times*. Ben H. Bagdikian, "Newspaper Mergers,"
      Columbia Journalism Review, March/April 1977, 19–20.

163   Reader's Digest Association. *Publishers Weekly*, 17 June 1968, 49.

164   "Most newspaper real estate." "We were surprised." Housing Research
      Group, *For Sale or for Rent* (Washington, D.C.: Center for Responsive
      Law, 1978).

165   In 1980 John Brooks. *Editor & Publisher*, 18 October 1980, 20.

165   A survey in 1977. "Food Section Survey," Food Editors Conference, Chicago,
      October 1977.

166   "We do nothing controversial." *Editor & Publisher*, 31 March 1979, 11.

166   Even when the market basket surveys. *Editor & Publisher*, 29 March 1980,
      15. Jospeh N. Uhl, director of the project, said that papers stopped carrying
      the reports after complaints from grocers.

166   In 1980 the *Washington Star*. *Washington Journalism Review*, October 1980,
      46–47.

166   More than forty newspapers and magazines. *Los Angeles Times*, 24 October 1977, 1.

167   "Cannot be taken." *Editor & Publisher*, 31 January 1981, 7, 44.

167   Camel cigarettes. *Editor & Publisher*, 15 August 1981, 7; *Columbia Journalism Review*, November/December 1981, 26.

167   Another ingenious method. *Editor & Publisher*, 11 November 1978, 4.

169   Six of them carried nothing. George Seldes, *Never Tire of Protesting* (New York: Lyle, Stuart, 1968), 62.

170   In 1963, for example. *New York Times*, 22 July 1963, 35.

171   When R. C. Smith. R. C. Smith, "The Magazines' Smoking Habit," *Columbia Journalism Review*, January/February 1978, 29–31.

171   In 1980. *Mother Jones* carried articles on smoking hazards in its issues of April 1979 and January 1980, after which all its advertisements from tobacco companies were canceled. From interviews with publisher of *Mother Jones*.

171   Elizabeth Whelan reported. Press release of American Council on Science and Health, San Francisco, 29 January 1980.

172   "To me that documentary." "The Deadly Balance," *Columbia Journalism Review*, Fall 1965, 13.

173   "Much lineage." *Editor & Publisher*, 24 July 1954.

173   It is not surprising. Meyers, Iscoe, Jennings, Lenox, Minsky, and Sacks, *Staff Report of the Cigarette Advertising Investigation* (Washington, D.C.: Federal Trade Commission, May 1981), 5.

173   "Sure the *News*." *Consumer Reports*, May 1964, 247.

10. Democracy and the Media (pages 174–92)

174   "Experience is kaleidoscopic." James Britton, *Learning and Language* (London: Penguin, 1970), 26.

174   Voters in communities. Bureau of the Census, *Statistical Abstract of the United States, 1981* (Washington, D.C., 1981), 297–98.

175   In 1900, for example. Bureau of the Census, *Statistical Abstract, 1981*, and *Historical Statistics of the United States*, vol. 2 (Washington, D.C., 1975), 11.

177   In 1920 there were. Bureau of the Census, *Statistical Abstract, 1981, Historical Statistics*.

177   In 1900 newspaper subscribers. *Historical Statistics;* American Newspaper Publishers Association; Frank Luther Mott, *American Journalism* (New York: Macmillan, 1972), 220; Alfred McClung Lee, *The Daily Newspaper in America* (New York: Macmillan, 1937), 259–64.

181 Many competent journalists. Edwin R. Bayley, *Joe McCarthy and the Press* (Madison: University of Wisconsin Press, 1981).

181 Some distinguished reporting. Erik Barnouw, *Tube of Plenty* (New York: Oxford University Press, 1975), 28–38.

183 Nothing in the history. *Television and Growing Up: The Impact of Television Violence,* Report to the Surgeon General of the United States Public Health Service (Washington, D.C., 1971); periodic reports of Dr. George Gerbner, University of Pennsylvania (see Harry F. Waters, "Life According to TV," *Newsweek,* 6 December 1982, 136–40B).

184 The American Association of Advertising Agencies found. "Ten-Year Contrast in Opinions About Advertising," *Broadcasting,* 24 March 1975, 29.

184 In 1977 a survey. *Broadcasting,* 9 January 1978, 28.

185 One firm advises. Another firm uses. John Mariani, "Can Advertisers Read—and Control—Our Emotions?" in *Television Today,* ed. Barry Cole (New York: Oxford University Press, 1980), 107.

185 "Advertising is the art." *Broadcasting,* 21 September 1981, 36.

185 "The propaganda arm." Billie Wahlstrom, "Sex Stereotypes in Advertising: Geritol Days and Aviance Nights," *Interface* (1980): 39.

185 The American Association of Advertising Agencies has estimated. Jack K. Stuart, "How to Get Extra Mileage from Advertising," *Broadcasting,* 16 June 1969, 18.

186 That answer has been contradicted. *Television and Growing Up.*

188 The average television station. Ben H. Bagdikian, "Media Scale and Community Boundaries," paper delivered at the American Association for the Advancement of Science, Washington, D.C., 15 February 1978, 5–6.

189 "When a town grows." Lee, *Daily Newspaper in America,* 77.

189 Today 43 percent. Leo Bogart, *Press and Public* (Hillsdale, N.J.: Lawrence Erlbaum Associates, 1981), 269.

190 A candidate for the U.S. House. *Broadcasting-Cablecasting Yearbook, 1982.*

191 The thirty-second political ad. Advertising department, WBBM-TV, Chicago.

191 (In Ronald Reagan's 1980 campaign.) Herbert Alexander, "Making Sense About Dollars in the 1980 Presidential Campaign," research report to the American Enterprise Institute, 12 April 1982, 39.

191 A major Chicago newspaper. *Circulation 1981/1982.* Ad cost estimated from rates of a Chicago daily.

192 Abraham Lincoln. Herbert Alexander, *Financing Politics* (Washington, D.C.: Congressional Quarterly Press, 1980), 11.

192   In California. State of California Fair Political Practices Commission, *Campaign Costs, 1958–1978*, 1980.

11. Mass Media without Masses (pages 195–207)

195   "By 1990." *Editor & Publisher*, 10 April 1982, 48.

195   "It was an axiom." *Collier's*, 4 February 1911.

195   The best quantitative measure. Bureau of the Census, *Historical Statistics of the United States* (Washington, D.C., 1975), 809; Bureau of the Census, *Statistical Abstract of the United States* (Washington, D.C., 1970–81).

196   In 1980 the average paper. *Statistical Abstract, 1981*.

197   The *Los Angeles Times* averages. *Wall Street Journal*, 9 August 1982, 27.

197   Radio began the change. *Statistical Abstract, 1970–1981; Historical Statistics*, vol. 2, 7.

198   Before World War II. *Historical Statistics*, vol. 1, 224, 381; *Statistical Abstract, 1981*, 144, 429.

198   Another positive change. *Historical Statistics* and *Statistical Abstract*.

199   In 1979, families. *Statistical Abstract, 1981*, 435, 26–27.

202   When the Magazine Publishers Association. *Public Relations Journal*, November 1978; *The New Yorker*, 5 October 1981, 159.

202   In 1982 a study commission. *Broadcasting*, 15 November 1982.

203   According to the 1982 edition. *World Press Encyclopedia*, vol. 2; *Facts on File*, 1982.

204   The main difference. In the 1970s and 1980s there were some signs of public alienation with the news media. In 1961 when the Gallup Poll asked adults if they would approve "placing greater curbs or controls on what newspapers print," 31 percent said yes and 14 percent had no opinion. A 1974 Gallup Poll asked high school students, "Would the nation be better off, in your opinion, if every news article sent out of Washington was checked by a government agency to see that the facts were correct?" In that case, 63 percent said yes. An analysis by the Libel Defense Resource Center, representing major media companies, showed that most large punitive judgments (many over $500,000) were made by juries rather than judges. Of fifty-four cases studied, only one punitive damage was invoked by a judge, twenty-nine by juries. *Editor & Publisher*, 4 September 1982, 16–17. Juries probably come as close to a cross section of the population as any randomized selection of organized groups and may reflect the degree of indifference or hostility among the public toward their media.

204   "The world of fact." In Michael Rice, ed. *Reporting U.S.-European Relations* (New York: Pergamon Press, 1982).

205   Until the 1960s. Ben H. Bagdikian, "How Editors Pick Columnists," *Columbia Journalism Review*, Spring 1966, 40–45.

206   When sterility of news writing. See James Britton, British thinker and writer, who discussed this concept in his book *Language and Learning* (London: Penguin, 1970).

206   RCA chairman David Sarnoff. Leo Bogart, *Press and Public* (Hillsdale, N.J.: Lawrence Erlbaum Associates, 1981), 248.

12. The Growing Gap (pages 208–22)

208   "It appears to have." Oliver Sacks, *The Man Who Mistook His Wife for a Hat* (New York: Summit Books, 1987).

208   In 1986 when. Form 10-K, Securities and Exchange Commission, General Electric, for fiscal year ending 31 December 1985.

209   In 1932, for example. Jerry de Muth, "GE: Profile of a Corporation," *Dissent*, July/August 1967, 502ff.

209   In 1982. *Washington Post*, 16 March 1982, A1.

209   In 1985. *Washington Post*, 27 March 1985, A1.

209   Over the years. *Dissent*, above.

209   It is still. *New York Times*, 10 December 1986, 1.

210   Another question. *Washington Post*, 16 March 1982.

211   That was too much. Harvey Swados, ed., *Years of Conscience: The Muckrakers* (New York: World Publishing, 1962), 513.

212   Today a majority. *Statistical Abstract of the United States, 1986*, 134. Median school year completed for persons twenty-five years old and over in 1984 was 12.6.

215   Too often. Oliver Sacks, above.

215   Exaggerated dependence. Edwin R. Bayley, *Joe McCarthy and the Press* (Madison: University of Wisconsin Press, 1981).

220   During the same period. *Statistical Abstract*, above, 15. Number of urban places in 1980 was 8,765.

220   But newspapers are. Ben H. Bagdikian, "How Good Are California Newspapers?" *California Magazine*, November 1984, 89ff.

220   There are 19,000. *Statistical Abstract*, above, 285. Number of municipal governments in 1982 was 19,076.

13. To Undo Excess (pages 223–37)

226 Today, for example. The newspaper chain with the largest aggregate daily circulation is the Gannett Company, whose nespapers have a daily circulation of 6,100,000, or 9.5 percent of the national total of 62,766,00.

227 Yet two corporations. Gannett Company and Thompson Newspapers each own more than ninetly daily newspapers in the United States.

Afterword (pages 239–252)

240 On the national social scene. *New York Times*, 28 February 1993, Sec. 3, 13.

240 There is a similarly. *New England Medical Journal of Medicine*, 2 April 1992, 962–67; *Facts on File*, 8 February 1996, 70.

240 Congress once passed. *Los Angeles Times*, 8 January 1995, Part D, 1; *Fortune*, 9 May 1992, 48.

242 Resistance to. Milton and Rose Friedman, *Free to Choose* (New York, Harcourt Brace Jovanovich, 1980).

242 There is no need. Life Jensen, "On Our Perception of History" (Oakland, Life Jensen, 1996), 44.

243 For example, the level. George Gerbner, *The World and I Journal*, "Television Violence: The Art of Asking the Wrong Questions."

243 Even a majority. Survey by *Electronic Media*, 2 August, 1993.

244 The basic answer. Ben H. Bagdikian, *The Information Machines*, New York (Harper & Row, 1970), Chapter 9.

244 With that content. *Statistical Abstract of the United States, 1998*, Table 728.

247 Broadcasters have successfully. *Les Brown's Encyclopedia of Television*, 3rd Edition (Detroit, Gale Research, 1992), 180.

248 The reality, of course. *World Press Encyclopedia* (New York, Facts on File, 1982), Vols. I and II.

249 The objection of. *Statistical Abstract of the United States*, 1995, Table 9, p. 576.

250 Within the United States. *Les Brown's Encyclopedia of Television*, above. p. 94.

251 Today NHK is. *World Press Encyclopedia*, Vol. I, 559.

INDEX

ABC (American Broadcasting Company), xxxiii, 7, 13, 18, 23; lead of, in audience size, 113-14
Abilene National Bank, 37
Accuracy, in media, 65
Advertising: alteration of media content to enhance, xiii, xxxiv, 8, 154-73; corporate, 58-64; cost of, to newspaper readers, 135-36; development of, as big business, 149; fraudulent, 144-45; importance of demographics to, 109-10, 115-17; industry expenditures on, 146; influence of, on American culture, 184; manipulation of, on television, 183-87; newspapers without, 147; in *The New Yorker*, 105-7, 109, 113; on radio, 138-40; symbols in, use of, 187-88; tax on, 231
— mass, impact of: on economy, 150; on magazines, 131-32, 137-38, 161; on media in general, lvi; 239-242; on newspaper content, 163-68; on newspaper industry, 119-31; on television, 131-33, 140-41, 183-87
Advertising Age, 75, 162
Advertising Council, 52, 56
Air Canada, 167
Alien and Sedition Acts (1798), 101, 223
Allen, Robert, 93-94

Aluminum Company of America, 50
Amalgamated Clothing Workers, 42
Amazon.com, xi, xxxviii
America Online, xxxvii. *See also* AOL–Time Warner, proposed merger; AOL Time Warner
American Association of Advertising Agencies, 55, 184, 185
American Booksellers Association, xli, 31
American Cancer Society, 169, 173
American Can Company, 57
American Council on Science and Health, 172
American Express, 25
American Journalism Review, xxv, xxx
American Magazine, The, 216
American Management Association, 57
American Medical Association (AMA), 169
American Newspaper Publishers Association, 54, 92, 99
American Petroleum Institute, 65
American Society of Newspaper Editors, 30, 82
American Sociological Association, 33
American Tobacco Company, 171
Anglo-Iranian Oil Company (AIOC), 39

Microsoft, xi, xxxix
Military-industrial complex, 11, 49
Miller, Colin, 93-94
Miller, Jonathan, 92
Miller, Paul, 70-71, 72, 73, 76, 87, 150
MIT Press (publisher), 59
Mobil Oil Company, 25, ads of, against
 news media, 59-61, 62-63, 64; and oil
 industry taxes, 61-64; sponsorship of
 The Genius of Arab Civilization, 59
Modern Medicine magazine, 163
Money magazine, 95
Monopolies, 74-75, 118-33
Montgomery Ward, 61
Morgan, J.P., 211
Morgan Guaranty Trust, 25
Mossadegh, Mohammed, 39
Mother Jones magazine, 171
Motion picture(s), xxxiv-xxxv, 3, 4, 17,
 222; corporate control of, 21, 24; stu-
 dios, 29, 100, 228. *See also* Buena
 Vista Films; MGM; Paramount Com-
 munications, Inc.; Time Warner;
 20th-Century Fox
"Motorola TV Hour," 159
MS. magazine, 172
MSN, xxxix
MSNBC, xi
Munsey, Frank, 72
Murdoch, Rupert, x, xxii, xxxv, 18, 21,
 41; takeovers by, 4, 6, 23
Music, xxxv
Mussolini, Benito, 197
My Lai massacre, 108. *See also* Viet-
 nam War
Mythology, 67

Nader, Ralph, xliii, 52
Napoleon Bonaparte, lii
Nation, The, xxxii, xxxviii, 33
National Academy of Sciences, 145
National Association of Broadcasters,
 11, 92, 202
National Cable Television Association,
 11

National Geographic magazine, xxxiii,
 61
National Industrial Pollution Control
 Council, 51
National Petroleum Council, 51
National Public Radio, xxxiv, 249
NBC (National Broadcsting Company),
 xxxiii, lv, 13, 18, 23, 113; acquisition
 of, by General Electric, 7, 11, 23,
 208-10; "Camel News Caravan" on,
 156; News, 11, 209-10
Needham, Harper & Steers/Issues and
 Images, 54
Nelson, W.R., 118
Neuharth, Allen H., lv, 67, 72-89
New Deal, the, 91
Newhouse and Thomson, 18, 20, 21,
 24, 95, 162
Newhouse Newspapers, xxxii, 22
New Mexican, The (Santa Fe, N.M.),
 87-88
New Orleans Times-Picayune, 165
New Republic, The, 33
News, as first rough draft of history,
 xxxi; international, xxx
News Corporation Ltd., x, xi, xxiii,
 xxxii, xxxvii, xxxviii, 21, 22, 23
Newspaper Advertising Bureau, 129,
 136-37
Newspaper Preservation Act, 91, 98,
 100
Newspaper(s): without ads, 147; competition among, xxxi, 122-23; control
 of readership, 199; corporate control
 of, xxxii, 3-9, 17, 21, 22; daily, ranking of countries in numbers sold,
 203; decline in public loyalty to, 195-
 99; development of, in America, 174-
 79; ideal ownership pattern for, 226-
 27; impact of advertising on content
 of, 163-68; monopoly among, 123-
 24; profit levels of, xxxii, 201; social
 role of, xxxii; on tobacco and disease, 172-173; weekly, xxxii
Newsweek magazine, xiv, 171-72